# Indian Theatre in English
# and
# Literary Feminism

## Politics of Gender, Identity and Authenticity

Arvind M. Nawale
Nibedita Mukherjee

AUTHORSPRESS

Worldwide Circulation through Authorspress Global Network
**First Published 2013**
by
**Authorspress**

*Editorial*
Q-2A Hauz Khas Enclave
New Delhi-110 016

*Marketing*
E-35/103, Jawahar Park
Laxmi Nagar, Delhi-110 092

e-mails: authorspress@rediffmail.com; authorspress@hotmail.com
Website: www.authorspressbooks.com



**Indian Theatre in English and Literary Feminism:**
**Politics of Gender, Identity and Authenticity**
**ISBN 978-81-7273-706-1**



Printed in India at Tarun Offset, Delhi.

Dedicated to Our Gurus

Dr. Harihar Kulkarni and Sri Shailendra Sharma

For Their Blessings

# Preface

The politics of gender which determines everything, including language and literature, and the recent trends in feminist criticism has moved towards gender studies. Elizabeth Abel argues, "Sexuality and textuality both depend on difference" and realizing the fact that the entire consequence of female oppression is caused by female "difference" these critics have decided to move beyond "difference", itself. So now the politics of gender identity has come into the scenario, replacing the entirely female perspective, and it serves as an umbrella term providing coverage to other areas too. Now male critics, who desire to pursue feminist criticism, and even the "Queer Study" group come under this broader concept.

Julia Kristeva has provided an adequate analysis of how feminism has progressed through stages to finally reach the fluidity of gender identity. She states that feminism began with liberalism when women demanded equality; then came the radical feminists who rejected patriarchy and called for separatist matriarchy, and finally they rejected both concepts and was asking for "gender identity". Thus, feminism starting in true sense with Beauvoir's *The Second Sex*, proceeded through varied phases to reach the phase of Judith Butler (*Gender Troub* 1990).

The present book desires to address the politics of gender identity from the authentically Indian perspective, and that too in the arena of English theatre. Indian drama and theatre have always exhibited a close symbiotic relation between genre and gender though literary feminism was quite late in evolving. The reason obviously was that theatre was a more public arena and hence a restricted medium for the females. The males, of course, took up the cudgel on behalf of the females, and we have early playwrights like Krishna Mohan Banerji (*The Persecuted*), Michael Madhusudhan Dutt (*Ratnavali, Sermistha, Is This Called Civilization?*) who presented women as iconic images of perfection and subjugation. They were followed by Tagore and Sri Aurobindo who in the truest sense propagated the cause of women. Bharati Sarabhai and Swarnakumari Devi were the earliest of female dramatists though their voices remained muffled.

But female centred issues began to occupy the stage with the development of the IPTA (Indian Peoples Theatre Movement) which became operative since 1943, and it preceded an era of theatre festivals and workshops committed to the cause of women. Few examples are *Yavintika*, a women's theatre festival organized by a Hyderabad-based group, "Voicing Silence", Gendered Theatre by M.S. Research Foundation, *Akka*, the National Women's theatre festival held in Mysore, and so on. All this interest focused upon the feminist cause resulted in a plethora of plays being written with women at the centre. Vijay Tendulkar and Mahesh Dattani are two great names in this perspective. They wrote and are still writing plays which expose the hypocrisy and mistreatment meted out to the female population through generations.

Female directors, once a rarity, now occupied the forefront, and names like Ipsita Chandra, Chama Ahuja, Usha Ganguli, Sheila Bhatia, B. Jayashree, Arundhuti Raje, Nadira Babbar, Anuradha Kapur, Amal Allana became household names. They were supplied with regular plays by another female brigade comprising names like Polie Sengupta, Dina Mehta, tripurari Sharma, Uma Parameswaran, Manjula Padmanabhan, Zahida Zaidi etc. Thus Indian Theatre and Literary Feminism both became the demand of the hour and it all propagated the "politics of gender identity".

The essays in this book address these multiple aspects of gender identity and feminism, and open up doors for varied speculations. The dramatists considered are from Kalidasa to Dattani, and provide as broad a spectrum as possible. Like the first note in an orchestra the first paper in this book "Gender Politics in Mahesh Dattani's *Tara*" lays the tone of the entire volume. The play revolves around the theme of favouring the boy and depriving the girl with exceptional originality of conception. The playwright presents arguments against the parents' preference for the male child at the cost of the girl child. The paper points out aptly the significance of the play in today's context when we still fight gender issues, when still the female foetuses get killed, and when our country faces the dipping in the female to male child ratio.

The next essay presents the concept of the "other" in the Dattanian perspective where it deals with problems faced by both women and the hijras who both live at the periphery of the patriarchal society. This essay "Feminizing the 'Other': A Critical Survey of Dattani's *Seven Steps Around the Fire*" portrays how the popular medium of language used in a radio-play can become the evidence of hetero-homo dialectic.

As already pointed out, *Tara* is an exceptional play by Mahesh Dattani, and the next three essays by Daxa Thakor, Anisha N. and T. Sasikanth Reddy all deal with the same play. The themes are varied – mother-daughter relationship, patriarchy and feminism – yet, the focus is the same. The sixth essay is also on Dattani though here the writer, Bhavesh Kumar draws our attention to another extremely powerful play *Bravely Fought the Queen*. Violence against women is a heinous crime and yet a persistent reality in Indian society, and this article draws our attention towards it.

Any study of Indian literature is incomplete without Rabindranath Tagore, and Dr. Bina Biswas exerts a pull towards the issue of feminism in the lyrical drama of Tagore. The essay deals with the popular dance dramas such as *Chitrangada; Chandalika* and *Natir Puja*, and shows how in the ancient period too women continued their battle against all sorts of discriminations – gender, class and religion. The next essay by Dr. Nirmala S. Padmavat is a deeper study into one play of Tagore in particular, i.e. *Chandalika.* Daughter of a Chandal, untouchable by birth, Prakriti had loved Ananda because he was the one who unleashed the real identity of her being a human first and not an untouchable. Prakriti was moved by this act of the monk and fell in love with him without realizing that making people recognize their true inner self was the duty of a monk, which he had performed. Similarly, the female-male consciousness in Tagore's *Chitra* is studied in depth by Dr. S.D. Sasikiran.

In Kalidasa's *Sakuntala* : The Next Trailing Stereotype in the Cult of Ahilya, Sita And Sati, Dr. Sonali Anand studies at depth the position of women in ancient society. This is followed by a study of Sri Aurobindo's women by the poet- author Aju Mukhopadhyay. Ankur Konar deals with the problems of female subjectivity in Mahasweta Devi's *Mother of 1084*, a novel which was later transformed into a play.

The next great name in our list is that of Vijay Dhondopant Tendulkar who is one of the greatest Indian playwrights, screen and television writers, literary essayists, political journalists, and social commentators of the twentieth century. He played a vital role in the modernization of India and his plays focus largely on women-centric issues. The next essays in our book by Dr. Ulka S. Wadekar, Miss Sapna Chaturvedi and Dr. Seeme Mahmood focus on the varied aspects of Tendulkar's plays and their gender-related issues.

Next comes the essay by Kamalakar K. Askar on Asif Currimbhoy which is a lone attempt to represent gender politics in the work of this great dramatist.

The next seven essays in this book deal with another great dramatist India has produced, i.e. Girish Karnad. He writes mainly in Kannada but seven of his plays have been translated into English. Here his plays like *Nagamandala, Hayavadna,*

*Yayati, Bali: The Sacrifice*, etc. are studied in detail by scholars like Ajit Kumar, Vithal Jaybhaye, K.S. Thirunavukkarasu, Hasibuddin, S. Somasundari Latha and Madhavi Paul, and they minutely reflect the evolving situation of women in a predominantly patriarchal society reflected in Karnad's plays. Deepali Patil takes Habib Tanvir's *Charandas Chor* with Karnad's *Hayavadana* in her gender study while Abhinandan Malas takes Mahesh Dattani with Karnad in his study of the rise of new women in the modern Indian English drama.

The remaining essays by Rupali Bhave, N. Sumathi and Seema Dhoble deal with the overall critical survey of Indian dramas in English through feminine perspective and socio-political studies of the suppressed position of women as portrayed in Indian English drama.

True to the process, the pattern of evolution from ancient times to the postmodern period is studied in depth, and it proves Indian English theatre to be a powerful aspect of literary feminism. The politics of gender and identity is the *mantra* of modern India, and its authenticity is the gospel of this book. It is our firm and ardent belief that the readers of this book will enjoy and benefit from these essays, and the book itself will prove to be a substantial contribution to the study of politics of gender, identity and authenticity of feminism and Indian theatre in English.

We are grateful to the publisher of this anthology, Mr. Sudarshan Kcherry, Managing Director, and the whole team of Authorspress, New Delhi for encouraging us to bring the present volume, and for helping our project to reach teachers and students internationally. Thanks are also due to our Management and Principals for their inspiration. We are grateful to our family members for allowing us to work together and their stimulation and constant support.

**Dr. Arvind M. Nawale**
**Dr. Nibedita Mukherjee**

# List of Contributors

**Abhinandan Malas**, Department of English, Ramananda College, Bishnupur, Bankura, (West Bengal).

**Ajit Kumar**, Assistant Professor in English, Maharani Lakshmi Bai College for Girls. Bhiwani Rohilla, Hisar (Haryana).

**Aju Mukhopadhyay**, poet, author and critic, and bilingual writer of fiction and essays, Pondicherry (India).

**Anisha N.**, Institute of English, University of Kerala.

**Ankur Konar**, Assistant Professor of English, Burdwan Raj College, Burdwan (West Bengal).

**Bhavesh Kumar**, Research Scholar, English and Foreign ·Languages, Hyderabad. (Andhra Pradesh).

**Nibedita Mukherjeee**, Assistant Professor of English, Bankura Chrisitian College, Bankur (West Bengal).

**Arvind M. Nawale**, Head, Department of English, Shivaji Mahavidyalaya, Udgir, Dist: Latur (Maharashtra).

**Bina Biswas**, Professor of English Language and Communications, TRR Engineering College for Women, Jawaharlal Nehru Technological University, Hyderabad. (Andhra Pradesh).

**Daxa Thakor**, Associate Professor, Shah N.H. Commerce College, Valsad (Gujarat).

**Deepali Rajshekhar Patil**, Associate Professor, Department of English. S.B. B alias Appasaheb Jedhe College of Arts, Commerce and Science, Shukrawar Peth, Pune (Maharashtra).

**Hasibuddin**, Reader, Department of English, GLA University, Mathura (Uttar Pradesh).

**K. S. Thirunavukkarasu**, Assistant Professor in English, Government Arts College, Tiruvanamalai (Tamil Nadu).

**Madhavi S. Paul**, Faculty, Department of English, Arts Commerce & Science College, Tukum, Chandrapur (Maharashtra).

**Nirmala S. Padmavat**, Assistant Professor of English, MIT, Aurangabad (Maharashtra).

**S.D. Sasi Kiran**, Vice–Principal, Mahatma Gandhi Degree College, Guntur. (Andhra Pradesh).

**Seeme Mahmood**, Assistant Professor in English, Institute For Excellence In Higher Education, Bhopal (Madhya Pradesh).

**Sonali Anand**, Guest Faculty, Govt. Maharaja College, Chhatarpur (Madhya Pradesh).

**T. Sasikanth Reddy**, Academic Consultant in English, YSR Engineering College of Yogi Vemana University, Proddatur Town, YSR Dist. (Andhra Pradesh).

**Ulka S. Wadekar**, Reader. Department of English, Smt. K.L. Mahavidyalaya, Amravati (Maharashtra).

**Jaybhaye Vithal Khandujji**, Assistant Professor in English, L.R.V.College, Sonpeth, Parbhani (Maharashtra).

**Kamlakar K. Askar**, Assistant Professor in English, Dhanwate National College, Nagpur (Maharashtra).

**N. Sumathi**, Head of the Department, Department of English, New Horizon College, Kasturinagar, Bangalore (Karnataka).

**Rupali S. Bhave**, Faculty, Department of English, Smt. R.S. College, Anjangaon Surji (Maharashtra).

**S. Somasundari Latha**, Assistant Professor, Department of English, R.V. Govt. Arts College, Chengalpattu (Tamil Nadu).

**Sapna Chaturvedi**, Ph.D. Scholar, Barkatullah University Bhopal (Madhya Pradesh).

**Seema Dhoble**, Research Scholar, Navi Mumbai (Maharashtra).

19. *Hayavadana:* A Mirror of the Society 224
— *Hasibuddin*

20. Attitude of a Patriarchal Society towards a Woman in the Plays of Girish Karnad 230
— *Madhavi S. Paul*

21. Rani's Empowerment in Girish Karnad's *Naga-Mandala* 243
— *S. Somasundari Latha*

22. Dialogues on Gender: A Study of Girish Karnad's *Hayavadana* and Habib Tanvir's *Charandas Chor* 251
— *Deepali Rajshekhar Patil*

23. The Rise of New Women in the Modern Indian English Drama: A Study of the Plays of Girish Karnad and Mahesh Dattani 259
— *Abhinandan Malas*

24. Indian Dramas in English: A Feminine Perspective 277
— *Rupali S. Bhave*

25. Indian Drama in English: A Feminine Outlook 297
— *N. Sumathi*

26. Reflection of Suppressed Status of Woman in Indian Drama in English: A Socio-Cultural Study 310
— *Seema Dhoble*

**Index** **325**

# Contents


Preface vii

List of Contributors xiii

1. Gender Politics in Mahesh Dattani's *Tara* 1
   — *Arvind M. Nawale*
2. Feminizing the "Other": A Critical Survey of Dattani's *Seven Steps around the Fire* 10
   — *Nibedita Mukherjee*
3. Influence of Patriarchy in Moulding Mother-daughter Relationship in *Tara* 19
   — *Daxa Thakor*
4. Patriarchy and Gender Preferance in Mahesh Dattanis's *Tara* 29
   — *N. Anisha*
5. Feminist Articulations in Mahesh Dattani's *Tara* 36
   — *T. Sasikanth Reddy*
6. Locating Shades of Violence: Assessing Function of Violence against Women in Mahesh Dattani's *Bravely Fought the Queen* 47
   — *Bhavesh Kumar*
7. Feminism in the Dance Dramas of Tagore 69
   — *Bina Biswas*

8. Feminism in Rabindranath Tagore's *Chandalika* 82
— *Nirmala S. Padmavat*

9. Interpreting Female-Male Consciousness in Tagore's *Chitra*: An Empirical Study 88
— *S.D. Sasikiran*

10. Kalidasa's *Shakuntala:* The Next Trailing Stereotype in the Cult of Ahilya, Sita and Sati 98
— *Sonali Anand*

11. The Coquettes and the Winners of the Hearts: Women Characters in Sri Aurobindo's Dramas 109
— *Aju Mukhopadhyay*

12. Altercation of Ideologies and Topography of Identities: The Agency of Women Subjectivity in Mahasweta Devi's *Mother of 1084* 132
— *Ankur Konar*

13. *The Vultures*: A Vestige of Venomous Vengeance 143
— *Ulka S. Wadekar*

14. Female Status, Their Roles and the Psychological Situation as Depicted in the Plays of Vijay Tendulkar 151
— *Sapna Chaturvedi* and *Seeme Mahmood*

15. Women in Asif Currimbhoy's Socio-Realistic Plays 167
— *Kamlakar K. Askar*

16. Feminine Perspective in the Plays of Girish Karnad 195
— *Ajit Kumar*

17. Girish Karnad's *Yayati*: A Play of Unheroic Filial Sacrifice 209
— *Jaybhaye Vithal Khandujj*

18. Feminine Perspective in Girish Karnad's *Hayavadana* 215
— *K. S. Thirunavukkarasu*

# 1

# Gender Politics in Mahesh Dattani's *Tara*

— Arvind M. Nawale

Any art achieves cosmic value when it truly reflects human experience and emotional response. By the virtue of its stage performances and potentials to facilitate direct communication between the artistes and the audience, theatre has emerged as a forceful literary mode of expression of human sensibility that is universal and is beyond any limitations of time and space. It is the most authentic, oldest and the most appealing form. The Indian tradition maintains that roots of all art are laying in the *Pranav nada, Om*. The dance of Lord Shiva is often said to be divine or cosmic play. Our great epics like the *Ramayana* and the *Mahabharata* also attempt to define drama and dramaturgy. The *Mahabharata* defines drama as a mixture of poetry, story, action etc. The great ancient Indian poet and the creator of the *Ramayana*, Valmiki uses the word 'Nat' or 'Narataka'-meaning an actor or a performer.'

The word "drama" has its origin in Greek. It originated from word "dra" meaning "do". In this way, 'doing' or 'action' is column beam of the whole dramatic premise. Aristotle has also acknowledged "action as the predominating component of drama." Narrative holds much importance in fiction, but action and dialogue hold paramount significance in drama. Compton-Rickett defines drama "as an articulate story presented in action."

M.K. Naik observes that "Drama is a composite art in which the written word of the playwright attains complete artistic realization only when it becomes the spoken word of the actor on the stage and through that medium reacts on the mind of that audience. A play, in order to communicate fully and become a living dramatic experience, thus needs a real theatre and a live audience." (Naik.1995:36). Thus, the text of the play is meant for the stage performance.

Indian English theatre finally got an independent character and standing in the last quarter of the twentieth century with the plays of Mahesh Dattani. With his strong dramatic vision Dattani understood that the tradition of Indian English drama as the mirror image of European traditions. He adopted to represent the profundity and strength of human experience in the Indian context. Therefore, it becomes necessary to contextualize his contribution to Indian drama in English.

Mahesh Dattani is the most dominant and compelling dramatic voice in the present Indian English dramatic world. He has developed and aggrandised the tradition of Indian drama with his bold experiments and innovations and very personalized stagecraft. His plays are characterized by very distinct theatrical and thematic innovations. He has not only logical power and prowess to produce a play in text but also has the ability to get it staged successfully. While commenting on his plays, John McRae calls him "the voice of India" and observes as follows: "They are the plays of today, sometimes as actual as to cause controversy, but at the same time they are the plays which embody many of the classic concern for world drama."

Dattani has an avant-garde approach towards drama. He looks at the theatre as the medium to voice the cause of the unprivileged segments of our society. His plays externalize the problems and pent-up feeling of the subalterns in a very authentic and realistic manner. In his plays, "Dattani visits untraversed and unexplored soil of homosexuals, HIV positive, eunuchs, physically challenged people etc. By touching up radical themes like gay themes, child sexual abuse, eunuch etc., he has greatly expanded new horizons in Indian English drama." He has dramatized problems and issues of the modern urban Indian society ranging from communal tension, homosexuality, child sexual abuse, gender discrimination, marriage and career, conflict between tradition and modernity, patriarchal social system, constraints of eunuchs, women, children, labourer, interpersonal relationship, workings of personal and moral choices, identity crisis of LGBT, revelation of past, the problems faced by HIV positives and terminally ill patients.

'Family' is the most important theatrical space in his plays as most of the plays have family as their locale. They are dealing with the stories or tales of various families. *Where There's a Will, Bravely Fought the Queen, Dance Like a Man, Tara* are some of his plays in which the painful tales of various families have gone into the fabric and texture of the plays. The dramatist depicts the battles being fought among the members of same family at home. "Home is the oft repeated arena of battle in his dramatic universe. The unrest eats up the happy and joyous atmosphere of the family curbing the personal development in them and necessarily embedded within the mechanisms of the middle class Indian family and this is the context from which he operates". (Kuthari 2008: 103)

*Tara* is the most touching two-act play by Dattani. The play revolves around the theme of favouring the boy and depriving the girl with exceptional originality of conception. The playwright presents arguments against the parents' preference for the male child at the cost of the girl child. The play is significant in today's context too when we still fight gender issues, when still the female foetuses get killed, and when our country faces the dipping in the female to male child ratio.

In his plays, Dattani takes on what he calls the 'invisible issues of Indian society'. *Tara* centres on the emotional cataclysm that grows between two conjoined twins following the discovery that their mother and grandfather had favoured the boy

(Chandan) over the girl (Tara) by giving the third limb to the boy instead to the surgically more deserving Tara. The play contests heteronormative sexual politics and shows Dattani's preoccupation with the margins that expresses through the problematics of the body which bears the scourging letterings of the multipart dynamics of the urban middle-class Indian society. Tara, a feisty girl who isn't given the opportunities given to her brother (although she is smarter) eventually wastes away and dies. Chandan escapes to London, changes his name as Dan and attempts to repress the guilt he feels over his sister's death by living without a personal history.

Chandan and Tara are conjoined twins, joined at the hip, with three lower limbs. Dr Thakkar puts it forth as 'United from chest downwards, breastbone down to pelvis.' There was a need for separation and Dr Thakkar says:

> Complications were expected. Our team of doctors were aware of that. The pelvic region, as I had mentioned before, was a problem. There was only bladder and it belonged to the boy. So did the rectum. We would have to have an artificial made for the girl. Later on, when she grows up, we can fashion one from her intestinal tissues. And the boy's lungs aren't fully developed. However, considering the magnitude of the work involved, this was a minor detail. The prognosis, on the whole, was favourable for both. Nature had done a near complete job. Medical science could finish it for her. Theoretically, the separation was possible. (45)

The play takes a look at the "battles, victories and the defeats of an Indian family coping with the trauma of freak children and their survival, while also exposing the existing patriarchal stereotypes of the Indian mindset which has always preferred a boy to a girl child." (Kuthari 2008:37)

The decision that was taken to give the third leg to the boy between the two conjoined twins has shown the hegemony of gender and class, and the play focuses openly on the age-old gender-bias of our patriarchal society where we deprive the girl child her basic rights to survive with dignity. The third limb is given away to Chandan and an unethical decision is taken by Bharati, the mother, and their powerful grandfather that leaves Tara crippled, though Bharati's guilt later drives her to insanity but that does not lessen the crime that was committed on Tara. Dattani's artistry lies in the depiction of social taboos and prejudices, gender discrimination against girl children and the all-devouring patriarchal mindsets in our society. His women characters are pitched against one another in his plays, and here, in *Tara*, too he shows Tara as a high-spirited, tough survivor with a sense of humour and delightful repartee while fighting against the prejudices and hurts that the society and family have inflicted on her by her mother Bharati, Roopa, Nalini et al.

The play successfully depicts that even scientific considerations are not free from social stereotypes. The surgeon's clinical commentary of the operation is also neatly pitted against the emotional turbulence brought about by the medical miracle. However, it is clearly shown that "Dr Thakkar's theoretical possibility fails to remain an essentialist proposition guided by the dictates of biology alone" (*Mulitiple Appropriations: Writing the Contested Body in Dattani's Tara* by Pathik Roy). The problems in the play begin when the secret is unravelled, "the unequal, unfair operation, with the mother, Bharati, her father and the surgeon collaborating to afford the male with better chances: physically- the second leg. Dr Thakkar, the God-like 'life-giver' is aware that the third leg would adhere better to the female half, and yet becomes party to the decision. God, it may well be observed, is male. In a sense he prolongs their lives through the surgery, but also leaves them physically mutilated and mentally traumatized, gaining notoriety as phenomenal freaks of science." (Kuthari 2008:71)

Dan at a later date, tries to define his other half, the feisty Tara: "She never got a fair deal. Not even from nature. Neither of us did. Maybe God never wanted us separated. Destiny desires strange things. ...But even God does not always get what he wants. Conflict is the crux of life." The single undivided body of

Tara and Chandan is claimed by phallocentric discussion that risks giving the third leg to Chandan instead of giving it to the more medically deserving Tara thus:

> Patel, Your grandfather and your mother had a private meeting with Dr Thakkar. I wasn't asked to come. That same evening your mother told me of her decision. Everything will be done as planned. Except– I couldn't believe what she told me– that they would risk giving both legs to the boy. (349)

The conjoined body becomes a site of patriarchal dominance, the consequence of which ultimately results in slow but sure physical elimination of Tara and psychological obliteration of Chandan. The politics of class also stakes its claim on the body of the twins as the power games are played out in terms of money and political influence:

> Patel: He had acquired three acres of prime land – in the heart of the city – from the state. Your grandfather's political influence had been used. A few days later the surgery was done. (350)

With Dattani it is never a watertight compartment for any situation, he doesn't blame one squarely or absolve the other totally. On the usual split level stage that is a Dattani trademark, the realistic level is the bed-sitter of Chandan in London, now playwright Dan. The set below is the stark zone of memory where Bharati's father, though physically absent, remains an omniscient presence, at once most powerful and devastative along with the God-like Dr Thakkar.

In the play Dr Thakkar represents science; Bharati's father represents the patriarchal ideology that neutralizes science even; while Bharati represents the typical female psyche of our society where one prefers a male child over a girl child. In a sense, politics is played on the body of Tara/Chandan and it becomes a site of contradictions, a site of mutilation of scientific ethics and massacre of God and Nature.

There is a difference between sex and gender. Sex is a biological term, whereas gender is societal. Dattani has depicted the perspectives of the gender of the characters in this play. Right from the beginning one can see the gender politics in the play. Like, in one of the scenes, where Bharati has finished her puja and Patel is getting ready to go to work depicts stereotypical gender roles in the Indian society, and Dattani makes full use of them to bring home his point. Now, here, we can observe his use of those stereotypical roles of man and woman. This thing also shows the gender perspective of the Indian society. Another example is where we can see the Indian gender perspective when Tara explains to Roopa about the conversation between the father and son. She says:

> The men in the house were deciding on whether they were going to hunting while the women looked after the caves.

One can explicitly find the Indian gender perspective that it is man's duty to earn for his family, whereas a woman has to work only in the house. Her work is to look after her house, husband and children. This is her world. She can't break this rule. Patel goes about trying to push his male and female children into separate troughs, into the stereotyped gender roles that would help fit into society while actually hurting them both, since Chandan wants to become a writer and Tara wants to follow her father's profession. Patel becomes furious with Bharati and accuses her of "turning him into a sissy – teaching him how to knit!". This is suggestive of Patel's hegemonic patriarchy when he insists that 'proper' division in the gender roles be made – with different set of plans for the boy and the girl. He seems much beleaguered and says to Bharati, "Yes, call me a liar, a wife beater, a child abuser. It's what you want me to be! And you. You want them to believe you love them very much". And again he tells Tara: "Tara, please believe me when I say that I love you very much and I have never loved you less or more than I have loved your brother. But you mother..." but Tara was always led to believe that it is she who has always been discriminated against by her father, and always gained the extra bit of affection from her mother. This revelation brings Bharati to the brink of insanity and hysteria. Tara learns the truth that it was Bharati's decision that deprived her of what she wanted more than anything else in the world – second leg. It shatters her and she says: "And she called me her star!"

Tara could have made her deficiency her strength and fight the society to carve a place of her own. She is discouraged openly, notwithstanding her feelings in the matter, even though she is more intelligent, sharp and witty, and would perform well if given opportunities in life. Economic and cultural factors have been responsible for the antipathy against and inferiorization of the girl child. Tara is killed by social system, which controls the minds and actions of the people.

Again there is intense focus on the body, and a climactic moment is reached when Bharati decides to donate her kidney to Tara. This is an attempt towards a psychological redemption and she contests the politics of patriarchy that marks women's bodies as sites of ownership and domination, and Patel exercises his ownership on Bharati's kidney now. The 'kidney' becomes a metaphor for psychological purging for Bharati. For Patel, Bharati's kidney donation would absolve her and he cannot allow that to happen since he has a phallocentric hold on her body. He gives in when she overturns the hierarchy model and threatens disclosure.

*Tara* is narrativization of the body – gender politics and problematics – constructed and deconstructed through dramatic expression, and the body of the conjoined twins and later the 'kidney' of Bharati are the contested sites in the play.

Dattani ends the play with metatheatrical objectives rightly explored, with projection of 'wholeness' in the identity, without any handicap or congenital disabilities. Dan escapes to anonymity in London and remains 'without a personal history', not able to make any progress with his writing career as a playwright, "alive but divorced from all his realities" while Tara is dead.

Despite the surface of 'medical improbabilities' and unrealities in the subject of this play, Dattani has successfully explored the questions of gender, body politics, the family and its relationship with the self.

## Works Cited

Chakraborty, Kaustav [ed]: *Indian Dram in English*, PHI Learning Private Ltd, New Delhi 2011.

Dattani, Mahesh, *Collected Plays*, Penguin, New Delhi.

Kuthari Chaudhuri, Asha: *Contemporary Indian Writers in English*, Mahesh Dattani, Foundation Books, 2008.

Naik, M. K. *A History of Indian writing in English*, New Delhi. Sahitya Akademi, 1995.

Nayar, Pramod K. *Postcolonial Literature: An Introduction*, Pearson, 2011.

Subramanyam, Lakshmi (ed). *Muffled Voices: Women in Modern Indian Theatre*, New Delhi, Shakti, 2002.

# 2

# Feminizing the "Other": A Critical Survey of Dattani's *Seven Steps around the Fire*

— Nibedita Mukherjee

Mahesh Dattani's illustrious career deals with themes which are often considered to be a taboo in the orthodox Indian society. The collective unconscious of the Indian urban majority is highlighted and exposed in powerful verbal battles where the readers and spectators are forced to encounter issues which are generally relegated to the periphery of the conscious mind. So great is the impulsion to expose the dark, the hidden and violated issues that even when Dattani writes an investigative radio play *Seven Steps around the Fire* it is the marginalised 'Hijra' community who come to the limelight and the play transcends its narrow boundary and becomes a universal saga of love, hatred, pain, death and agony.

However, in course of the play the hijras are almost united with the other most neglected section of society, i.e., the females. The names adopted by the hijra's in Dattani's plays such as Anarkali, Champa, Kamala are feminine in origin and in no way different from Uma, the Commissioner's daughter-in-law. The treatment meted out to them, i.e. the hijras and Uma, are also the same. Both are subject to mercy of the patriarchal society which considers as "other" anyone who is not male. So, if *Seven Steps around the Fire* is a play highlighting the suffering of the hijras then it also portrays the suffering of the female.

Jane Flax, while studying gender relations, had commented, "Through gender relations two types of persons are created – man and woman. Man and woman are posited as exclusionary categories. One can only be one gender, never the other or both" (628-629).

From this perspective both the hijras and the female are "devoiced". They both fall under the category of the derogatory "other" and are both relegated to the periphery of social existence. Both in feminism and psycho-analytic criticism, the word "sexuality" has multiple interpretations, but here it has been used in two basic concepts, i.e. biological and social. 'Gender Identity" or "gendered subjectivity" brings within its compass not only the biological females but also the "not males". Lacan's abstract and abstruse theory also supports this social construct of "other than male" and speaks of the rejection of self. This is also presented as "social castration and "penis envy" and has been strongly challenged by Simone de Beauvoir (411).

In Dattani's plays language works an intrinsic pattern through which the invisible becomes visible and margin comes to the centre. "The ideological apparatus" (Louis Althusser) comprising of the "voices" of society, i.e., the media and the literatures invariably operate to maintain silence about the de-voiced of society, i.e the subalterns (women and the hijras) who are forever neglected. But for Dattani, this language whose silence had become a tool of oppression becomes a medium of voicing a protest against the heterocentric milieu. His stage setting, his dialogue and even sound – all work together in weaving a pattern of protest against the politics of "invisibilisation". In discussing about this language of protest in post colonial literature, Bill Ashcroft, Gareth, Griffith and Helen Tiffin comment:

> Language is a fundamental site of struggle for post-colonial discourse because the colonial process itself begins in language. The control over language by the imperial centre – whether achieved by displacing native languages, by installing itself as a 'standard'

> against other variants which are constituted as 'impurities', or by planting the language of empire in a new place – remains the most portent instrument of cultural control (283).

Quiet naturally, language proves to be the sight of native struggle even after the end of the colonial rule. The colonisers were now replaced by the "mimic men" and men with "black skin/white faces" (Franz Fanon) who took upon themselves the onus of ruling the society. Those at the margin, i.e., the females, the tribals, the hijras, the criminalised and downtrodden, remained at the margin and language (or the absence of it) became the medium of oppression. But mere invisibility of issue does not make it disappear "but of [these] we would rather not talk about; issues we would conveniently coverup with a rug and act as though they do not exist" (Saraswati 2).

Mahesh Dattani's play *Seven Steps around the Fire* was first performed as *Seven Circles around the Fire* in 1999 and symbolically begins with the sound of a Hindu marriage being performed:

> Sanskrit mantras fade in, the ones chanted during Hindu wedding.
> Fire. The soundo of the fire grows louder, drowning the mantras.
> A scream. Flames engulf the scream (7).

Here three sounds together form a language collage. The sound of Vedic mantras and that of the crackling fire symbolises the main stream heterogeneous society. It silences the scream of the hijras who stand outside this main stream. They are needed to make marriage a success but they have no power to transgress the dictums of society and enter within. But does the scream speak only of the hijras? Or does it speak of the other non-male entity that is brought under male subjectivity through the Vedic ritual of marriage. According to Hindu marriage concept women are needed to carry the family line forwarded, so they are important only for biological reason and the patriarchal society does not allow them an identity or individuality. Uma, the researcher-sleuth of the play, has a strong personal identity as she reveals to Anarkali, "I teach at Bangalore University...I teach Sociology" (12). But such commendable identity does not have any value for the patriarchal society, there she is only known as, "the daughter-in-law of the Deputy Commissioner and the wife of the Superintendent" (7). The sense of being identified by male identity is so powerful and deeply embedded that even Uma herself resorts from time to time, "I am DCP Rao's daughter-in-law" (30) or "Could you put me through to the Vice-Chancellor's office?...This is his daughter, Uma Rao" (19).

Both Uma and the hijras stand as a strong contrast to the male section of society and the dramatist introduces the "it-she" dialectic to highlight the hypocrisy imminent. For the researcher-sleuth Uma the hijra is a "she" but to Munswamy a hijra is merely a nonentity and he addresses her as "it". Here Munswamy, though a mere constable, represents the peatriarchy who believe in binding the society with iron rules. Uma desires to meet Anarkali, a hijra accused of killing one of her brethren but Munswamy tries to draw her attention elsewhere:

> Uma: Will she talk to me?
> Munswamy: (chuckling). She? Ofcourse it will talk to you. We will beat it up if it doesn't (7).

Munswamy fails to understand Uma's interest in a hijra who is supposedly even forsaken by God and therefore misformed. He offers Uma a number of other cases, "man killing wife, wife killing man's lover, brother killing brother. And that shelf is full of dowry death cases" (7) all of which he considers much superior to the murder of a mere hijra. The atrocity is so profound that despite having feminine preference, Anarkali is put in the male section of the prison where the prisoners get pleasure out of violating her existence.

Both the hijras and women are objects of sexual desire (however perverted it may be) and their own wish does not really matter to the males. In sheer disgust Anarkali comments, "After servicing all these sons of whores, my mouth is too tired to talk"(8). Uma's situation is certainly no better though she has to serve as a whore within the sphere of marriage. In a poignant scene seething with undercurrents, Dattani writes:

> Interior. The bedroom of Suresh and Uma.
>
> A Hindi movie fight scene blaring from a TV set in the next room.
>
> Suresh. That is just the sort of name a hijra would fancy.
>
> (*Chuckles*) Anarkali!
>
> Uma. Why do they put her in a male prison?
>
> Suresh. They are as strong as horses. Wear the purple one.
>
> Uma. I wore it last night.
>
> Suresh. Again.
>
> Silence. Uma opens the wardrobe.
>
> Good.
>
> ..........
>
> Suresh. Look, it is one thing that I am allowing you to go through these cases for your thesis, but don't feel any compassion for them. They will take advantage...Keep your soft heart for me.
>
> Uma. What is the evidence against Anarkali?
>
> Suresh. Come here.
>
> *Silence. Uma lies down on the bed. Suresh moans with pleasure as he kisses her* (9-10).

This existence of violation is here powerfully portrayed by Dattani in this scene where Uma's feminity is violated by Suresh, her husband and patriarchal prototype. Here the class-gender based power implication achieves a different status altogether. The female and hijras both become sites for male domination. It is probably for this reason that Uma and Anarkali decide to call each other "sisters". This relationship exhibits the similarity of the male torture inflicted upon both the women and the hijras and Anarkali comments, "Maybe you are more unhappy than I am" (14).

But who are the hijras? This is a question Uma tries to trace in the course of her sociological study. The term hijra, she points out, is of Urdu origin. It is derived from the Arabic root "hijr" in the sense of "leaving one's tribe". The Indian usage is translated into English as "eununch" or "hermaphrodite" where "the irregularity of the male genitalia is central to the definition". They usually lead a closely knit community life and their day-to-day affairs are bounded in secrecy. Whether they are homosexuals, transvestites, or transgender remains a matter of debate. Though debarred from society their blessing remains essential to the wellbeing of society. Their origin can be traced back to Hindu myths and Uma in a "voice-over" thinks:

> Another legend traces their ancestry to the *Ramayana.* The purpose of this case study is to show their position in society perceived as the lowest of the low, they yearn for family and love. The two events in main stream Hindu culture where their presence is acceptable – marriage and birth – ironically are the very same privileges denied to them by man and nature.
>
> Not for them the seven rounds witnessed by the fire god, eternally binding man and woman in matrimony, or the blessings of "may you be the mother of a hundred sons"(11).

Thus victimised by both man and nature the hijras remain a mystery to all – the patriarchal, heterogeneous society fails to comprehend their nature and therefore use abusive language in referring to them. Munswamy considers them to be a matter of "shame"(8) while Suresh calls them "liars". He feels that they can have no human relationships – "what's that you said? Sister? There is no such thing for them. More lies. They are all just castrated degenerate men"(10). They have no human identity for a successful male like Suresh, the Superintendent of Police and he refers to Anarkali as "the thing", a mere "bud of pomegranade". Uma feels a strange kinship with them and wonders:

> Nobody seems to know anything about them. Neither do they. Did they come to this country with Islam, or are they a part of our glorious Hindu tradition? Why are they so obsessed with weddings and ceremonies of childbirth? How do they come to

> know of these weddings? Why do they just show up without being invited? Are they just extortionists? (16).

But for Uma, who in a way also represents the "subaltern" (for she is silently fighting a battle against male domination and patriarchal concepts), the hijras like Anarkali and Champa are "also" a part of society. Here "also" has specific significance for it indicates not a parallel social institution but rather a intermingling, an association within the heterogeneous society. So Dattani's use of language indicates a social inclusion for the "other" and he goes on to highlight the close-knit, hierarchical structure of the hijras. Champa points out that she is the "Guru" or the "head hijra" and has the right to decide the next Guru. Similarly, the hijras do not support marriage for it highlights social inclusion and therefore Anarkali scars the face of Kamala, the beautiful hijra who wanted to marry Subbu. There is infighting but at the same time love and relations exist between them. Anarkali comments:

> We make our relations with our eyes. With our love. I look at him, he looks at me, and he is my brother. I look at you, you look at me, and we are mother and daughter (11).

But society holds a taboo against them and even Uma wonders whether they are after all, mere criminals. But this is again negated by Dattani when Champa says, "Are you mad? Hold the bag tightly. You should not bring so much money in to such places" (24).

Motherhood is a blessing which the hijras confer upon the newly wedded couple and motherhood is biologically the result of the union between the male and female. But in this patriarchal society it is the woman who are alone held responsible for the lack of motherhood. Uma's foster mother had failed in this regard and she blamed the hijras for it. Uma voices her thoughts about this matter:

> Is it true? Could it be true what my mother used to say about them? Did they really put a curse on her because they did not allow them to sing and dance at their wedding? Or was that their explanation for not being able to have children of their own? Or...a reason to give to people for wanting to adopt me (17).

If not being able to give birth is a curse then Uma too bears it. Being a modern woman she is well aware that the fault can be with her husband too but he declines to get himself checked. She implores her husband but to no avail:

> Uma. I went to the doctor again. Your mother insisted she take me.
> Suresh. What did they say?
> Uma. Nothing...They want to see you.
> Suresh. I don't think so.
> Uma. Just a test for your sperm count.
> Suresh. I don't have to go...(32).

So Suresh, being a male enjoys the privilege of deciding whether he goes to the doctor or not while society goes on blaming his wife for her childlessness. But Dattani's woman is certainly different from her predecessors. She has the courage to take independent decisions and in a telephonic conversation, Uma tells her father:

> I wish I could come back and live here with you...I just might...Well, you taught me to do exactly what I want to do, and one day I just might...(19).

So freedom for the New Woman appears at the horizon but no such independendence is visible for the "other", the hijras. Forit is not the heterogeneous society alone which has closeted the hijras. They themselves believe in this demeaning role and hence come to bless the marriage of the minister's son who in reality was responsible for the death of Kamala, the beautiful hijra. This is revealed in a final voice-over. In stoical, powerful language Uma comments:

> They knew. Anarkali, Champa and all the hijra people knew who was behind the killing of Kamala. They have no voice. The case was hushed up and not even reported in the newspapers. Champa was right. The police made no arrests. Subbu's suicide was written off as an accident. The photograph was destroyed. So were the lives of two young people...(42).

## Works Cited


Althusser, Louis. *On Ideology (Radical Thinkers)*, Trans. Ben Brewester. London: Verso, 2008. Print.

Ashcroft, Bill, et al. *The Empire Writes Back*. 2nd Ed. London: Routledge 2002. Print.

Beauvoir, Simone de. *The Second Sex*. 1949. Reprint. Harmondsworth, England: Penguin, 1972. Print.

Dattani, Mahesh. *Collected Plays*. New Delhi: Penguin, 2000. Print.

Fanon, Franz. *The Wretched of the Earth*. New York: Grove Weidenfeld, 1963. Print.

Saraswati, L. "Deconstructing Gender in Mahesh Dattani's Tara and Dance Like a Man". *The Quest*. 20.2 (Dec 2006). Print.

# 3

# Influence of Patriarchy in Moulding Mother-Daughter Relationship in *Tara*

— Daxa Thakor

## Introduction

Women constitute about one-half of the global population, but they are placed at various disadvantageous positions due to gender differences and bias. Women in Indian society have been victims of humiliation, torture, exploitation and discrimination in spite of legislative measures, spread of education and economic independence. They are still relegated to second class status that makes them more vulnerable to abuse and less able to protect themselves from discrimination.

In the Indian culture, since the very early periods, women as a group have been dominated by men, and their status has been low in family and society. Such attitude of society in Third World developing countries also exist. Different schools look at it differently. The most popular approach is of the feminist school. They argue that women are oppressed within the household is due to the dominance of patriarchy. They argue that patriarchy is a form of social system characterized by men dominating over women within and outside the household. The women are bound by different laws, institutions and beliefs formed by rishies and brahmins which are made by the patriarchy for that on benefits. For the low status of women, most often, brahmanical austerities on the entire society is responsible. They try to influence the whole society that it is the son who can give them 'moksha'. Parents without a male child feel guilty about it. They say that their stars are not in their favour, maybe because of their past misdoing. It is the son who only can give name and fame to their families.

In addition to all this, some parts of *Garudaquran or Manusmruti* force the uneducated or low profile women to surrender themselves to whatever is written on the religious pages. A woman is taught to respect all the males in the family. Hindu tradition is such that a woman's life is hemmed in by a web of duties to her husband, her 'pati-parameshwara' and where she is conjoined to stay faithful to him irrespective of his character or treatment of her.

The Law of Manu, 5.154, says that a virtuous wife should constantly serve her husband like a God, even if he behaves badly, or freely indulges in his lust, and is devoid of any good qualities. Woman having relations with more than one person is considered as characterless or 'kulkalankini' while people have no concern at all with the man who has illicit relationship with more than one woman. In creating such attitudes among people, females also sometimes play an important role in giving respect to other women. There is need of sisterhood concept among females of the society. Especially, a mother has to change her attitude towards her daughters or daughters-in-law. They must not be oppressed by the mother-in-law. She must not oppress them by banning them from doing this or that but should be given freedom and courage to fight against the injustice heared on them by the male section.

The important thing is that there should be a balanced attitude for both males and females. If required, there should be a good combination of tradition and modernity to create a healthy society. The tradition-modernity gets further complicated on account of the heterogeneity of our society and the asymmetrical growth and development among different regions and sections of it. What may be modern in a rural setting may be traditional in a city. The whole question is highly complex and can best be studied not in terms of tradition-modern dichotomy, but in terms of social and cultural change and interaction between the two. Woman with traditional virtues suffers from subordination, dharma, sexual purity and silence. The subordination or acceptance of male authority, whether of father, husband or son, sexual purity, both premarital virginal and merital fertility and silence are all cherished Indian values sanctified by tradition and particularly enjoined upon women.

Today to some extent, women are seen moving towards autonomy, personal goals, sexual emancipation and speech under the impact of new ideas but somewhere somehow still women are influenced by traditional thinking. They can't be rid of them. An Indian woman's self-perception as also the society expectations from her have for long been largely determined by the complex of ideas, values and beliefs codified in the *Manusmruti*. Still, most of the women, as per the laws of Manu, 5.148, are in childhood under their father's control, in youth under their husband's and when their husband dies, under their son's care. A woman is not entitled to have an independent life. Now it is expected from the women to change their attitude at least while looking at other females with some positivity, constructivity, sensitivity, understanding, confidence and love. To transform the present society, many people have tried their best by using different media like television, newspapers, periodicals, ICT tools, etc. Literary work is also considered as one of the strongest media to mirror and reflect the contemporary society in their different forms of literature like short stories, novels, poetry, drama to teach the way of life to the readers. The novel is considered the best form of it. But during the post-Independence period in India the drama played an important role in awakening the sleeping society from a deep slumber to change their traditional thinking adopting new attitudes.

## Dattani's Concept about Women

Mahesh Duttani is one of the best playwrights to have mirrored the threatening aspects of the society to force the readers to think over the issues to be solved. His profile by Anita Nyre says, "I believe in justice and fairness and something that doesn't make me angry. Just as prejudices too." His opinion is that women should also be treated with equality. They should be also given the respect given to the male section of the society. To depict women's mentality, the real position in his plays, the traditional women as the mother is portrayed with some contempt, be it Sonal of *Where There is a Will*, Prema in *Do the Needful*, Baa in *Bravely Fought the Queen*, Aruna in *Final Solutions*, Bharati in *Tara*, etc. Mahesh Duttani belongs to the pro-feministic attitude, which passes a favourable attitude towards women. So far as the perception of women is concerned, he is quite unconventional. He tries to discover different facets of feminine psyche. His works depict constant battle between the feminine psyche and patriarchal order. He replies to Lakshmi Subraminiam when being interviewed, "They are humans. They want something. They face obstacles. They will do anything in their power to get it. All eyes focus on in the powerlessness of sensibility for political correctness either. My only defence is to say that I am not biased against women".

The mother-daughter relation is considered one of the best relations among other human relations as each one of them feels incomplete without the other. Generally a mother loves her daughter a lot. But the mother, who is highly influenced and affected by patriarchal hierarchy, hates her girl child or does not give that much care that she gives to her son. She always advises her, what to do and what not. Normally she gives all the freedom to her son which he expects. Perhaps, this bias leads the girl child to hate the 'male-dominated society.' She wants equal treatment from society, at least, from her mother.

## Mother's Decision and Tara's Life

This paper presents how Mahesh Duttani has described the influence of patriarchy in moulding the mother's mentality and the mother-daughter relationship in his third play *Tara. Tara* is the most touching three-act play by Duttani. It presents a tale of Siamese twins, namely, Tara and Chandan. The play oscillates between the past and the present events. Chandan is the narrator in the play. The story of the drama moves out from his memory. The playwright has used the 'stream of consciousness'-like technique as many modern novelist have used to make the movement of the story of their work more authentic, more forceful. A sense of guilt grips his conscious, so Chandan has changed his name to Dan to free himself from the burden of Tara, his sister, and shifted to London. But there also he is not free from past memory.

Tara and Chandan are Siamese twins. They are separated after three months of their birth. Actually, they were conjoined at the chest and had three legs. The chances of survival of the third leg was more with Tara. The medical report was in favour of Tara. But as a woman's life is always structured and governed by patriarchy since time immemorial, in the play, the mother is proved the worst enemy of her daughter Tara. The mother, Bharati, prefers the male child to be operated with the third leg against the medical report and strengthen the chain of injustice. With the difficult operation that separates the twins the third leg has to be given to one of the babies, leaving the other crippled for life. The twins' mother persuades her wealthy politician father to bribe the doctor to give the third leg to her son. Accordingly, the doctor goes against the decision dictated by medical evidence and gives the leg to the boy. As most of the blood supply actually came from the girl, the leg dies a few days after the operation, leaving both the children instead of one crippled for life. If the leg had been given to Tara, she might lived a better life. Dr. Thakkar insists on it, but the mother wants to make her son perfect. Not the daughter. She knows very well that a physically or mentally disabled girl has to suffer a lot. Directly Tara's father, Mr. Patel, is not involved in the decision but he never utters a single word against his wife's decision. So he is also as much responsible as Bharati for making Tara's life miserable.

Every girl child born in an Indian family suffers from some kind of exploitation. Even by her mother and if there is a male child in the family, the mistreatment to the girl child is visible as consciously or unconsciously all the privileges are offered to the son. If the family is financially sound, such things are rare. But if it is middle class or lower class, it happens often.

The play symbolizes the modern society which claims to be liberal and advanced but in fact has a cripple mentality. It is a society where mothers are educated. Still they have typical a Indian mindset which differentiates the girl child treatment from a male child. All the promises of equality between male and female are false. If an Indian mother is asked about her first expected baby, definitely, she would prefer a male child. Mahesh Duttani reveals in one of his interviews with Lakshmi Subramaniam, "I see *Tara* as a play about the male self and female self. The female self is being preferred in all cultures." Whereas the famous theatre director Erin Mee writes in the note of the play, "*Tara* centers on the emotional separation that grows between two conjoined twins following the discovery that their physical separation was manipulated by their mother herself and grandfather to favor the boy."

In the play, it is shown that the socio-cultural myths and conventions control and construct the course of the human life. Sometimes they damage the bond of familial relationship. Despite the civilization and development in the human field, we are still rooted to the past in our mind. Bharati's love for her daughter is pure. She loves her very much. She knows that in society, a physically handicapped girl child has no right to live. Nobody respects her. Bharati is quite fearful about the future of her daughter. She says, "It's all right while she is young. It is all very cute and comfortable when she makes witty remarks. But let her grow up. Yes, Chandan, the world will tolerate you. The world will accept you but not her! But let her grow up. Yes, Chandan, the world will tolerate you. The world will accept you but not her!... when she sees herself a eighteen or twenty, thirty is unthinkable and what about forty and fifty! Oh God!" But we can see that in the play the mother-daughter relationship proves secondary to the orders of patriarchy. Tara's father is a symbol of male domination by society. He holds absolute power in taking decisions for the family. Bharati has no right to interfere in it. She has to follow her husband's wishes. Such kind of family background has, perhaps, made her give preference to the male child, even though she loves her daughter very much.

Dr. Thakkar is God-like. If he wishes he can strongly support Tara by following natural justice. But he has done an unfair operation by collaborating with Bharati and her politician father, and gives the male child, better chances physically. He, the life giver, is aware of the fact that the third leg would adhere better to the female half and yet goes against his better judegement. The question is: why is she denied the privilege of the good leg even though it is her right? It is only because she is a girl child.

In our society, it is a curse to be a girl. The order of society is such that she can be trapped and blackmailed anywhere by anyone. Perhaps, this is also one of the biggest reasons why the Indian mother dislikes a girl child. In our country, so much partiality and differentiation is there for women. No doubt, there might be some families where thay might be treating both male and female children equally. But they are very few. In most of the cases, it has not happened. First of all, they think only about their son's better prospects and future and then only think about the girl child. In doing this, the mother is also playing an important role. Bharati symbolizes such an Indian mother.

No doubt, Bharati feels guilty for doing this injustice to her daughter. She tries to come out from this anguish by offering her kidney to Tara. She tries to shower more love on her. She always thinks about her future. All these reveal that just like the mothers of Shashi Despande's novels, this mother is by nature not the worst enemy of her daughter. She decides to give a better chance to Chandan. But for her, it does not mean that she will leave Tara at her fate. She takes all possible care of her. Tara's father has always done injustice to Tara. But he wants to escape from this fact, so whenever he gets chance, he tells Bharati that she is responsible for the tragic condition of Tara. Actually, not only the mother, but also the father is equally responsible for the misfortune of Tara. Otherwise he might have come forward and stood against Bharati's decision. When Bharati tries to donate one of her kidneys body to Tara and craves satisfaction out of this, Mr. Patel disapproves of her idea. To conceal the worst mentality of Mr. Patel, Bharati tells lie that it will involve expenses. She tries to assert her moral superiority over her husband. They have a conversation…

> Bharati: (pleadingly) why won't you let me do it?
>
> Mr. Patel: (Controlling) Need I tell you? Because I do not want you to have the satisfaction of doing it.
>
> Bharati: I will do it.
>
> Mr. Patel: You will have to obey me. It's my turn now.
>
> Bharati: I want to give her a part of me! (*CP* 344)

This dialogue reveals that Mr. Patel wants to prove that now it is his turn to take a decision for Tara. It proves that one turn to take a decision regarding Tara was already given to Bharati when she decided to give the third leg to Chandan. As that decision was as per Mr. Patel's mentality, he had not taken any objection in implementing it. If she had not taken the decision, it might have been taken by her husband because he always nurtured the patriarchal ideology and liked other to follow his decisions. It also shows that now as a mother of Tara, leaving patriarchal dichotomy aside, she wants to take a decision and she firmly tells Mr. Patel that she will do what she wants to do. Her firmness shows her pure motherly love for Tara. She wants to make the right decision this time. Her excessive care for Tara and immense exposure of her love for Tara is the result of her past grave blunder. She is quite conscious of her past wrong deed and feels the full pressure of her guilt. Her efforts to compensate for the loss caused to Tara by her, causes a conflict with her husband that ultimately leads her to a mental breakdown.

When Bharati is hospitalized, Tara wants to see her personally. But, her father does not allow her to do so. So, she begins to hate her father. She thinks that her mother wants to tell her something about her father which he prevents from disclosing. To win a place in Tara's heart, he discloses to her the truth, "Your grandfather and your mother had a private meeting with Dr. Thakkar. I wasn't asked to come. That same evening, your mother told me of a decision. Everything will be done as planned. Except... I couldn't believe what she told me... what a grave mistake they made." No doubt, the decision was taken by Bharati, but he was also as responsible as Bharati. Otherwise after that he might have thought about Tara's future and intervened on her behalf.

When Tara comes to know that it was her mother who had made such a decision, she is unable to bear this truth and the shock takes away her life. She was more intelligent, sharp and witty and would have performed much better than the male child would, if only she had been given a chance. Before the exposure of the truth, she thought, "I will spend the rest of my life feeding and clothing those... starving, naked millions everywhere. Maybe I can start an institution that will... do all that. Or I could join Mother Teresa and sacrifice myself to a great cause. That may give... purpose to my existence."(370)

If her parents had given her moral support, she might have done all the good deeds which a normal girl does but the father's revelation of truth made her lose interest in life altogether. She did not want to survive and that's why she refused to have any physiotherapy treatment or to go to college.

In the play, Duttani shows how women feel suffocated under the evil clutch of patriarchy and gender bias. For a healthy society to survive, a sound position of family life is necessary unlike Mr. Patel's family life where the foundation of the future was weak to make it stand strongly forever. Mothers are basically good. Educated mothers are capable enough of doing good to their children but in this male- dominated society, their mentality can't be free from this gender bias because since their childhood, they have been dependent upon their male siblings. If this continues, our society will not survive longer and tragedies like those in Tara's life will continue to occur forever.

## Works Cited

Das, Bijay Kumar: *Postmodern Indian English Litrature*, Nice Printing Press, Delhi, 2006

Dattani, Hahesh: *Collected Plays*. Panguin Edition, New Delhi, 2000.

Fareed, Sadaf: Tara: a voice of Voiceless (article) Interview with Mahesh Dattani.

Kuthari, Chaudhuri, Asha: *Contemporary Indian Writers in English Mahesh Dattani*, New Delhi, Foundation Books Pvt. Ltd., Cambridge House, 2005.

Mehrotra, Arvind, *History of Indian Literature in English*.

Nyre, Anita, *Profile of Mahesh Dattani*.

Parmar, B.R: *A Critical Study of Mahesh Dattani's Stage Plays*. (article) Shodhganga in flibnet. ac. in

Raina, Rita: 'A note on the play, *Where There is a Will' in Collected Plays Mahesh Dattani*, New Delhi, Penguin Books, 2000.

Sharma, Laxmi: Mahesh Dattani's *Where There is a Will*, www literaryindia.com

Sharma, Ram: Social issues in the plays of Mahesh Dattani. Article posted on net 11/7/2008. www.amazines.com

Shriram, Review: *Where There is a Will www.johetimes.com*

# 4

# Patriarchy and Gender Preferance in Mahesh Dattanis's *Tara*

— N. Anisha

> The patriarchal construction of the difference between masculinity and femininity is the political difference between freedom and subjection.
>
> (Pateman 207)

Patriarchy is a "social organization marked by the supremacy of the father in the clan or family, the legal dependence of wives and children, and the reckoning of descent and inheritance in the male line; broadly: control by men of a disproportionately large share of power" (Merriam-Webster). Gender is also a social construct specifying the socially and culturally prescribed roles that men and women are to follow. According to Gerda Lerner in *The Creation of Patriarchy*, gender is the "costume, a mask, a straitjacket in which men and women dance their unequal dance" (238).

Western female thought through the centuries has identified the relationship between patriarchy and gender as crucial to the women's subordinate position. For two hundred years, patriarchy precluded women from having a legal or political identity and the legislation and attitudes supporting this provided the model for slavery. In *Patriarchy, Structure and Gender Inequality* Walby reveals how patriarchy operates to achieve and maintain the gender inequalities essential for the subordination of women. Kate

Millet in *Sexual Politics* explores the term patriarchy and finds it the cause of women's oppression.

Mahesh Dattani's play *Tara* questions the society that treats the children of the same womb in two different ways. The play *Tara* was first performed as *Twinkle Tara* at Chidian Hall, Bangalore on 23 October 1990 by Playpen Performing Arts Group. Dattani's *Tara* is a powerful play about two children (twins) born with three legs between them—two on the girl's side with regular blood flow and one on the boy's side. The family took a decision to operate them giving two legs to the boy and one to the girl. Tara died and Chandan was crippled. Erin Mee writes in the note of the play:

> *Tara* centers on the emotional separation that grows between two conjoined twins following the discovery that their physical separation was manipulated by their mother and grandfather to favor the boy [ Chandan] over the girl [ Tara]. Tara, a feisty girl who isn't given the opportunities given to her brother [although she may be smarter ] eventually wastes away and dies. Chandan escapes to London, changes his name to Dan, and attempts to repress the guilt he feels over his sister's death by living without a personal history. Woven into the play are issues of class and community, and the clash between traditional and modern lifestyles and values.
>
> (*Collected Plays* 319)

*Tara* is the story of every girl child born in Indian family, where patriarchal conventions have a strong hand to silence female members. We can clearly make out that Tara's family consciously propounding privileges to their male child alone. The play throws light on the gender prejudices prevalent in our society. "To tell you the truth,I had even forgotten I had a twin sister." The play opens with the monologue of Dan where he ingeniously speaks about the male mindset of 'othering' one's female sister.

*Tara* brings in front of us the strict gender roles that we practice in our day today life. Right from the beginning we can see the difference between male and female in the scene where

Bharati has finished her *pooja,* and Patel is getting ready to go to work. Gendered roles are accepted by the society as natural and hardly does anyone bother to go beyond those norms. Thus Patel finds it strange when Chandan is helping his mother to sort out her mistake in knitting

> PATEL. Let Tara do it.
> CHANDAN. It's okay.
> PATEL. Give it to her.
> CHANDAN. Why?
> PATEL. Chandan, leave that damn thing alone!...
> PATEL (to Bharati). How dare you do this to him?...you can think of turning him into a sissy teaching him to hit! (*CP* 151)

These words of Patel highlight how certain roles have been confirmed as feminine in the society and how the society opposes any sort of reversed role. Under patriarchy, women's identity is defined by men.

Another example is that when Tara explains to Roopa about the conversation between father and son, she says that, "The men in the house were deciding on whether they were going to hunt while the women looked after the caves" (*CP* 328). Now, here, we can see explicitly the Indian gender perspective that man's work is taking care of his family, where as women have to work only in the house. Her work is to look after her house, husband and children and the important family decisions are taken by the male members.. In her essay, Asha Kothari says, "Dattani plays with the idea of female infanticide that is prevalent among Gujarati's through the various intimations that Roopa makes, and also suggests Patel's hegemonic patriarchy when he insists that 'proper' division in the gender roles be made with different sets or plans for the boys and the girls" (*Mahesh Dattani* 89).

Roopa, Tara's neighbour in Bombay, explained to Tara how **the Patels would drown their newborn girl child in bowls of milk:**

> Roopa: (to Tara) Since you insist, I will tell you. It may not be true. But this is what I have heard? The Patels in the old days were unhappy with getting girl babies—you know dowry and things like that-so they used to drown them in milk.So when people asked them how the baby died, they could say that she choked while drinking her milk (*CP* 349).

Chandan and Tara's maternal grandfather is a wealthy man who could hardly see his grandson standing on single leg. Thus he bribes the surgeon for doing the unethical job of transplanting the third leg to Chandan's body, which had a better chance of survival with Tara. Bharati agrees to his father's wishes and even Patel too does not protest. But the operation is unsuccessful and both the twins have to depend on an artificial leg. Tara is denied the chance of having both natural legs only because she is a girl child. Dan tries to define Tara, "She never got a fair deal. Not even from nature. Neither of us did. May be God never wanted us separated. Destiny desires strange things... But even God does not always get what he wants. Conflict is the crux of life" (*CP* 330).

In one of the conversations between Patel and Chandan, Dattani probes into the patriarchal mindset of Tara's grandfather.

> PATEL. He [grandfather] left you a lot of money.
>
> CHANDAN. And Tara?
>
> PATEL. Nothing
>
> CHANDAN. Why?
>
> PATEL. It was his money. He could do what he wanted with it (*CP* 360).

This will is a product of strict patriarchy. Despite her intelligence and optimism Tara has been rejected by the male community because of her physical deformity. Here patriarchal mindset is visible, where money spent on girls is considered to be a meaningless act. Bharati knows her daughter's intelligence and courage. She says:

> She…she must make more friends. Chandan is all right-he has his writing, but she… He is different, he is sort of self contained, but Tara…she can be very witty and of course, she is intelligent. I have seen to it that she…more than make up in some ways for what she …doesn't have (*CP* 340).

Tara herself knows that Chandan cannot stand without her support. "What would you do without me?" (*CP* 334). Her words justify Dan's incompleteness after his separation from Tara.

Tara is an intelligent girl but Patel thinks only about the education and future of Chandan. The fact that the male is always given the greater privilege is obvious from Patel's planning for Chandan's education and future career. He says to Chandan, "I was just thinking… It may be a good idea for you to come to the office with me" (*CP* 351).

> PATEL. Chandan is going to study further and he will go abroad for his higher studies.
> BHARATI. And Tara?
> PATEL. When have you ever allowed me to make any plans for her? (*CP* 352)

The relationship of Bharati and Tara is subordinated to her subjugation to the expectations of the society. She has no free will and her compassion for Tara proves weak in her preference for her son Chandan. In *Of Woman Born,* Adrienne Rich makes a clear distinction between two meanings of motherhood: "The potential relationship of any woman to her power of reproduction and to children, and the institution, which aims at ensuring that potential-and all women- shall remain under male control" (13).

Throughout the play we can feel that Tara feels some kind of aversion towards the male-dominated world. She questions, "How do you expect me to feel anything for anyone if they don't give me any feeling to begin with? Why is it wrong for me to be without feeling? Why are you asking me to do something that nobody has done for me?" (*CP* 371). These words of Tara bring in front the silencing of female voice and feelings.

And she continues, "... I have the right to be selfish, like everyone else!" (*CP* 370). She realizes that her alienation and suffering is a part of the selfishness of male members in her family.

The secret of her invalid situation is revealed to her by her father that upsets the innocent child:

> Your grandfather and your mother had a private meeting with Dr. Thakkar. I was not asked to come. That same evening, your mother told me of her decision. Everything will be done as planned. Except.... I couldn't believe what she told me—that they would risk giving both legs to the boy (CP 378).

Tara's last words on the stage reflect her painful surprise at the role taken up by her mother: "And she called me her star!" Bharati, who even calls her daughter as her 'star', under the authority of her father, did injustice to her daughter. She was subordinated to the expectations of patriarchal society. In this story the mother prefers a son to a daughter that finally results in the death of the girl. The play in a sense speaks about female masochism, where Bharati, Tara's mother, feels a kind of satisfaction while practising patriarchy. In a male-dominated society Chandan enjoyes greater preference and Tara is left to enjoy the position of the 'other'.

Mahesh Dattani mentions in one of his interviews with Lakshmi Subramanyam," I see *Tara* as a play about the male self and female self. The male self is being preferred in all cultures. The play is about the separation of self and the resultant angst" (*CP* 134).

The final confession of Dan, "Forgive me Tara, forgive me, for making it my tragedy" (CP 380) gives us the feeling that the tragedy happens only in Chandan's life and not in Tara. Thus Chandan can be seen as a follower of the age-old male- centred system. Unlike her mother, Tara finds the reality that 'men and women are equal'—a reality that no other individual in her family fails to see.

TARA. You. Me. There's no difference.
CHANDAN. No difference between you and me?
TARA. No! Why should there be? (CP 361)

Tara is killed by the age-old social system, which controls the minds and action of the females, where men is the norm, the rule. Men are granted the power to define, interpret, judge and represent the world on their own terms and women are to be defined, interpreted, judged and represented by them. The word "separated" which has been used repeatedly all through the play underlines the main theme of *Tara*-gender separation. It is clear that the identities, roles and relationships that are associated with gender comes about as a result of human agency. They are neither innate nor given but are constructed, made and remade by human beings.

## Works Cited


Anselmi, L. Dina & Ann. Law.*Questions of Gender: Perspectives and Paradoxes*.Virginia: Mc Graw Hill,1998.Print.

Butler, Judith. *Undoing Gender*. New York: Routledge, 2004. Print.

_______. *Gender Trouble: Feminism and Subversion* of *Identity*. New york: Routledge, 1990. Print.

Choudhuri, Asha Kuthari. *Mahesh Dattani*. New Delhi: Foundation Books Pvt. Ltd, 2005. Print.

Dattani, Mahesh. *Collected Plays*. New Delhi: Penguin Publishers, 2000. Print.

Kumar Das, Vijay. *Form and Meaning in Dattani's Plays*. New Delhi: Atlantic, 2008. Print.

Lerner, Gerda. *The Creation of Patriarchy*. New York: OUP, 1986. Print.

Mee, Erin B. "A Note in the Play". *Collected Plays*. New Delhi: Penguin Books, 2000. Print.

Multani, Anglie, ed. *Mahesh Dattani's Plays: Critical Perspectives*. New Delhi: Pencraft International, 2007. Print.

Pateman, Carole. *The Sexual Contract*, Stanford University Press,1988. Print.

Rich, Adrienne Cecile. *Of Woman Born: Motherhood as Experience and Institution*. New York: Norton, 1995. Print.

Subramanyam, Lakshmi, (ed.) *Maffled Voices: Women in Modern Indian Theatre*, New Delhi: Shakti, 2002. Print,

# 5

# Feminist Articulations in Mahesh Dattani's *Tara*

— T. Sasikanth Reddy

Mahesh Dattani is one of the promising Indian English playwrights vocalising for the marginalized victims through the experimental fragmentary settings in his theatres. Most of his plays are a true reflection of his time, place and socioeconomic background. When he won the Sahitya Akademi award for his *Final Solutions and Other Plays,* the Akademi commended that his plays "probe tangled attitude in contemporary India towards communal differences, consumerism and gender... a brilliant contribution to Indian Drama in English."[1]

Dattani's plays are the postmodern attempts that try to map the cultural shifts occurring in the urban India. Some of his major plays *Tara* (1990), *Final Solutions* (1993) and *On a Muggy Night in Mumbai* (1998) depict the impact of the new money power on this urbanized society. Also, he draws the attention of his audience towards the socio-political and cultural conflicts existing in contemporary pluralist India through his stages. Sudha Rani in her critique on Mahesh Dattani, considered him: "a society and... chooses expressionism to illustrate the continuous struggle of urban Indian in familial, social and cultural modernist artist who in such a critical cultural situation selects different forms other than realism to depict the spheres to treat his individual identity".[2]

Dattani's plays can be analyzed through the poststructuralist perspectives like gender theories. Hence, the gender schema approach born out of sex role theories of the mid-80's has been chosen to study the major characters in Mahesh Dattani's *Tara*, reflecting the gender issues as social trauma. As *Tara* is the stage play of multilevel sets the gender issue discussed as content is also multilayered. Sandra Lipsitz Bern, one of the cognitive psychologists of Cornell University, popularizing the gender schema theory views as "the process by which a society transmutes male and female into masculine and feminine is known as the process of sex typing".[3] From this point of view the author tries to discuss the characters of Tara and Chandan born as conjoined twins representing both female self and male self, and explaining how the male has more privileges over the female self in all cultures, and this sex typing is deeply rooted in man-woman psyche of Indian cultures. Tara, the play's title character, is to be studied as the victim of this collective consciousness of the social system.

Dattani has presented the bizarre reality of the woman playing second fiddle to man. This play opens with Chandan changed into Dan in order to absolve himself from the guilt of his sister. He has to bear the brunt of his grandfather's cruelty. He considers himself responsible for his sister's death. In this play Dattani plays with the idea of female infanticide that is prevalent among the Gujratis and also suggests Patel's hegemonic patriarchy when He insists that proper division in the gender be made. *Tara* gives us a glimpse into the modern society which claims to be liberal and advanced in its thought and action. In a society which claims that its mothers are educated today have "Devis" like Durga, Kali, Saraswati, Lakshmi etc. whom not only women but men also pay obeisance, differentiate between a male child and a female child. All the propagandas of equality be male and female, equal opportunities to women in all the fields are belied.

Dattani's deep preoccupation with gender issues leads to the emergence of the idea of the twin side to one's self—quite literally embodied in one body and the separation that follows. He mentioned in one of his interviews with Lakshmi Subramanyam: "I see Tara as a play about the male self and female self. The male self is being preferred in all cultures. The play is about the separation of self and the resultant angst."[4] Erin Mee writes in the note of the play: "Tara centres on the emotional separation that grows between two conjoined twins following the discovery that their physical separation was manipulated by their mother and grandfather to favour the boy [Chandan] over the girl [Tara]. Tara, a feisty girl who isn't given the opportunities given to her brother [although she may be smarter] eventually wastes away and dies. Chandan escapes to London, changes his name to Dan, and attempts to repress the guilt he feels over his sister's death by living without a personal history, woven into the play are issues of class and community, and the clash between traditional and modern lifestyles and values."[5]

*Tara* is the play about a female self viewed through a male self, and the irony is both selves are born as conjoined twins, medically called 'Siamese twins' but they were miraculously separated to survive. The physical separation is made through the surgery. As Dan recollects: "like we've always been Inseparable. The way we started in life. Two lives and one body in one comfortable womb. Till we were forced out - and separated."[6] The story line clearly indicates that when Chandan and Tara turn 15 they start realizing the adulthood as man and woman constructed on them by their parents, Patel and Bharati, who are educated but the social thrust of sex typing phenomena drives them to be discriminating between their children favouring the male child. Bharati's father is also an influencing factor in this misdeed. The twins are conjoined from the chest down though they do not share any vital organs. The conjoined twins are about to be separated but there is a complication as there are three legs. Bharati and her father influence the doctor by bribing him with three acres of prime land in the heart of the city, Bangalore, so that Chandan might have two legs, the weaker third leg would survive on the girl. Yet, Chandan's body rejects the second leg that is later amputated. Dattani has well pointed out that the biologically conjoined twins never experience natural or sex favouritism but socially nurtured gender favouritism. The mother, her father and the surgeon have collaborated to afford the male with better chances. They reflect the social milieu that is always male specific.

Bern's gender schema theory discloses the intricacies of patriarchal society under which both sexes are cognitively schematic to influence any individual to favour the particular gender, male. There is a paradigm in the collaboration of mother, father, grandfather and the male Doctor, Thakkar in favouring the boy, Chandan against the girl, Tara. The system still prevails to treat Tara as subaltern. Bern states: "A schema is a cognitive structure, a network of associations that organizes and guides an individual perception. Schematic processing is thus highly selective and enables the individual to impose structure and meaning onto the vast array of incoming stimuli."[7] She further views it as a "constructive process where in what is perceived is a product of the interaction between the incoming information and the perceivers preexisting schema".[8] This perception would help one know the subtleties of gender construct occurred among the characters of Patel's family and so is the society at large.

Bharati tries to shed her burden of guilt by showing maternal love and concern for her daughter and to assert her moral superior over her husband. She also tries to expatiate by the act of donating kidney to her daughter which was ultimately futile. Dattani establishes that mother and daughter relationship is ultimately subordinated to the directives of patriarchy. All cultures and all countries by establishing values, roles, gender perception, prescribe unequal means to achieve. Dr. Thakkar occupies the one on the highest level throughout the play. Tara and Chandan are conjoined, Siamese twins who must be separated to survive. The dichotomy between the twin 'gendered' selves is recognized, and a physical separation is made through surgery "Like we've always been inseparable. The way we started in life. Two lives and one body in one comfortable womb. Till we were forced out –And separated."[9]

Mr. Patel, an emblem of male chauvinism, maintains his absolute authority in the decision making about the family. Bharati is a pathetic victim of patriarchy. She is exceptionally conscious for her safety for Tara, not for the sake of Tara but for her own sake. It is an irony of fate that Chandan and Tara are entwined in such a way that their separation is impossible. Chandan enjoys greater preference and Tara is left to enjoy the position of a subaltern. The effort to separate them through surgery leaves Tara a cripple for life. The suffering of Tara and Chandan is a symbolic justification to the perception that the grace of the relationship exist not in their separateness but in their moving in a coordination or interdependence. The famous theatre director Erin Mee writes: "Dattani sees Tara as a play about the gendered self, about coming to terms with the feminine side of oneself in a world that always favours what is 'male', but many people in India see it as a play about the girl child."[10]

Tara is more enthusiastic and full of jest and spark of life. She has high aspirations which she cannot accomplish because of her handicapped state while the boy is comfortably ensconced and has come to terms with his handicapped life. Why is Tara then denied the privilege of the good leg. Why? Is it because she is a girl? Is being a girl in the society a curse? Why so much partiality and differentiation done to women in the country which has rich heritage and where women are otherwise placed on the pedestal? Dr. Thakkar belies his godly profession and leads himself to be bribed by Bharati's father into becoming an accomplice in the bizarre act of severing the leg. He should have upheld his profession by denouncing the decision at his inception whereas he in a way took Tara's life by severing the leg. His wise decision could have given Tara a safe, secured and complete life. Patel meanwhile seems much beleaguered: "Yes, call me a liar, a wife beater, a child abuser. It's what you want me to be! And you.You want them to believe you love them very much."[11] Again he tells Tara: "Tara, please believe me when I say that I love you very much and I have never in all my life loved you less or more than I have loved your brother. But your mother...."[12]

This is why the play generates a death like response from Tara when she learns the truth, she is discriminated against, because of her gender, but not by her father — it is Bharati's decision that deprives her of what she wants more than anything else in the world—a second leg. Bharati's father further strengthens his indulgence for a male grand child by leaving his property after his demise to Chandan and not a single penny to Tara. Patel's attitude has also been negative. He blames his wife and father-in-law, for the damage done cannot be denied. The fact that a male is always given the greater chance is obvious from Patel's planning for Chandan's education and future career. No consideration whatsoever for her feelings! Tara is the victim of this collective social system. Her father, Mr. Patel, is not much different from his wife, though Bharati is guilty of a more serious crime against Tara. He continuously and doggedly favours Chandan when it comes to giving him higher education abroad, and a career.

> PATEL: You are turning them against the whole world,
>
> BHARATI: I am doing that.
>
> PATEL: Yes! Look at the way you treat Tara.As if she is made of glass. You coddle her, you pet her, you spoil her, She's grown up feeling she doesn't need any one but you.!
>
> BHARATI: What d'you want me to do? Just tell me in plain simple words what you want me to do and I'll do it!
>
> PATEL: Let me go. Just let me go. And let me handle them.
>
> BHARATI: All right. You stay at home then! You stay at home and watch what they can do and what they can't. You remind them of what they can't be. It's easy for you to talk about their future and your plans. But tell them what they should do now. This day, this hour, this minute. Tell them! I want to hear!

> PATEL: Chandan is going to study further and he will go abroad for his higher studies.
>
> BHARAT1: And Tara?
>
> PATEL: When have you ever allowed me to make any plans for her?[13]

But Tara could have made her defiance, her strength and fight the society to etch a place of her own. She is discouraged openly, not withstanding her feelings in the matter, even though she is more intelligent, sharp and witty, and would perform well if given opportunities in life. Economic and cultural factors have been responsible for the antipathy against and inferiorization of the girl child. All these factors combine to create the social system in which the girl child has to live and die. Tara is killed by the social system, which controls the minds and actions of the people. The trauma of coming to know the role her mother has played in her life, and the discrimination become too much for her. And why is she killed? Tara is not wanted. Girls are not wanted.

> TARA: Oh! What a waste! A waste of money. Why they spend all the money to keep me alive? It cannot matter whether I live or die. There are thousands of poor sick people on the roads who could be given care and attention, and I think I know what I will make of myself. I will be a crer for those people. I.... I will spend the rest of my life feeding and clothing those.... starving naked millions everywhere is talking about. May be I can start an institution that will... do all that. Or I could join Mother Teresa and sacrifice myself to a great cause. That may give... purpose to my... existence. I can do it. I can do it, can't I? I will be very happy if I could, because that is really what I want.That really...[with emotion].Oh!, bullshirt! I don't care. I don't for anyone except mummy!.[14]

The above statement shows that Tara is not deterred by the injustice done to her by her parents but she presents herself as an empowered lady to face all the hurdles. She also shows sympathy towards the downtrodden. She is bubbly and energetic girl who has all the qualities of a normal girl. If she has been given moral support by her parents, she might have shone like a star as her name signifies. Her life is a burden on this earth. This makes her lose interest in life altogether. Further she refuses to have physiotherapy or fill forms for college.

> TARA: How do you expect me to feel anything for anyone if they don't give me any feeling to begin with? Why is it wrong for me to be without feeling? Why are you asking me to do something that nobody has done for me?[15]

Tara is a bright and shinning star which is a source of cheerfulness and happiness of the family. A complete life could have done wonders and she would have scored the limits which her brother Chandan couldn't have. Tara's potentiality is sacrificed on the alter of gender. Identity crisis becomes a chain with which a female is fettered when the question of choice between male and female arises.

> TARA: The hospital staff. At the reception, they asked me who I wanted to see. I told them. They asked me to wait. One of the nurses passing by recognized me. She drew the receptionist aside and spoke to her in a low voice. She thought I couldn't hear what she was saying. But I heard! She told her that she had received strict instructions from our father that I shouldn't on any account be allowed to see mummy on my own.[Pause] Now tell me I'm imagining things. Tell me that he doesn't hate me![16]

The play, *Tara*, is of multilevel setting; one level depicts older Chandan, referred to as Dan, in a suburban of London, trying to write his story as a drama in two acts, that he intends to repent for his twin sister Tara; it is the realistic level in which he attempts to create his history but futile. And on a higher level, Dr. Thakkar seats a chair throughout the play reporting to an interviewer about that historical surgery of separating Tara-Chandan, the conjoined twins. The major portion of the lowest level represents Patel's house, revealing the family politics as reflecting the gender politics prevailing in the society. The construct of multilevel setting is as complex as the gender schema functioning in the minds of the adults irrespective of their sexes. Thus, "gender schematic processing is itself derived from the sex-differentiated practices of the social community."[17] Aristotelian opinion "the female is a female by virtue of a certain lack of qualities"[18] that continues to exist in the various communities of the world is deeply rooted in Patel's family too. What is attributed to femininity leads men to commit female infanticide. It is obviously cited through Roopa, one of the neighbour's of Tara, saying "The Patels in the old days were unhappy with getting girl babies - so they used to drown them in milk."[19] It is noteworthy that discrimination against Tara continues even after her death. Chandan, who was always interested in writing, and who has come to England for higher studies, has transferred into Dan. He turns the story he writes into his own tragedy. Dan apologises to Tara for doing this, "Forgive me, Tara. Forgive me for making it my tragedy."[20]

To conclude, the central idea of the play is that the society can accept and tolerate male though he is physically challenged and when Tara turns 15 she becomes the victim of gender biased system promoted by male dominant generations. The tragedy is that she could not survive. The play ends with the note of failure on the part of Dan, saying: "I move. I move, without meaning. I forget Tara. I forget that I had a sister - with whom I had shared a body, In one comfortable womb, till we were forced out - and separated."[21] But Dattani seems that he didn't content with such a note that the male self is very much privileged over the female self and, hence, he just idealistically intends to anticipate the better understanding among the gendered sexes on the basis of humanist perception, as Dorothy Parker has written, "My idea is that all of us men as well as women, should be regarded as human beings."[22] At last the play extends a little to show, "Tara walks into the spot without limping. Dan also appears without limp"[23] and Dan speaks to Tara, "Forgive me for making it my tragedy. Tara embraces Dan... they hug each other tightly."[24] This fantasy scene implies that Dattani's creative consciousness longs for the reunion of all the sexes at a single point of humanism. It would be fruitful if gender study thus expands beyond feminist consciousness to assert the socialist need of humanism. For, this gender study must transcend all sexual and cultural politics to promote the humanist concern among the people of different sexes.

## References


1. Mangayarkarasi, T. "Tensions and conflicts: A Critical Responses to Mahesh Dattani's Final Solutions" published in the Proceedings of National Seminar on *Indian English Literature: Theme and Techniques*, St. Xavier's College, Palayamkottai, p 222.
2. Rani, Sudha. "Expressionism on Contemporary Indian English Stage". *<http://www.museindia.com/showfeature3.asp?id=669>*
3. Bern, Sandra Lipsitz. "Gender Schema Theory: A Cognitive Account of Sex Typing", *Psychological Review*, 1981, Vol. 88. No. 4. p. 354.
4. Subramanyam, Lakshmi, ed., *Muffled Voices: Women in Modern Indian Theatre*, New Delhi: Shakti, 2002, p.134.
5. Mee, Erin, "A Note in the Play", *Collected Plays, Mahesh Dattani*, New Delhi: Penguin, p. 320.
6. Dattani, Mahesh, *Collected Plays*, New Delhi: Penguin, p.325.
7. Bern, Sandra Lipsitz. "Gender Schema Theory: A Cognitive Account of Sex Typing", *Psychological Review*, 1981, Vol. 88. No. 4. p. 355.
8. Ibid., p. 228.
9. Dattani, Mahesh, *Collected Plays*, New Delhi: Penguin, p.325.
10. Mee, Erin, "A Note in the Play", *Collected Plays, Mahesh Dattani*, New Delhi: Penguin, p.320.
11. Dattani, Mahesh, *Collected Plays*, New Delhi: Penguin, p.354.
12. Ibid.
13. Ibid. p. 352.
14. Ibid. p. 370.
15. Ibid. p. 380.
16. Ibid. p. 373.
17. Bern, Sandra Lipsitz. "Androgyny and Gender Schema Theory: A Conceptual and Empirical Integration" (ed.) Theo B. Sonderegger. *Psychology and Gender*, USA: Nebraska University Press. 1984. 186.
18. Beauvoir, Simone De. "Woman and Other", (ed) Dennis Walder, *Literature in the Modern World: Critical Essays and Documents*, New York: Oxford University Press. 2004. pp. 282.

19. Dattani, Mahesh, *Collected Plays*, New Delhi: Penguin, p.371.
20. Ibid. p. 380.
21. Ibid. p. 381.
22. Beauvoir, Simone De. "Woman and Other", (ed) Dennis Walder, *Literature in the Modern World: Critical Essays and Documents*, New York: Oxford University Press. 2004. pp. 280-285.
23. Dattani, Mahesh, *Collected Plays*, New Delhi: Penguin, p.354.
24. Ibid. p.380.

6

# Locating Shades of Violence: Assessing Function of Violence against Women in Mahesh Dattani's *Bravely Fought the Queen*

— Bhavesh Kumar

This paper is intended to locate violence against women within the family unit by examining the role, reasons and forms of violence through the discussion of Mahesh Dattani's *Bravely Fought the Queen*. "The play", Anju Bala Agrawal justly views "is the picture of women from affluent homes fighting against patriarchal dominance as it prevails in India" (7). The function and operation of violence occupies the focus of the discussion in this paper. It is primarily aimed at a close discussion of the embedded violence meted out to women in the domestic settings. An attempt is also made to demonstrate how women and violence are inextricably intertwined, and why violence is frequently used as reliable weapon to subjugate, oppress and undermine them so as to perpetuate certain normative function of the society and the family.

A close examination of suffering, anguish, pain, frustration, anxiety, complexes, guilt and experiences of protagonists would reveal both subtle and gross reasons and both visible and invisible forms of domestic violence directed against women within the urban Indian household through detailed analysis of the dilemma of the female protagonists, their sense of defiance, ability to conform to and go against the ingrained social norms, their experiences and exploitation. The thrust of the discussion lies in the revelation and divulgence of invisible shades of violence against women that lead to bizarre sufferings to women in contemporary Indian urban family.

## Concern and Focus

*Bravely Fought the Queen* discerningly unmasks the institution of patriarchy in operation in the two successive generations (enacted in the one night episode though). The play is centred on women and their suffering, oppression and suppression through the institutions of marriage, inheritance and through a series of acts of violence of different semblances. Rozario Ignatius has pertinently pointed out, "*Bravely Fought the Queen* questions the male and female roles in society... [I]n the play, Dattani depicts the plight of helpless women victims of male tyranny" (108). The issues range from the child abuse to the violence against women to suffering of women on account of homosexuality. The striking feature of the play is to show how women are made victim owing to the homosexual orientation of their spouse—an area almost untouched in the history of Indian English theatre.

Though the play is conventionally engaged in dealing with the continuation of the patriarchal societal norm, it provides a glimpse of unmatched marriage travails and connotes the common urban dissatisfaction towards the marital life. Erin Mee writes in *Contemporary Indian Theatre: Three Voices* about the core subject and characters of Dattani's plays. She remarks, "Mahesh Dattani...takes as his subject the complicated dynamics of the modern urban family. His characters struggle for some kind of freedom and happiness under the oppressive weight of tradition, culture constructions of gender, and repressed desire" (4). This is particularly unravelled how the suppressed and surreptitious life of the homosexual results in the devastating conjugal mishaps.

*Bravely Fought the Queen* is mainly a family play concentrated on the travails of its members and the fragmented relationships of those who are the part of it. In a sense, the women have often seized the spotlight (as female characters exceed) since the play seems to be more oriented towards the women's concern. Subir Dhar aptly avers, "A powerful domestic tragedy, this play highlights the circumstances of a woman fighting against all the odds that the forces of patriarchy have piled up against her" (83). Here, Dattani has sprucely portrayed the modern urban conjugal life encapsulated in the microscopic representation of the Trivedis and that of the couple of Lalitha and Sridhar.

The play is divided into three acts: 'The Women', 'The Men' and 'Free for All'. Such watertight compartmentalization of the woman and the man worlds and eventually their merging into one reveals that there is skilled plot in the play and those acts are intricately and seamlessly interwoven. Asha Kuthari Chaudhuri puts it rightly, "The claustrophobic 'female' world of Act I is pitted against the 'male' world of Act II and the characters stand exposed in Act III where two worlds clash and collapse, with the home as the site for the battle" (32). Each act has vivid and complete actions that foreshadow the further actions. But the dexterous interweaving of first two acts juxtaposes them within parallel time-frame. Here, the dramatic techniques of Dattani excel the acumen of other playwrights.

Though at the onset the actions skilfully conceal the violence, the play starts unfolding it with the advancement of the plot. Violence against women can be located from the beginning to the end of the play. In other words, the act of violence is an apparently embedded element in the entire realm of the play since this would hardly be difficult to locate instances and incidents of violence in any chosen Act. Apparently, all those instances fall into the gamut of the domestic violence - the family violence to be more precise. Wife beating, child abuse, eve teasing, psychological torture, physical aggressions, etc. are some of the prominent forms of violence to be found in *Bravely Fought the Queen*. This has been ubiquitous that women are always potential victims of violence if all men are not potential perpetrators. Women in the play are closely related to the violence because the plot allows it reflect through a series of interconnected actions.

## Theme and Issues

*Bravely Fought the Queen* has multiplicity of themes ranging from patriarchy to homosexuality. But among these dominant aspects, violence against women has been central to the play. The entire gamut of the play is blended with oppression, subjugation and suppression of women within the family dominated by the men. Gauri Shankar Jha aptly synthesises:

> In *Bravely Fought the Queen* he (Dattani) presents the same picture, traditionally bound, organised and manipulated by patriarchy in all ages by established values, norms, roles and gender perceptions, they are guided by idealism that prescribes unequal means, methods and routes to achieve the so-called 'wholeness' for women, motherhood and wifehood being the dual crowns of womanhood. (155)

The family is shown fractured and its fragmentation serves as Dattani's design as far as the theme of the play is concerned. But the complex connection of violence and women is inescapably and repetitively stressed in the play.

Apart from those reiterated themes, *Bravely Fought the Queen* adroitly deals with several other issues and social evils. Since the protagonists and other characters are married, their troubled conjugal lives and fractured relationships are the major preoccupation of the playwright. In the introduction of *Contemporary Drama: India*, Erin B. Mee firmly accentuates that "Dattani's plays are not mindless fluff: he takes as his subject the complicated dynamics of the modern urban family. Dattani's characters struggle for some kind of freedom and happiness under the oppressive weight of tradition, cultural construction of gender, and repressed desire" (3-4). The pretentious and feign lifestyle of the upper middle class urban people is brought into the question and the emerging trend of the closeted expression of homosexuality is well pitted against the strict heteronormative society (heteronormativity is a term for a set of lifestyle norms that hold that people fall into distinct and complementary genders—male and female—with natural roles in life. It also holds that heterosexuality is the normal sexual orientation, and states that sexual and marital relations are most—or only—fitting between a man and a woman.). In the conversation with Ranu Uniyal, Mahesh Dattani himself, in general, unravels the crux of his plays, "There are these recurring issues in my plays basically to do with gender inequality, the battle between the genders or in egalitarian position. The individual versus society, I guess, is a theme that's in all my plays" (183).The outline of the ingrained social hierarchy based on gender can effortlessly be traced by considering how women are accorded to the secondary position in the patriarchal family and the society at the broad level. Chaudhuri aptly observes, "The play dramatizes the emptiness and sham in the lives of its cloistered women and self-indulgent, unscrupulous men, blurring the lines between fantasy and reality, standing on the brink of terrible secrets, deception and hypocrisies" (32). Sexual difference, gender discrimination, inequality and imbalance in power relations, unfulfilled desires and women's experiences in the family, society and urban areas are also given special attention in the play.

## The Female World

### *Baa: The Prosecutor and Victim*

Baa is the oldest family member (the oldest in the play) in the Trivedi family who belongs to older generation with her horrible experiences of married life. She is an aging and bedridden old woman and most of time "keeps talking to herself" (244). Her calling someone through ringing her bell constantly suggests that she is keen to wield her authority and seek undue attention from others. The bell is symbolic of her decaying control on her family and thus, she is often less cared. Since "[S]he is an invalid who has been ditched by her husband" (Ignatius 109), Baa has a quite troubled past. She is thoroughly tortured by her cruel husband when she is young and in turn, she develops a strong hatred against him. She is beaten, maltreated, harassed and intimidated by her husband and is never cared well throughout her married life. As Baa intermittently revisits her past life, she clearly visualizes her marriage day when it is rained. John McRae subtly notes about the technique of fragmenting time between the past and present, "This is indicative of his (Dattani) playing with time (too)—none of his plays is static with time frame. They move between past and present, even between life and death, with the ease with which a character enters and leaves the stage" (8). She vividly reminds of the stinking smell of the tobacco from the mouth of her husband and of her being beaten. Her recounting of the horrible past is evident to suggest that Baa was brought up in traditional and conservative family and social settings. This may be manifest in the instance when she was asked to sing. She is stereotypically represented as a traditional Indian woman:

> BAA.... It rained on my wedding day. He asked me before marrying him if I will sing! He knew that I could sing! You want me to sing only for you?...I will sing for everyone! Why are you so angry?...We must not see each other before the marriage, it is bad!... I saw him! He is dark! Dark! And I am so fair! My children will be dark, like him!...Two sons! I have given you two sons! The younger one is beautiful, like my father! He has my blood! Don't kiss him! You will leave tobacco on his cheek. Don't spit! Oh, the whole house smells of you! I have married such a villager! Aah! You slapped me? Never, never slap me. Nobody has hit me. The men in our family are decent.... (288)

Now she lives with her two sons and two daughters-in-law who are morally and socially entrusted with the responsibilities of looking after her as the part of their familial duties. This may be meaningful to make out through Baa's utterances that there is certain detestation for Jiten in her heart simply because he seems to be reminiscent replica of his father—his dark skin; violent behaviours are determinative factors for that matter. But the younger one Nitin is the apple of her eyes for the obvious reason that he is fair like her. Baa is clearly able to see her shadow in and identify herself with Nitin.

Baa is shown paralyzed and unable to carry out any physical movements. She is now taken care of and respected only because she possesses the immovable property - the ancestral house. She is frequently given pills for sleep because Jiten instructs Dolly to "[G]ive her a Calmpose... every day. It will help her sleep better" (284) and pacify and make her virtually silent. This is quite noticeable that like older generation women, Baa bears no proper name, instead known by the existence of her relationship with the rest of the family members. She is virtually nameless, and is never shown and appears on the front stage. She remains fixed at the back stage- motionless, unheard, and neglected. Since this negligence of the old falls in the ambit of violence against women, Baa is real victim of this form of violence. But she seems to be keen to prove her identity and agency through her hold on the ancestral property. She is far-sighted woman because she names her will against the youngest in the family- Daksha: her granddaughter. At this point, this can easily be made out from this stance that her sense of insecurity in term of Daksha's future is genuine.

Baa seems to be much concerned with her granddaughter because she does not want that deformed girl to be a victim of such immeasurable sufferings that may arise out of violence in her absence and after her death. She, therefore, makes Daksha the owner of that valuable properties and Praful trustee, though he is not her son or a blood relation. She is a far-sighted woman who does not name Nitin as the inheritor of the ancestral house. It seems that Baa has a déjà vu that "[N]obody loves Daksha in this (the Trivedis) house" (305). She has already sensed the selfish motive and inappropriate behaviour of her sons in everyday life.

Though Alka and Dolly have alternately been attending and taking care of her, she has developed certain grudge against Alka simply because her marriage with Nitin was against Baa's will. Baa's warning is apparent to her younger son, "Nitin! Don't marry her! Your friend Praful is fooling you! The older one is good for Jitu, but beware of the younger one! She is like her mother!" (285). The mother of Dolly, Alka and Praful was discovered as a keep mistress since their father abandoned them all. Therefore, Nitin as per Baa's wish threw Alka out of the house earlier. But this time, she is not willing to hand over the house to Nitin even if he kicks Alka out of the house by snapping all relationships.

After discussing Baa as the victim and a good old grandmother, it would not be irrelevant to point out that she is also a prosecutor of violence, as shown above in Alka's case, against her daughter-in-law. Ignatius crisply pinpoints, "Embittered- that she is, she sets up her sons against their wives" (109). Jiten, for instance, is provoked to hit Dolly when she was expecting Daksha.

> BAA. Jitu, throw her out of the house as well. Whore!
>
> DOLLY. And you hit me! Jitu, you beat me up! I was carrying Daksha and you beat me up!
>
> BAA. No! Jitu, hit her on the face but not on the...stop it Jitu! On the face, only on the face! Enough! Stop! (311)

Her cruel and brutal intention to intimidate and inflict violence on Dolly is manifest through her blatant instructions of the spot where Jiten was to hit. Hence, this can be well pointed out that Baa can periphrastically be held responsible for the birth of deformed Daksha.

Thus, Baa is a mysterious but dubious character in *Bravely Fought the Queen*. Even though she is not appeared directly before the audience and remains distant, she seems to be a virtual nexus of all happenings in the play. She does not only serve as the background of the present status of the Trivedis, but also represents the entire gamut of their experiences. Baa's life is painfully coloured with the stains of violence both against and by her. It may be relevant, here, to quote Alka Tyagi's observation on the role of the old:

> In most of Dattani's plays, the past is a constant presence in the character's consciousness; mostly past is relived in the memory or narrated in dialogues of characters. Old people are there in every play. They are neither stereotypically revered, morally perfect beings, nor downright victimized beings. They are normal human beings with very real shortcomings and vices and virtues. In fact they are the carriers of the past with which they interact or cleanse the mind of the progeny. (122)

She is a symbol of accomplishments but also possesses failures. Baa is the great but old remindful duplication of the 'Queen', fighting a losing battle for years. This is quite noticeable that Baa is often grossly ignored by the literary critics.

### *Dolly: The Moderate Fighter and Prudent Lady*

Dolly is the most considerate and shrewd of all the female characters. The entire plot of the play hinges on her; it unfolds and gears up only when Dolly is allowed to open her. Being the wife of the elder son and the elder daughter-in-law in the Trivedi family, Dolly has one more responsibility - her daughter. She is the epitome of the tolerance who combines the feature of urban woman and her down-to-earth nature. Dolly is sophisticated, reserve and self-conscious and tries to conceal some 'guarded' secrets from others. In the play she, it seems, emerges victorious at the end by overcoming a host of odds with strong will and greater tolerance. If the title role of *Bravely Fought the Queen* is judged in term of its suitability, Dolly Trivedi may be acknowledged as 'the Queen', though suggested ironically in the play. Dattani hints the origin of the title that reflects the protagonist too:

> ...[W]hat I had witnessed at somebody's house, was some form of battle between the woman and her husband and immediately something triggered off and the poem come to my mind, that she was fighting very bravely. And then I immediately got this setting of a woman fighting a losing battle and the title just came to me and is reflective of Laxmibai's fight against the British and it was a losing battle but she never gave up.
>
> (Uniyal 183)

The implicit dialogues of the play are arguably potential enough to reveal that Dolly is most often suggested for the title role in the play. This may be further argued that Dolly, a virtuous wife, is wholeheartedly committed to her husband and compromises most of times whenever feuds occur in the family. For instance, she does not react when Jiten cancels the outing programme, though she is fully dressed up and made up. In fact, she has put up an invisible mask so as to conceal her frustration, pain and suffering. Her trajectory of struggles may pass unnoticed before the eyes of the most of audience/ readers, but the power of her blanketed silence remains intact till the last moment of the action in the play. At length, unable to withstand the worst of the past she gives vent to her anger and Jiten inevitably and justifiably becomes her target.

> DOLLY. No! Oh no! I will not let you get away so easily! They were your hands hitting me! Your feet kicking me! It's in your blood! It's in your blood to do bad! (312)

Dolly is emotionally too strong to reveal her private life. She often tries to shield the secrets of her private and family life, but it is Alka who bursts out the dark secrets. Dolly is relatively a responsible daughter-in-law as she genuinely takes care of Baa. She is justly sympathetic towards both Baa and Alka. It may always be considered a strong point in her character that Dolly does want a united and peaceful family by balancing her anger and suffering. Her battle is greater than Alka because she simply does not give up things and let them go astray. She optimally manages to keep the family run undisturbed. In short, Dolly's persona appears to be diametrically opposite of Alka's, because they have their temperament extremely opposite.

The life of Dolly has been a devotion to the family, particularly as a mother. Daksha is born deformed because Dolly was hit right in the stomach in advanced stage of her pregnancy. Dolly squarely accuses Jiten because, "...Daksha was born – two month premature. With the cord around her neck!" (312). This is a brute form of violence against women both as a mother and as a wife. Her past life has been extremely perturbed and chronically plagued by both Jiten and Baa. The premature delivery conspicuously afflicted deformity to the newborn Daksha. Here, Dattani is at his best when he tries to expose very subtle form of violence meted out to the pregnant women that affects both the child and its mother. This act of violence does not only accentuate women as victim in the role of wife, but also underlines the instance of the child abuse. But through her strong and determined character and sustained struggle, Dolly infallibly tries to bind the family and overcome the odds in her battles of life.

Seen in the social spectrum, Dolly is a sophisticated urban woman who likes to attend parties and has keen interest in doing make ups. However, she often attends party, but seldom likes to be mixed with the crowd. She not only prefers to stay aside, but also shows disinterestedness in drinking. Alka sarcastically tells Lalitha, "She is neither interested in the so-and-sos of this world, nor unfortunately, in the bottle. Poor Dolly, sitting all by herself, looking pretty and...wasted" (260). Unlike Alka who normally breaks down under the influence of alcohol and starts speaking in unconcealed and explicit manner, Dolly never allows herself anything that may create a feud in and out of the family. Though she has scores of complaints, grudges and agonies to speak out, Dolly does not take recourse to the liquor that supposedly helps suppress tension. She is well aware of dubious character of her husband, but never entertains that to matter in their connubial life.

Unfortunately, Dolly and Baa share similar fate and parallel past- they are victims of violence perpetrated on them by their respective husbands. This is commonplace to observe that Dolly has learnt to lead her life according to the particular norm of the family and tries to conform to patriarchal system of the society. Unlike Baa, she is wise enough not to develop hatred for and bitter relationship with Jiten. She generally avoids abusing the unmatched marriage and respects the institution of family to a great extent by observing it in every effort. A comparison with Baa's experience and that of Dolly reveals that though the society has changed and 'modernized', its norms and orthodox traditions remain unchanged and intact. In other words, patriarchy still rules and even in the changed socio-economic scenario, compliance to it is imperative for women whatever class they belong to. Gauri Shankar Jha comments on the role of patriarchy:

In *Bravely Fought the Queen*, he (Dattani) presents the same picture, traditionally bound, organised and manipulated by patriarchy in all ages by established values, norms, roles and gender perceptions, they are guided by idealism that prescribes unequal means, methods and routes to achieve the so-called 'wholeness' for women, motherhood and wifehood being the dual crowns of womanhood. It is the man who has defined this unequivocal term, as motherhood is disciplined by males and they further justify themselves through religions, myths, science, politics, economics, etc. (155)

Dattani, here, tenders a fine example of this circumstance through the family of the Trivedis, since they all are educated (Baa is doubtful) and live in a big city. It is, thus, easy to conclude that even in the 'progressive' and 'cultured' society, the evil of patriarchy remains intact and that in turn, helps perpetuate, flourish and nourish violence against women. The violence against women in the play is shown in continuity from the time of Baa to that of Dolly.

Dolly is the embodiment of forbearance since she valiantly endures both physical and psychological tortures. Many instances from Jiten's behaviour demonstrate that Dolly as a wife, has been perpetual victim of her husband's violent nature. The mode of nagging between wife and husband does not remain confined to the verbal argument only, but it extends to the psychological limit. Disrespect for women, oblique outlook for them, abusing and wife beating are a few forms of violence that Dolly as a life partner copes with Jiten. Jiten's sexually obsessed nature degrades him to the extent that he hires call girls for his sexual gratification. Consequently, sexual dissatisfaction arises on the part of Dolly who fantasizes of sexual pleasure with a fictional Kanhaiya. Dolly's sexual fantasy is manifest in her own words: "All I'm aware of are two powerful black arms around me and the beautiful sound of the heartbeat of a warm gentle soul" ( 262). The fantasy of sexual pleasure with invisible Kanhaiya accentuates the fact that Dolly is not happy with her married sexual life with Jiten. Though she dimly admits that she is fighting a losing battle against Jiten, violence and patriarchy by adopting a unique modus operandi of silence, she is greatly hopeful about the agreeable future time once she manages to win it. Dolly by annihilating the literal meaning of her name, wishes to establish her own identity.

### *Alka: The Innocent Rebel and Deprived Wife*

The character of Alka Trivedi is informed with extremity-alcoholic, outspoken, rebellious. Alka is a compulsive boozer and an outspoken woman. It seems that a rebellious spirit possesses her because she follows her heart and cares a fig of others. Alka is being accused for unworthy wife and constant alcoholic. Jiten's pressurizing but truthful words to Nitin are remarkable that provoke the younger brother and put a question mark on his male sexuality as well.

> JITEN. Throw her out of the house. This time, for good. Damn Praful's money! The property is more important. You want to get even with Praful? This is your chance. Say damn to his money

> and damn to his sister. Your marriage never worked. She is a drunkard. An alcoholic. Your wife is a boozer and you still keep her? What kind of a man you are? (290)

As a daughter-in-law, Alka is not successful and responsible because the old Trivedi has developed certain repulsion for her. Baa's abhorrence is palpable when she declares: "I don't forget bad deeds. It is in your blood to do bad!" (283). She, in fact, lacks the soft and caring touch of her sister that every time leads Baa back to Dolly's house (as they strike a verbal obligation of Baa's stay in alternate at their respective houses). As a result, Alka has also developed certain dislike in return. The trickery that is played on her by Praful to marry her off with Nitin pains her since the day she discovers the homosexual orientation of her husband. Thus, in order to suppress the frustration and agony, she turns to be alcoholic and gradually grows to be rough, disrespectful and the cynosure of hatred for one and all in the family.

Unlike Dolly's conjugal life that is grimly disturbed by sexual preoccupation of Jiten, Alka's marital relationship is marred by Nitin's surreptitious homosexual doings because "Nitin is homosexual and consequently is unable to satiate his wife's desire which is also a source of pain for Alka" (Das 115). Whatever reasons may be, Alka's position in the Trivedi family is of nominal wife for Nitin and of an acting daughter-in-law for Baa. Her life is more complicated and troublesome than her counterpart. Her existence in the family might be seen as negligible and objectified entity. Hence, her direction of life is lost somewhere in oblivion. A childless mother, a nominal wife, a 'characterless' sister (to Praful), and a heavy alcoholic for the society, Alka is leading a feign life divorced from happiness and pleasure. In short, Alka has been literally deprived of any fruit of marital and sexual life.

Like Baa and Dolly, Alka also carries the cross of her painful past to the unknown direction. She became the victim of her brother's sadism and finally was tricked in marriage with Nitin so that the homosexual relationship between those two men could be continued. In other words, her marriage with Nitin is both the inevitable and fine pretext to continue closeted relationship and the by-product of such relationship that is in turn, the by-product of heteronormative society of India. Observed from the diverse angle, Alka's marriage serves as a clandestine bargain of the surreptitious homosexuality of the two males. Tyagi notes the point that, "Alka, who longs for her brother Praful's acceptance of herself, silently suffers a fruitless marriage with Nitin" (121).

In *Bravely Fought the Queen*, Dattani's observation of the contemporary urban trend towards gays finds an expression in discreet description of Nitin and Praful's relationship. This may be well argued that the violence cropped up out of such relationship is a bizarre phenomenon in the contemporary urban Indian social life. Prior to Dattani, it can be well established through a retrospective literary survey, no playwright has ever made an attempt to highlight this gray area of homosexuality—neither in evident nor in concealed manner in the annals of Indian English theatre. Most of the travails that Alka encounters can be well associated with the nexus of the homosexual relationship of Praful and Nitin. Consequently, the grotesque form of violence against women takes shape in such circumstances. Alka in this play is the exemplary figure of the representation of such women who confront that absolutely new form of violence that is making its monstrous presence felt in Indian heteronormative social setting.

Compared to Dolly, the suffering and experience caused by violence against Alka are entirely different in nature and scope, though both the sisters have been victim of their husbands. The violence against Alka, on a close observation, finds twin expression from two different men – Praful and Nitin. In other words, Alka has triple sources (including Baa) of violence meted out to her whereas Dolly has only two—Jiten and Baa. Thus, it would hardly be an exaggeration to state that the amount and stretch of violence the younger sister receives is, if roughly and abstractly measured, few times more than that of Dolly. The compass of Alka's experience of violence against her incorporates beating, harassing, eve teasing, hitting, abusing, intimidating, insulting and battering. Alka's agony is revealed in her account:

> ALKA....Nitin and Praful were home, talking. I came home from school with the neighbour's son on his scooter instead of walking with you (Dolly). I told him to drop me before our street came. He didn't understand and dropped me right at our doorstep. Praful saw. He didn't say a word to me. He just dragged me into the kitchen. He lit the stove and pushed my face in front of it! I thought he was going to burn my fair! He burnt my hair. I can still smell my hair on fire. Nitin was right behind us. Watching! Just...Praful said, 'Don't you ever look at any man. Ever'. (257)

These are some probable reasons that may be cited for her turning to alcoholism because she grossly is of opinion that she can deceive herself by drowning in the intoxication of liquor. It is remarkable at this point that she is not a boozer by birth, but she chooses to be so or is made boozer - more precisely. Her conversion from a social woman to constant alcoholic is the result of her wish to lead a life of oblivion and self-deception. Alka desires to sink in the world of intoxication willy-nilly.

Alka, unlike Baa and Dolly, has no hope left with her, though the old Trivedi has lived her life and the elder sister is optimistic of her happy future time. In that case, Alka is the representative of the most deprived women of her kind since she has no concrete expectations to live with any longer. This is very much clear when, at the end, Nitin comments on sleeping Alka:

> NITIN. He tricked you too, didn't he? How can you still love your brother after what he did to you...? That's right. Don't answer. Just sleep...You always were a heavy sleeper...He told me to get married...How could I? And to whom?... He told me that you knew. That he had told you...about me. And that it didn't matter to you. You only wanted the security of marriage. He...he told me everything would work out fine...But you didn't know! He tricked you! (315)

As a young woman, Alka is vibrant and full of life. But the unfortunate conditions she faces do not allow her to land on a solid ground. She cannot aim something like Lalitha who willingly does not want to have a child and is saving for a house to live a better and secure life thereafter.

### *Lalitha: The Cultivated Mind*

Though the character of Lalitha serves as a catalyst from the beginning to the end of *Bravely Fought the Queen*, she is a simulacrum of the stereotype of cultivated urban women with a trite determination and materialistic aim in life. Lalitha is meant to be fulcrum for the quickening and advancement of actions in the play and helps the plot unfold. Being an outsider to the Trivedi family, she plays a significant role in propelling the incidents of the play and in unravelling the dark secrets of the Trivedis. For a couple of times, she has been a vulnerable target of Jiten's outrage and wrath, but is shown to be utter daring lady who is inquisitive enough to ask questions to Dolly about Kanhaiya. Her fascination for bonsai and other occupations such as part time columnist, writing and poetry composition suggest that she embodies the emerging educated urban middle class woman with rational but closed mindset. She shares her occupations:

> LALITHA. Oh, I keep myself occupied. I do a bit of writing. Freelance. I write an occasional woman's column for the *Times*. Sometimes I review cultural events. I am into meditation. And, oh yes, I grow bonsai plants – I've been growing them for years. I do a bit of creative writing as well. You know, poetry and stuff like that. Nothing great but... (243)

Even after being hailed as an intruder to the Trivedi family, Lalitha dexterously manages to establish a good rapport with the sister duo. Thus, she seems to be the axel on which most of the actions unwind.

This is obvious by Lalitha's conscious nature that she has made a good wife to Sridhar, but yet to be a mother of a child.

She relatively enjoys more freedom than Alka and Dolly Trivedi. Lalitha exudes confidently, "Sridhar says it's typical of women to do exactly the opposite of what their husbands want, just to prove they are independent" (252). Though the freedom is claimed, the statement conceals an irony within. In such case, Lalitha may be taken as an example for a comparatively freer woman in the emerging clan of educated women in India urban society. Her pairing with Sridhar sounds perfect since both the spouses are caring for each other. But like Dolly and Alka, she is also duped and is made victim of the infidelity of Sridhar. In other words, she is camouflaged with a mask of having liberal husband in order to project happy conjugal life before the world, but she is, in fact, helpless. Lalitha's problem of not leaving Dolly's house alone and her apprehension of being raped by some auto rickshaw men are indicative enough to draw a conclusion that every woman like her is a potential victim of such crime prevalent in the urban locality.

As a finely carved and brilliantly streamlined character, Lalitha is a representative of the potential victim of violence against women- rape and manhandling both in and outside the home. This can be further illustrated by the instance at the Trivedi's house when Jiten abuses and misbehaves with her:

> LALITHA. What's going on?
>
> JITEN. If you open your trap once more, you will regret it.
>
> SRIDHAR. Be more polite! It's my wife you are talking to!
>
> JITEN. Screw your wife!
>
> SRIDHAR....Now listen you – I've had enough!
>
> JITEN. You want to protect your wife from whom? From me?
>
> SRIDHAR. Just don't talk to my wife, okay?
>
> JITEN. I wouldn't lay her even if she got me the ReVaTee account. (306)

Though the intervention of Sridhar for her rescue saves her at the last minute, it may be well concluded that such women represented by Lalitha are neither safe at home nor outside. In other words, all women seem to be potential victims of violence if circumstances go awry.

## Offstage Figures

This would not be wide of the mark at this juncture to discuss a couple of offstage female characters like Daksha and the old beggar woman. Being a deformed girl, revealed during discussion at the Trivedi's house, Daksha is the symbol both of the uneven relationships of her parents and of violence against female child (though her gender is taken for granted). Due to her deformity (she is a spastic—the mentally challenged child who has uncoordinated arm and neck movements), she is literally deprived of her normal and due share of happy life. The fact of spastic Daksha is conspicuous in her revelation of the truth to Lalitha. She reveals to her, "You want to see her dance? They teach her dance where she goes! Only they call it physiotherapy" (312). Moreover, her premature birth may hamper her normal mental, psychological and physical growth. Seen through the broad spectrum of child abuse, Daksha's life long suffering is the symbol of the manifestation of violence against both women and children invisibly present in the Indian social setting. In short, the violence against women may also indirectly cause the violence against their vulnerable children. Once the children are made victims, they have to bear that heinous brunt till the old age and that culminates with their death only.

The old beggar woman of the play, though distant from the stage, has no name, no identity, no shelter and no regular means of livelihood. This old age trauma, it seems, must be the product of negligence of the old women by their offspring. By taking account of negligence of old women, this may be considered one of the many forms of violence against women. Sridhar witnesses the brutal murder of her by Jiten. Shridhar screams out "He's running over her! He's running the car over a beggar woman!

Over and over!..." (313). The beastly and barbaric murder of the beggar woman is the case of extreme violence against marginal women in Indian society.

The discussion would certainly not be complete without taking account of two historical women from Indian history viz., thumari queen Naina Devi and the Rani of Jhansi, Laxmi Bai. In *Indian English Literature* M.K. Naik and Shyamala Narayan precisely notes the connection between the title and the significance of the name of the Queen of Jhansi, "Her name is evoked as an ironic parallel to the women in the play who are passive, helpless victims of male tyranny" (207). The historical narratives of two bold and courageous women are a constant source of inspiration for optimistic vision of all women since they wielded their power by defying and rebelling against the established social and patriarchal norms. Dattani sounds to be prophetic by incorporating two legends in the play because his intension may be to send a strong message to all women to rebel against the orthodox and patriarchal frames if they really desire to be free from the shackles of violence against them.

## Conclusion

Mahesh Dattani's *Bravely Fought the Queen* is not all about the patriarchy, the fragmented urban family, the troubled conjugal life, the mismatched marriage, the brute violence against women; it also brings out to notice the resilience of women in adverse circumstances. The play can be read as the documentary record of resolute women – optimistic and hopeful. Though the abrupt ending of the play does not suggest something concrete and traditional, this can arguably be made out that it is the manifestation of the sense of the recovery of the loss of the past. Chaudhuri aptly sums up, "The fissure between conventional and current cultures having thrown up a new social landscape, the play races towards a brave culmination, laying bare the gruesome truth that lie behind the pretence of conservative Indian morality" (32).

*Bravely Fought the Queen* also allows the reader/audience rebel voices to be heard. The most important speculation that can be formulated at this point is that the institution of patriarchy seems to be weakened with the force of anti-patriarchal voices. Neelam Gorhe in her article "Combating Violence against Women for Their Empowerment" prophetically avers, "A combination of awareness building and gender sensitization in society, better enforcement of laws and empower of women will aid the process of reaching a violence free world" (167). And that is what Mahesh Dattani's interest and effort lies in awareness building and gender sensitization. With the rapid urbanisation of India and quick modernization of the country and of polymorphous culture and society, Dattani's *Bravely Fought the Queen* exerts an indelible imprint on readers'/audience's mind. The play is very much relevant and contemporary and may well be contextualized in any urban society in India without problems.

## Works Cited

Agrawal, Anju Bala. "The Drama of Mahesh Dattani: A Study in Technique". *The Dramatic World of Mahesh Dattani: A Critical Exploration.* Ed. Amar Nath Prasad. New Delhi: Sarup Book Publishers, 2009. 1-19. Print.

Chaudhuri, Asha Kuthari. *Mahesh Dattani: An Introduction.* New Delhi: Foundation Books, 2005. Print. Contemporary Indian Writers in English.

Das, Sangeeta. "The Sensational Issues in the Plays of Mahesh Dattani". *The Commonwealth Review* 13.2 (2004): 111-18. Print.

Dattani, Mahesh. *Collected Plays.* New Delhi: Penguin Books, 2000. Print

Gorhe, Neelam. "Combating Violence against Women for Their Empowerment". *Empowering the Indian Women.* Comp. and ed. Promilla Kapur. New Delhi: Publications Divisions: The Ministry of Information and Broadcasting: Govt of India, 2001. 147-168. Print.

Ignatius, Rozario. "Contemporary Social Issues in the Plays of Mahesh Dattani". *The Commonwealth Review* 13.2(2004): 104-10. Print.

Jha, Gauri Shankar. "Dattani's Exercise in Postcolonialism". *The Commonwealth Review* 13.2 (2004): 148-57. Print.

McRae, John. "An Introduction to the Plays of Mahesh Dattani". *Final Solutions and Other Plays.* Madras: Manas, 1994. 7-12. Print.

Mee, Erin B., ed. "Introduction". *Drama Contemporary: India.* Baltimore and London. The Johns Hopkins University Press, 2001. 1-19. Print.

________. "Contemporary Indian Theatre: Three Voices". *Performing Arts Journal* 19.1 (1997): 1-5. *JSTOR.* Web. 13 May 2010.

Naik, M. K. and Shyamala A. Narayan. *Indian English Literature: 1980 – 2000: A Critical Survey.* Delhi: Pencraft International, 2001. Print.

Tyagi, Alka. "Diversity of Themes: The Plays of Mahesh Dattani". *The Commonwealth Review* 13.2 (2004): 119-22. Print.

Uniyal, Ranu. "Conversing with Mahesh Dattani". *The Commonwealth Review* 13.2 (2004): 176-84. Print.

# 7

# Feminism in the Dance Dramas of Tagore

— Bina Biswas

The world knows him as a poet, philosopher, thinker, painter, musician and social activist, but few know the Nobel Laureate Rabindranath Tagore as a feminist, with gender issues forming the underlying theme in many of his works. From *Chitrangada* to *Chokher Bali*, he was scornful in his comments against gender suppression. He has wonderfully celebrated womanhood in many of his works and his works are relevant even today.

Tagore's works—stories, novels, poetry, and drama—all have women characters in the kernel. As the plots thicken, the women characters emerge alive and the author's social perception is discovered. He does not cut any reformist image for himself; he is concerned with the umpteen ills that plague our society. He draws attention to the problems and then leaves the rest to the reader to comprehend.

Tagore was naturally sensitized over the predicament of women in Indian society; he wanted to establish the individuality of women because individuality ensures dignity, self-respect and sexual-independence of women. From the very beginning of the twentieth century Tagore conceptualized the newer complexities, various ideas and current thoughts of social life of Bengal. There were already signs of break-up of large Bengali joint families and community life. Sense of individual identity became firmer, there developed a need for determining the individual's relation with society.

Tagore advanced the women's cause by showing rebellion by his heroines. Individualism is the marker of his female characters. They are crusader of individual freedom. He campaigned for women's individuality ever since he wrote *Chokher Bali* (The Eyesore). He oscillates between traditionalism and bold unconventionality on the gender question in his works.

Tagore's heroines are not extravagantly traditional. They are the 'new woman'. They undergo emotional crises. They want love, affection, self-expression and freedom of thought. Tagore's progressivist thinking was vehemently protested in his age – but what the great seer could feel and write more than one and half century before what had to come true in modern times. The modern women are not only Feminists but are a kind of revolt against social conventions. Feminism is not only consciousness of females for equality with males but Tagore seems to be asking "new questions of old texts".

An attempt has been made to focus on the feminism reflected in Tagore's *Chitrangada*, *Natir Puja* and *Chandalika* in this paper and then evaluate these works as per Tuttle's Feminist Theories.

In the last decade of the nineteenth century, travelling through the rivers and plains of Bengal to look after the family estates, Tagore wrote many short stories, poems, plays and introduced a new form—*Natyakabya*/dance drama or the dramatic poem. In this genre, like play, there are verse dialogues between characters. This form was borrowed from Western literature. *Chitrangada* (1938) is unique. A proper play, in true Greek tradition, is divided into several scenes instead of one. The merit of all the dramatic poems lies in their poetry, and the roots of Tagore are deeply deep-seated in the Indian in the Indian tradition and culture.

Tagore's dance dramas enter into direct contact with his poetic material, between the intangible and the tangible. They occupy a position where religion, poetry, music and dance find a merger. In Tagore's dance dramas, plain speech progressively develops into finely tuned speech and then draws itself up into emotionally charged songs and the corresponding action is signifying the self: intersections of class, caste and gender issues. Songs and dances in these dramas are an extension of the dialogues and action, not having any separate role to play. In the dance dramas, dance becomes a part of the songs as the natural outcome of a literary culmination. The dance dramas illustrate Tagore's bold and perceptive trialling with various literary forms and techniques and the radical nature of his ideological orientation.

Unlike previous Bengali dramas, Tagore's dance dramas emphasize a fusion of lyrical flow and emotional rhythm tightly focused on a core idea. Tagore liberated dance from the shackles of formal, geometrical patterns of some set movements, tinctured new life and spirit in the dance forms and rendered a supple touch of graceful elegance to them. He conceived of mingling drama with dance in a subtle manner so that it would have a profound imprint on the psyche and mind of the audience. Theatre, songs and dances were finely blended in an unprecedented way in these dance dramas fusing in themselves Indian tradition and culture as well as western philosophies. Integrating several dance forms in his dramas, His dance dramas present a unique blend of music, rhythm and expressions. In them, he has freely adopted in his own way the style and techniques from Manipuri, Kathak, Bharat Natyam, Kathakali, folk dances and even European dances like the ballet. Tagore's dances are yielding, supple, graceful and spontaneous with a poignant effect.

In his dance dramas, the dances do not follow any strict convention or set pattern of the intricate classical dances of the past. Rather, these dances portray the inner worth or essence of the songs through the elegant gestures and expressions. In the dance dramas, Tagore lets the dances weave the story in an eloquent and poised way creating a elusive union of fiction with romantic imagination. The gestures and expressions of the dance-drama do not need the help of words or speech. The dances aptly express the essence of the songs. In these dance dramas, dance is seen as soul's mirror that gives expression to the soul's yearnings and aspirations, the ecstasies and agonies, the dreams and frustrations. The dance dramas of Tagore, a genre quite unique in his time and milieu, portray the radical nature of his conception of women and the maturation of their selfhood.

The story of *Chitrangada* is a simple one, narrated in 13 shlokas—11 in Adhyaya 207 and two more in Adhyaya 209—of the Adiparva of the *Mahabharata*. The timeframe of *Chitrangada* extends to one year. The imaginative pen of Tagore turns these short episodes of 13 shlokas into a dramatic poem of 1, 014, with 11 scenes, set in an unrhymed metre called payar – a numerical metre of 14 letters and regular rhyme.

On 25 February 1940, about the genesis of *Chitrangada*, Tagore said,

> Many years ago I was going by train from Santiniketan in the direction of Kolkata. I think it was the month of *Chaitra* (March-April). Along the edge of the railway tracks there was a forest of wild trees. Innumerable yellow, purple, white flowers were blooming. Seeing them it occurred to me that after sometime the sun will be quite hot and this colourful illusion of flowers will wither – then in the fields of the village, on the branches of the trees there will be mangoes – the very nature of the trees introduces its treasure of juice concealed within the fruits. Suddenly, it seemed to me that if a beautiful woman realised that she was loved for the illusion of her youth alone then she might hate her beauty as she would consider her a rival of her own self! A momentary infatuation calls for an external appearance procured as a blessing from *Basanta* (Spring) to fulfil biological need. A character within benefits the beloved and the lover and helps their voyage together. Such a character is the true introduction to the soul, which does not get tired and tarnished despite exposure to a dusty environ. The force of character is the primary sustenance of life; it does not depend upon the immediate purpose of the world.
>
> I felt giving a dramatic shape to this idea and I remembered the story of *Chitrangada* from the *Mahabharata*. This story with some

> modifications remained in my mind for quite sometime. Finally, I found time to write the same in a lonely town of Pandua I Orissa.
>
> (*Parekh, Shailesh, Chitrangada and Other Dramatic Poems*: Rupa & Co, 2007, p.9)

*Chitrangada* is a dramatic poem wherein Tagore, the poet, ever in quest of truth, expresses his views on truth and beauty in a poetic style and dramatic manner. Tagore's biographer, Krishna Kripalani rightly said regarding *Chitrangada*:

> ...a lyrical drama par excellence, the breath of spring blows through every line of it, making it languorous with the ecstasy of sensuous delight. Indeed, the theme is the enchantment of spring and the power of its spell on the senses, and Spring is itself one of the characters in the play, which is one of Rabindranath's best, and perhaps the only one that is flawless, if anything made by man can be called flawless. Not a line would one like to take away from it; one wishes it were longer – in the original Bengali where every utterance quivers with lyrical passion held in masterly restraint. The play is in blank verse, his last great experiment in that form.
>
> (*Parekh, Shailesh, Chitrangada and Other Dramatic Poems*: Rupa & Co, 2007 p.13)

The play is very characteristic of the author, in the sense that it does not embody a seasonal mood or idea which he outgrew but represents a basic and permanent attitude of his mind and philosophy—his unification of man and nature, the latter almost an active participant in the drama of life, and his concern with the perennial questions—what is beauty? what is love? what is true and enduring basis of man-woman relationship?

The play succeeds not much as a play but as enchanting and significant poetry. It succeeds because of the inner laws of art, the laws of beauty, and this beauty we encounter in the persistent veracity of the poet's vision and in the perfection of the structure as a whole. *Chitrangada* is great poetry because of its delicate but bold psychological construct, glorious description, tenderness and grandeur of the passion, evocative images and metaphors and for its music and melody.

Rabindranath Tagore challenges the traditional view of woman as the weaker sex. Tagore's *Chitrangada* is as strong as a man. She is an expert in riding, hunting, duel and war. She has an ambition to challenge Arjuna in a single combat. When Arjuna in the forest rejects her and when she narrates this to Basanta and Madana, one finds how beautifully she understands that she is a woman:

> One day, alone had I set out in search of a deer,
> in the deep forest, on the banks of the river Purna.
> tying up my horse with a tree,
> following the pug marks of a deer,
> I proceeded on a crooked forest path
> difficult to tread upon,
> darkness echoed ever
> with the chirping of crickets.
> Going on further down, suddenly I saw,
> obstructing the tapered path,
> sleeping on the ground,
> a man tousled but resolute.
> In a tone of scorn, I asked him to move away –
> neither did he move nor did he look at me.
> With anxiety, rage and conceit,
> I goaded him with the edge of the bow –
> with the speed of an arrow
> that straight and large body shot up
> and stood before me –
> like a fire resting in the ashes,
> at once flashing up in a flame when fuelled.
> He stared at my face for a moment –
> seeing this child-like figure of mine,
> the anger in the eyes vanished in an instant
> on the edge of the lips, danced a line of smile –
> serene, simple, concealing curiosity.
> I have learned the arts of men,
> adopted the dress of men, stayed with them,
> but seeing his face,
> seeing his self-confident and firm image,
> instantly I remembered that I am a woman.
> At that moment,
> Little did I realise that there stood in front of me
> a man!
>
> (Translation mine)

She does not go back home dejected. She tries to show her strength and power by gaining perfect beauty from Madana. She seeks revenge of her insult of rejection by making him to surrender before her borrowed beauty. But Tagore gave her strength by making her come out of her garb of a beautiful woman which she has donned to woo Arjuna, the moment she wins him over. The indomitable spirit in *Chitrangada* makes her immortal in Tagore's works.

*Chitrangada* is an ingeminating of Tagore's breakthrough feminist dance drama. Act I opens with the King and Queen of Manipur praying for a son and receiving Chitrangada, a daughter. They rear her as a son. In Scene II, the princess, now the ruler of her kingdom is out hunting in the forest with her friends, when she encounters the legendary hero, Arjuna, protagonist of the *Mahabharata*. She falls in love. Dressed as a woman, Chitrangada offers herself to Arjuna. He refuses her on grounds of vowed celibacy. Although Chitrangada is left in tears, the warrior in her is undefeated. She asks Madana, the God of Love, for the weapon she needs, Beauty, for one year. Act II opens with a transformed Chitrangada marvelling at her beauty, at feelings that she had never had before. Arjuna, bewitched by her beauty, breaks his vow of celibacy and declares his pride in his manhood. Chitrangada's rival is now her own body, and she realizes the bitterness of her victory. She also watches her hero belittles himself. In desperation, she goes to Madana who assures her that she needs to play the game a while longer. Arjuna also tires of this love when suddenly he encounters villagers getting ready to fight off prowlers. He learns from them of the woman who rules Manipur, one who loves like a mother and fights like a tigress, a King. He longs to meet his equal. It is time for Chitrangada to return her "stolen" beauty to Madana. In the last act, Chitrangada, the Warrior Princess, enters her own court and demands the right and power to be an equal in prosperity and adversity if Arjuna still wants to marry her. Arjuna accepts her on her terms. Chitrangada confessing the truth about her beauty, reveals herself as the princess and asserts:

> I am Chintrangada,
> Not a goddess, but not an ordinary woman either.
> Worth worshipping am I not;
> to be ignored and kept in the wings, that also am I not.
> If allowed to share
> the perilous path and perplexing worries,
> I would be helpful in all your difficulties.
> You will know me if I am your companion
> In all your joys and sorrows.

Vyasa's Chitrangada is not only brought up as a son but is also attractive enough to be appealing to Arjuna, who approaches her father for her hand in marriage. In spite of her being brought up as a successor to the throne, she does not have much of a role in the story as well as the matter of her own marriage, which is settled between the two men, on a condition set forth by the father of the bride Chitrangada is a woman who seeks and rules her own destiny and pursues her goal with the determination of a single-minded warrior that she is trained to be.

> In a sense, both Arjuna and Chitrangada as portrayed by Tagore as images of his own mind – modern but steeped in the traditions of the Indian culture. Both of them pursue their love on their own, seeking the help of the deities known to be kind, and eventually drifting towards the quest of truth, which is revealed at the end. The quest for truth (satya) of the self was a lifelong mission of Tagore, and a path he pursued was that of beneficence (shiv) and beauty (sundar).
>
> Tagore has a strong argument for gender equality in *Chitrangada*, where the princess makes it clear to the rather foolish, sexist and love-struck Arjuna that she will marry him only if he takes for what she is – neither a goddess nor a doormat but an equal in every way, a partner who will share joys and fears and stand shoulder to shoulder in all battles.

Tagore's *Chitrangada* conforms to Lisa Tuttle's feminist theory of asking "new questions of old texts." She cites the goals of feminist criticism as: (1) To develop and uncover a female tradition of writing, (2) to interpret symbolism of women's writing so that it will not be lost or ignored by the male point of view, (3) to rediscover old texts, (4) to resist sexism in literature, and (5) to increase awareness of the sexual politics of language and style.

A few years after the publication of *Chitrangada* some Bengali critics had found it obscene and corrupt and had held Tagore responsible for 'attributing glory to sin'.

In the touching tale, *Natir Puja*, Tagore relates about a young girl in ancient India, not too high on the social hierarchy, but resolute and brave enough to defy the royal diktat. She knew that she would have to pay a price for her deed. Yet she did not flinch away. She gave up her life for what she considered to be her duty. *Natir Puja* is a ballad, but its dramatic qualities have inspired people to act it out on stage and are still immensely popular. Bimbisara, the King of Magadha, had a stupa built in a corner of the palace garden, on a tiny toe-nail of Gautam Buddha. Prayers were offered there every evening and lamps were lit by the women of the Royal household. After Bimbisara, when Ajatashatru became the king, he ruthlessly put to sword all those who worshiped the Buddha and put to torch all sacred Buddhist scriptures. He banned the worship of the Buddha in his kingdom. Sreemati was a court dancer. She was an ardent follower of Gautam Buddha. She could not bear to see no lamps lit at the Stupa and resolved to do the Puja on her own. She went to all women of the royal household, to all the queens and intellectuals asking them to accompany her. All of them refused for fear of death. So she went alone and completed the Puja. Seeing the light of a lamp under the stupa, the guards rushed in and put her to death as per the Royal diktat.

Srimati in *Natir Puja* makes supreme sacrifice which is an incredible one. She has equalled herself with the males who sacrificed for the noble cause of religion. Thomas A. Becket in

Eliot's *Murder in the Cathedral* makes deliberate efforts to become martyr. If one compares his sacrifice with Srimati one may conclude that 'Srimati is superior.' He is a priest of high rank and she is a court dancer of low rank. Srimati becomes a model martyr. Her religious sense is superior to those who just pretend to be religious. I would like to draw a distinction between the 'real' Beckett and the 'real' Canterbury Chaucer's pilgrims went to, one that still exists and Eliot's Beckett which is Eliot's alter ego reflecting his inner spiritual struggle from whence comes the selfishness (the desire to be a martyr, of the fourth tempter)and the real Beckett was not like that and this is a well known fact now on the other hand the comparison between Srimati and Beckett in terms of position/class and gender and implicitly between Tagore and Eliot—if we grant the validity of literature and martyrdom at all, I think two primary issues must not be confused, the character with its historical genesis and secondly not to compare different historical contingencies and exigencies on the same plane – Srimati is caught in religious conflict, Beckett in a battle between religion and state – the two are different in its grounds – my view is that both Eliot and Tagore are actually (if the issue is considered to be ideology) hypocrites as Eliot subverts a system he adopted/converted to – Anglicanism – through his play and Tagore pretends to be for women, the untouchables and Buddhism through his writings when he was not for any of these things actually. I hold greater value for the brilliant lives of Srimati and Beckett for the motives of history and not that what Eliot ascribed to him.

Another point – it is understood that martyrs in their time and space as noble souls who died for what they believed right, what they thought with conviction but in today's world aren't they, when used by Eliot and Tagore, examples of retrogression – they did not want the world to change and tried taking it back into the past but why this fear of present – shown as degenerate – and the future as something that may be even worse in both of them, unless corrected by them – there is no healthy mix of the past, present and future outside of their works, according to them, no awareness that the day may come when historical wrongs will be righted by others or rather it is that fear that others may do it that makes them both typical patriarchal figures of authoritarian control, laying down how it should go in the future – whether Tagore in his essays like the collection, 'creative unity' or Eliot in his last two treatises on culture and Christianity; frankly Tagore could not predict what was to happen in the third front in India now that is slowly coming into being – made up of the Dalit, Communist, Muslim, Christian, Sikh, Jain, Buddhist, Sects, Techno-communities, Tribes, Atheist, Feminist, LGBT, poor and other unprivileged minorities or Eliot, the empty churches of Europe of today being replaced by vibrant idiosyncratic followers of Christ who do not care for religion or religions – and that is why they seem a bit outdated – the shape of future is going to be different and unfortunately these great writers couldn't see it – they only walked to the tune of an antiquated drum.

In his dance drama *Chandalika,* he explores the intimate links between dance and female self-construction. Tagore opts for the non-conformed icons–warrior, untouchable, and courtesan. The women who danced in Tagore's experimental dance-dramas in the 1930s in Bengal in full public view, were far from being confined to the inner precincts of their home, and were called 'impure', 'inauthentic', non-classical yet powerful alternatives of being modern Indians. This shows his feminist orientation in the politics of woman's emancipation in the nationalist era.

Dance dramas written by Tagore can be used as points of entry into a discourse on feminism. In *Chandalika* he uses dance as a subtle form of self-expression for Prakriti; without the dances the desire for expression in Prakriti would remain inarticulate. It is through the free and supple movements of the body that Prakriti as a woman expressly articulates her desires– emotional, physical and spiritual – at once liberating the female dancing body from the strict rules of classical dance as well as traditional society that viewed dance as impure and demoralizing. It is through dance that Prakriti gains her freedom from the constricting strictures of 'pure/impure, body/soul, ethical/unethical, self/other that bind her'.

Prakriti in *Chandalika* stands for the revolt against conventions. She proves that a woman has equal right to choose her life member. She does not care for caste, creed, and religion for the fulfilment of her ambition. Tagore's women characters are as conscious as modern ladies. They try to gain self - improvement. Tagore has given priority to his female characters. Her consciousness inculcates in her mind the strength to venture further to gain Ananda. She brings him under the control of black magic. She withdraws the magical effect from Ananda out of sympathy. Thus Prakriti becomes stronger than Ananda.

Tagore's 'Chitrangada' 'Srimati' and 'Prakriti' have significant status. They are shown self-sufficient and strong. They emerge victorious. Chitrangada proves her ability by defeating Arjuna in the battle of romance. Srimati proves her superiority by making supreme sacrifice for the noble cause of religion. Prakriti shows her strength by making Ananda to come to her door-steps begging for love. Thus Tagore's women characters are superior to other ordinary women in the society. They are role models for the women. Suffering women can improve their circumstances by imitating the women characters of Tagore. They may realize their strength and may improve their condition.

## Works Cited

Choudhuri, Indra Nath. "Theatric Form of Tagore's Dance Drama and Its Symbolism": in Chaudhuri, Bhudeb and K. G. Subramanyan (eds.) *Rabindranth Tagore and the Challenges of Today*, Shimla: Indian Institute of Advanced Study, 1988, p. 130

Chaudhuri, Sutapa: *Signifying the Self: Intersections of Class, Caste and Gender in Rabindranath Tagore's Dance Drama Chandalika* (1938) Dr. Kanailal Bhattacharyya College, India

Das, Sisir Kr.(ed.) *The English Writings of Rabindranath Tagore*, Vol. 1, Poems, New Delhi: Sahitya Academy,1994.

Iyenger K. R. S. 2001. "Prarthana Purkayastha, Warrior, Untouchable, Courtesan: Fringe Women In Tagore's Dance Dramas": *South Asia Research*, Vol.29 (3), Sage Publications Ltd., 2009, p. 255.

Naik M. K. 1995, *A History of Indian writing in English*, New Delhi. Sahitya Akademi.

Parekh, Shailesh, *Chitrangada and Other Dramatic Poems*: Rupa & Co, 2007

Rabindranath Tagore: *Religion of Man* (New Delhi, Rupa & Co., 2005)

Rao, Shyamala B. *Indian Writing in English, Tagore And His Chandalika. A Critical Study*. New Delhi: Sterling Publishers.

# 8

# Feminism in Rabindranath Tagore's *Chandalika*

— Nirmala S. Padmavat

## Introduction

Tagore is a well- known Indian English writer of Rennaissance age. He is the well-known philosopher, founder of 'Shantiniketan', a great poet, novelist, jornalist, musician, mystic and playwright. Talking about female, he views his women in his writing. Many of his dramas are dance dramas, among which *Chandalika* has a special place.

*Chandalika* is based on the theme of female desire of love and sacrifice of life of a female for daughter's love. "Tagore's 1936 essay Nari (Woman) urged women to step out of the precinct of their home to pursue an education and cultivate their intellect stressing the importance of their autonomous self development."[1] Feminism thus used by Tagore in his various writings, e.g., mother's love, can't be compared with anything, furthermore 'Mother' is the great creation of God. The same theme he has shown in *Chandalika*. There is only one male character is in *Chandalika*, having a less important role compared to female characters. He has given more importance to female characters.

## Theme of *Chandalika*

Chandalika (Name Prakrati) is an untouchable girl and the daughter of a magician. "This society is called as 'Chandal' in that age, and emerges as a voice of the silenced and marginalized in history. She is a rebel who questions societal norms that relegated her to an existence of a lesser being, an untouchable. She once meets Ananda, the Buddhist monk, who demands her to draw water from the well, and she rejects it due to untouchability. He opens her eyes and conveys to her that there is no caste differences and all humans are equal one. "This realization of Prakriti's selfhood is intermingled with the conscious negation of her socially imposed caste and class as well as as acknowledgement of herself as a women proud of her self worth."[2] After the realization of the self, she meets Ananda many times and falls in love with him, becomes possessive of him and asks her mother to use her magic power to get him as her lover. At first site, Maya, her mother refused to do it, as he was a Buddhist monk and it is wrong to one use magic. She warned her that when she stops her magic, she would die. This shows her possessiveness for Ananda, her love.

The mother's blind love motivats, her to use the magic power for Prakrati's love, Ananda. As the magic starts, Ananda starts to come back from his spiritual journey. " The magic powers of Maya contest with Ananda's spiritual power intil he is forced against his will to come back to Prakriti."[3] Now he looks paler and weaker. Prakrati is observing all these changes in Ananda and as he is near her door, she asks her mother to stop the magic. For this is the moment when she realizs her mistake and wants Ananda to go back on his spiritual journey. Mother stops the magic and dies immediately. Ananda goes on his journey and Pakrati remains alone.

Thus, Rabindranath Tagore has shown the sacrifice and greatness of females in his drama entitled *Chandalika*. The era in which he conceived *Chandalika* in the form of a dance drama was also an age in which untouchablility and narrow- mindedness prevailed in the society. "Tagore's women characters are superior to other ordinary women in society. They are role model for women. Suffering women can improve their circumstances by imitating the women characters of Rbindranath Tagore."[4] Through her dance movements, Chandalika (Prakriti) articulates her anger and love—anger, against a social status imposed upon her to which she found herself bound for life, and love for a monk who respected and acknowledged her as a human being.

## Chandalika Realises Her True Identity

One of the moments defining helplessness by Prakriti in the play is when Ananda, the monk and disciple of Lord Buddha pleads, "Give me some water," and she resists by voicing her powerlessness to quench his thirst. This is the moment of awakening for Chandalika. The monk tells her that she was not 'impure' but a child of the same Almighty like others. She is first a human being and a child of God. Now realization dawns upon Prakriti that all this time she has been a victim of society and its social stigma. Recounting this incident to her mother, she says, "This is my new birth. In satisfying his thirst, I feel baptized. I am aware of my 'self' now mother. I now know what freedom tastes like".

## Possessiveness of Females for Love

It is true that the monk appears as a symbol of freedom to Prakriti but he is not the protagonist of the play, Unlike the Buddhist legend describing Ananda's journey that Tagore modelled his play on. For Tagore, Prakriti's journey occupies centre-stage. Tagore, through his drama, has signified that the society's issues and their superstitions never bind humanity. It is, indeed, ironic to see how a girl named 'Prakriti' meaning 'nature' can be enmeshed in a web of class, caste and gender distinctions. Nature is meant to take in everything and is never victimized by the society, unlike 'Prakriti'.

Prakriti commits the mistake of keeping her mother's life at stake when her love for Ananda crosses all boundaries. Her blind love for Ananda makes her to plead to her mother, Maya, to bring him to her by chanting the fiercest magic spell of

'Nagpash Mantra'. Only in the penultimate scene does she realize her guilt of making a person suffer against his wishes. When she sees him standing in front of her in almost a mutilated state, she repents and surrenders in shame. She now realizes that Ananda has lost all his charm when she has forcefully tried to mean him away from the aura of his thoughts and positivity that he had to go through the journey of being a saint, a monk spreading humanity. In a battle of magical chants and spiritual power, she concludes that love can never be forced or possessed.

## Characteristics of Ananda

Ananda, as Tagore has placed him in the story as a monk, wanders across the world to make people realize their fate and their true being. He does the same to make Prakriti realize that she is a free being not bound by the allegations of society to be an untouchable. He is selfless and performs his duties as a monk to make people realize that they are all the same and in their hearts resides the soul of the Almighty and that they belong to Him first.

## Characteristics of Maya (Prakriti's Mother)

Maya has been shown here as a magician, though she does not believe in black magic. She performs magic for good. She is selfless and appears in the story as a pure, motherly soul by helping her child to get her love, Ananda. Even after her warning to Prakriti about her imminent death with the halt of magic in the process, without caring for herself, she risks her own life to brighten the life of her child. She is aware that the monk has his charm and positive aura due to his own sacrifice that he has made for the society. This shows nothing but the awareness of worldly things as a mother.

## Feminism in *Chandalika*

Tagore had written this drama in the era where a male- dominant society prevailed. However, this drama had female characters as the prominent ones. Tagore has projected a female to possess a sacrificing nature, as the magician Chandal did sacrifice her life for procuring the love for her daughter. A female as projected by Tagore is also shown as a person with infinite dedication and possessiveness for her love, be it the one-sided love of Prakriti for Ananda or be it the motherly love of Chandal for her daughter.

Men, considering women to be weak and subtle, overshadowed them in that era; in fact, Tagore has unmasked the true woman of the society, who fights for her love. A woman is that element in the society who will never endorse her gains at the stake of losing the real identity of her lover. This moment is signified in the story when Prakriti stops her mother during the magic of getting her love, Ananda, to fall for her. Prakriti realizes that Ananda has lost all the charm and beauty in this process. He has his positive aura as a monk who does not believe in falling in love with a person but only with God. Prakriti loves Ananda because he is the one who unleashes the real identity of her being a human first and not an untouchable. She is moved by this act of the monk and falls in love with him without realizing that making people realize their true inner self is the duty of a monk, which he has performed. "Prakriti shows her strength by making Ananda to come to her door-steps begging for love."[5]

## Atmospherics in *Chandalika*

Poetic speeches, mellifluous songs and artistic dance postures coupled with the fragrance of incense sticks placed at occasional junctures create an atmosphere that has the audience completely mesmerized.

## Tagore is Immortal

*Chandalika* has been performed and staged in many languages with multiple interpretations across the country, proving only one thing—'Tagore shall never die.' He continues to live in his literary works and music that will never cease to have relevance across decades. The ongoing cultural festival will stage some of Tagore's most popular plays that one can't afford to miss.

## Conclusion

Thus, Rabindranath Tagore's women characters in *Chandalika* are superior with more strength and self-realization, and with a conscious mind. A mother's sacrifices for her daughter, and Pakriti's sacrifice for Ananda's love show the greatness of females in this drama.

## References

1. Pathan, M.D. "Feminism Reflected in Rabindranath Tagore's Plays: *Chitra, Natirpuja* and *Chandalika*" *RNI* Feb. 2011 Volume-I Issue-17.
2. Chaudhary, Sujata "Signifying the self: Intersections of class, caste and gender in Rabindranath Tagore's Dance Drama *Chandalika" (1938). Rupkatha Journal*, Vol.2 No.4.
3. Ibid.
4. Pathan, M.D. *op.cit.*
5. Ibid.

## 9

# Interpreting Female-Male Consciousness in Tagore's *Chitra*: An Empirical Study

— S.D. Sasikiran

Among the literary genres, drama stands alone as the most peculiar, appealing and delightful, since man is projected from several dimensions. In Indian Literature in English the contribution is very meagre here when compared to the other genres like poetry or fiction. The birth of Indian drama emphasizes that it is an integral part of our society and culture.

Though the first drama was by Krishna Mohan Banerjee (1813–1885) *The Persecuted* (1831), the real journey of Indian drama started in 1871 with the emergence of Michael Madhusudan Dutt's *Is this Called Civilization.* Sri Aurobindo sketched the western personalities in Indian traditional garb with a different treatment to each play. Harindranath Chattopadyay's plays projected the brighter and nobler aspects of man in his The Five Plays – *The Window, The Parrot, The Sentry's Lantern, The Coffin and Siddhartha, Man of Peace* that reveal his socialistic approach. In *Yama and Yami* (1948), Manjari S. Isvaran who is a well known Indo- Anglian writer voices a happy synthesis of realism and idealism. G.V. Desani, a talented Indian novelist and short story writer, penned an entirely different 'poem play' *Hali* which is an attempt to project Hali's confrontation of creation and destruction. He received high praise for its originality. Lakhan Dev's *Tiger Claw* (1967) is a historical verse play in three Acts on the controversial murder of Afzal Khan, the Muslim General of Bijapur, by Shivaji. Mahesh Dattani is one of India's best and most serious contemporary playwrights, writing in English. He is the first playwright in English to be honoured with the Sahitya Akademi Award. A director, actor, dancer, teacher and writer, Mahesh Dattani has a long chain of plays written by him, such as *Tara, Night Queen, Final Solutions, Dance like a Man* and many more. His plays deal with the social and contemporary issues. All these playwrights have made a mark and enriched the drama in India. Tagore also did the same.

The play, *Chitra (*1914*),* a lyrical drama divided into IX scenes, written by Ravindranath Tagore, is based on a humble episode from the grand Indian epic – *The Mahabharata.* In the course of his wanderings in the length and breadth of India during his term of exile, in fulfilment of a vow of penance, Arjuna came to Manipur in the eastern Himalayas, an almost mystic kingdom renowned for its natural beauty. There he saw Chitrangada, the beautiful daughter of Chitravahana, the king of the country. Her father demurred on the plea that, according to the matrilineal customs of his people, the children born of Chitrangada were heir to Manipur; he could not allow his heirs to be taken away from Manipur by their father. Arjuna agreed to the stipulation that he would take away neither his wife Chitrangada nor any children borne by her from Manipur, and wed the princess on this premise. The king had, always treated her as a son and had made her his heir. Continuing, he said:

> The one son that will be born to her must be the perpetuator of my race. That son will be the price that I shall demand for this marriage. You can take her, if you like, on this condition.

Arjuna promised and took Chitrangada as his wife, and lived in her father's capital for three years. When a son was born to them, they named him Babruvahana. Arjuna embraced her with affection, and taking leave of her and her father, set out again on his travels.

Chitrangada is very much like a modern-day musical with the story put to music and with the characters acting out the parts in dance. Tagore's story differs a bit from the story of Chitrangada in the *Mahabharata*. He expands on the character and gives her new life. In Tagore's story, Chitrangada is the only child of the King of Manipur. Being the heir to the throne, she dresses like a man and is the protector of the land.

> ... thy father brings thee up as his son. He has taught thee the use of the bow and all the duties of a king.

Her people look to her to keep them safe. One day, she meets Arjuna and seeing him in action as he hunts in the forest, she falls in love with him.

> Then for the first time in my life I felt myself a woman, and knew that a man was before me.

Arjuna is impressed by her fighting abilities but all along believes her to be a man. Chitrangada falls madly in love with Arjuna but believes he could never love her the way she is. She receives a boon from Madana, the Hindu god of love, and transforms herself into a beautiful ladylike woman.

> For a single day make me superbly beautiful, even as beautiful as was the sudden blooming of love in my heart. Give me but one brief day of perfect beauty, and I will answer for the days that follow.

When she meets Arjuna again, he can't help but fall in love with her.

> ...there came out from the folding darkness of foliage an apparition of beauty in the perfect form of a woman, and stood on a white slab of stone at the water's brink. It seemed that the heart of the earth must heave in joy under her bare white feet. Me thought the vague veilings of her body should melt in ecstasy into air as the golden mist of dawn melts from off the snowy peak of the

> eastern hill. She bowed herself above the shining mirror of the lake and saw the reflection of her face. She started up in awe and stood still; then smiled, and with a careless sweep of her left arm unloosed her hair and let it trail on the earth at her feet. She bared her bosom and looked at her arms, so flawlessly modelled, and instinct with exquisite caress. Bending her head she saw the sweet blossoming of her youth and the tender bloom and blush of her skin. She beamed with a glad surprise. So, of the white lotus bud on opening her eyes in the morning were to arch her neck and see her shadow in the water, would she wonder at herself the livelong day. But a moment after the smile passed from her face and a shade of sadness crept into her eyes. She bound up her tresses, drew her veil over her arms, and sighing slowly, walked away like a beauteous evening fading into the night. To me the supreme fulfilment of desire seemed to have been revealed in a flash and then to have vanished...

Though she believes that she has everything she wants in life, deep down she wishes that he could love her for her true self. When marauders come into her kingdom to take over the villages, Arjuna learns from the people of the kingdom that their princess is the greatest warrior around and they wonder why she isn't there to help protect them now. Arjuna is impressed by the story of this woman who seems to be his equal when it comes to fighting and longs to meet her. "They say that in valour she is a man, and a woman in tenderness." Chitrangada appears and saves her kingdom before revealing her true self to Arjuna. No longer in love with her just for her beauty, Arjuna marries her. They have a son named Babruvahana.

Modern age is considered to be the age of feminism. The women in the modern period have crossed the barriers of society. They have proved their equality to their male counterparts. Feminism is a kind of revolt of women against social conventions. Feminine consciousness is, of course, consciousness of females for equality with males. An attempt has been made to focus on the feminism reflected in Tagore's *Chitra*, in this paper.

In the good old days, a woman was considered as a subordinate and a parasite. She was not independent to lead her life. The rights of a woman were completely neglected. Rabindranath Tagore has brought out his women out of the kitchen and placed them in the active stream of life.

Feminism in Rabindranath Tagore challenges the traditional view of woman as the weaker sex. Tagore's Chitra is as strong as man. She is an expert in riding, hunting, duel and war. She is a type of terror for the evil-doers in the state. She has the ambition to challenge Arjuna in a single combat. When Arjuna in the forest rejects her, she does not go home weeping. She tries to show her strength and power by gaining perfect beauty from Madana. She seeks revenge against her insult of rejection by making him to surrender before her borrowed beauty.

Chitra lived in the olden days but she had a sense of feminism as a modern lady.

Rabindranath Tagore has described the journey of his women characters from ignorance to knowledge. Self-consciousness in all the characters play a vital role in their development. Chitra has no consciousness as woman, she is just the princess of the land. When she sees Arjuna, she is aware for the first time of her womanhood. Physical attraction enhances passion in her heart for Arjuna. She makes an experiment of penance, and borrows beauty due to her self-consciousness. Arjuna violates his vow of celibacy under the impression of Chitra's heavenly beauty. Chitra takes courage and inspiration out of her self-consciousness and acts further. Rabindranath Tagore's women characters are as conscious as modern ladies. They try to gain self-improvement.

> Arjuna, tell me true, if, now at once, by some magic I could shake myself free from this voluptuous softness, this timid bloom of beauty shrinking from the rude and healthy touch of the world, and fling it from my body like borrowed clothes, would you be able to bear it? If I stand up straight and strong with the strength of a daring heart spurning the wiles and arts of twining weakness, if I hold my head high like a tall young mountain fir, no longer

> trailing in the dust like a liana, shall I then appeal to man's eye? No, no, you could not endure it. It is better that I should keep spread about me all the dainty playthings of fugitive youth, and wait for you in patience. When it pleases you to return, I will smilingly pour out for you the wine of pleasure in the cup of this beauteous body. When you are tired and satiated with this wine, you can go to work or play; and when I grow old I will accept humbly and gratefully whatever corner is left for me. Would it please your heroic soil if the playmate of the night aspired to be the helpmate of the day, if the left arm learnt to share the burden of the proud right arm.

Tagore has given priority to his female characters. Chitra has never thought herself inferior to male. So she learns the duties of the male. The modern women have entered several sectors and working respectfully equal to their male counterparts. Chitra's desire of challenging Arjuna in a single combat shows her modernity. She loves her people like her children. As modern women are serving the country joining defence services, she too is defending her people. Rabindranath Tagore's 'Chitra' has a significant status. She is shown as being self-sufficient and self-centred and remains victorious. Chitra proves her ability by defeating Arjuna in the battle of romance.

> I am Chitra. No goddess to be worshipped, nor yet the object of common pity to be brushed aside like a moth with indifference. If you deign to keep me by your side in the path of danger and daring, if you allow me to share the great duties of your life, then you will know my true self. If your babe, whom I am nourishing in my womb be born a son, I shall myself teach him to be a second Arjuna, and send him to you when the time comes, and then at last you will truly know me. Today I can only offer you Chitra, the daughter of a king.

Thus Rabindranath Tagore's Chitra is superior to other ordinary women in the society, and thus a role model for the women. A suffering woman can improve her circumstances by imitating Rabindranath Tagore's Chitra. The modern woman may realize her strength and may improve her condition.

Feminist writings cover all aspects of writing for women, by women, and about women and the issues that concern them. Different writers have expressed their ideas about feminism in unique and groundbreaking ways. Some of the most important works of feminist literature have also been controversial and banned—for their concepts of awakenings to new ways of thinking, feeling, and being. In exploring the world of literature, these heroines come immediately to mind: Edna Pontellier (Kate Chopin), Madame Bovary (Gustave Flaubert), Moll Flanders (Daniel Defoe), Anna Karenina (Leo Tolstoy), Lily Bart, Jane Eyre (Charlotte Bronte), Hester Prynne (Nathaniel Hawthorne), Elizabeth Bennet, Daisy Miller, and Murasaki Shikibu. Tagore's Chitra is par exceltence as she has shown the shades of male and female; love and marriage; daughter and mother; spiritual and worldly desires.

All through the human documentation, woman has been portrayed as an icon of fertility or an idol representing the motherland or even as an individual whose best place is in the kitchen and within the home. Tagore continuously tries to place the central female character as being very independent and with an individual mind *A Vindicaton of the Rights of Woman* by Mary Wollstonecraft who was influenced by the ideas of the French Revolution (1792) lettered the first modern awareness of women's struggle for equal rights. Therefore Tagore's work in the Indian literature of drama is the first milestone for the equality of the sexes.

Seventy-seven years later, in *The Subjection of Women* (1869), John Stuart Mill (1806-1873), a British philosopher, expressed it very powerfully: "All men, except the most brutish, desire to have in the woman most nearly connected with them, not a forced slave but a willing one, not a slave merely, but a favorite. They have therefore put everything in practice to enslave their minds" (Norton Anthology Vol.2, 991). Tagore utilizes the importance of the idea of Swami Vivekananda, who highlighted the importance of women as he makes us realize that the history of India is incomplete without any understanding of the trials and tribulations of women. Women constitute half of India as a nation of people.

As seen in the great Indian epic written by Veda Vyasa, *The Mahabharata* presents social, religious, political, and philosophical discourses through the dynamics of a few members of a large family. Tagore does the same thing with the present work in projecting the title—character from these shades. Virginia Woolf's *A Room of One's Own* (1929) developed and enhanced these views with a strong female sensibility and criticism. *A Room of One's Own* became an important precursor of feminist literary criticism. Here, Virginia Woolf argues that the male-dominated ideas of the patriarchal society prevented women from realising their creativity and true potential.

According to Betty Friedan (1921–2006), an American writer, activist and feminist, in the 1950s women had gone back to the house abandoning their jobs to men who came back from the war to claim their positions, and a feminine mystique was created in the media making the housewife and the mother the ideal models for all women. Promoting women's ideal reality within the domestic realm, this mystique had reduced the identity of women to sexual and social passivity. Tagore attempted to demystify this false feminine mystique, which Betty Friedan described as "a world confined to her own body and beauty, the charming of man, the bearing of babies, and the physical care and serving of husband, children and home" (155) in order to renew the woman's own identity. Tagore had started a new consciousness raising movement, and undoubtedly played a central role in developing the new discipline of women's studies.

The study of a female tradition in literature has transgressed the boundaries of the traditional canon in its theoretical, political and literary assumptions. A rereading of critical theories and methods of the literary tradition is possible only if those theories and methods are challenged from within their own assumptions. This is what French feminist criticism aimed at starting with Helene Cixous who has challenged the binary opposition of man/ woman in the value system. Cixous has subverted the logocentric logic behind the underlying paradigms of male/female opposition in culture and literature. Binary systems validate logocentricism so convincingly that "to decentre logo centricism would invoke re-versing the values placed on each component in the binary terms which constitute it" (53). Once the binary opposition of male/female is reversed, the signifying supremacy passes on to the once- secondary term in the hierarchy: "female." The supremacy of the privileged term, female, cannot remain in its privileged position to create new values and meanings. This goes on infinitely. Therefore, it is necessary to study the female literary tradition in relation to its male counterpart, and to deconstruct all the binary oppositions that have been falsely created and accepted over the centuries as universal and privileged meta-narratives. For this, Tagore keeps himself from making his feminine players superhuman beings.

The present play has been ever contemporary to the times. Tagore uses psychological realism to paint a better picture of freedom—a freedom without any chains. He successfully webs the life of feminism in a unique unadulterated fashion. He shows through the characters of Chitra's father, Chitravahana and her husband, Arjuna all that is needed to be provided for the woman in order to establish her independence in the human world. Both of them helps Chitra to grow and shape herself in spite of the constant guarding they extend her. They have not compelled their selfish desire – her as the heir or the beloved - as the goal of her but facilitate her to rise to their expectations so naturally and majestically. The drama engrosses from the narrowness of the institutionalized marital practices to the understanding of the spirit of humanism in the Hindu way of life, in which there has been a liberal streak, always trying to assimilate the other ways of living, thinking and relating.

## Works Cited


Dhawan, R.K., *Flowering of Indian Drama*. Prestige Books, New Delhi, 2004.

Eagleton, Mary (ed.), *Feminist Literary Theory: A Reader*, Basil Blackwell, 1986.

Hawthorn, Jeremy, *A Concise Glossary of Contemporary Literary Theory*, 1992.

Iyenger, K.R.S. *Indian Writing in English*, New Delhi: Sterling Publishers, 2001.

Naik M. K., *A History of Indian Writing in English*, New Delhi. Sahitya Akademi. 1995.

Natesan, Sharda Iyer, *Musings on Indian Writing in English: Drama*. Sarup & Sons: Delhi, 2007.

Selden, Raman, *A Reader's Guide to Contemporary Literary Theory*, Harvester Wheatsheaf, 1989.

Sherzer, Dina, "Postmodernism and Feminisms", in Edmund J. Smyth (ed.), *Postmodernism and Contemporary Fiction*, B.T. Batsford Ltd., 1991.

Showalter, Elaine, "The Feminist Critical Revolution", in Elaine Showalter (ed.), *The New Feminist Criticism: Essays on Women, Literature and Theory*, Virago Press, 1986.

_________, *A Literature of their own: from Charlotte Bronte to Doris Lessing*, Virago Press, 1977.

Subramanyam, Lakshmi (Ed.), *Muffled Voices: Women in Modern Indian Theatre*, New Delhi, Shakti, 2002.

Tagore, Rabindranath, *Chitra*, Madras, S.G. Wasni, Macmillan India Ltd. 1992.

Woolf, Virginia, *A Room of One's Own*, Harvester, 1981.

# 10

# Kalidasa's Shakuntala: The Next Trailing Stereotype in the Cult of Ahilya, Sita and Sati

— Sonali Anand

India is an abode of various customs and traditions, rites and rituals, gods and goddesses, religious and languages. Thus its culture is diverse. In any corner of the country the ideal of womanhood is Ahilya, Sita and Sati. Ahilya (the wife of *Rishi* Gautam) had to turn into a stone because of her seduction by Lord Indra. It was her unconscious fault. Sita (Lord Rama's wife) had to pass through an ordeal of fire in order to prove her chastity. Sati burnt herself for the sake of her husband's respect. The basic tenet behind all the three tests which the ideal woman had to take was their chastity, love, respect and faithfulness to their husbands. Their lives were not more important than their husband's honour.

Kalidasa, one of the greatest Indian poet, has introduced one more stereotype to the cult of ideal womanhood, i.e., Shakuntala. She is the heroine of drama *Abhijnana Shakuntalam.* The research paper aims to give an exhaustive study of the position of Shakuntala in her society and a deep insight of her character by vindicating her honour as a 'pure woman'. The story of Dushyanta and Shakuntala has been derived from the epic *Mahabharata.* It has been revived by Kalidasa as a drama. In order to find Shakuntala's position in her society the time period of society has to be analysed. "Pargiter closely examines the chronology of the *Puranas* a nd on the basis of his findings asserts that the *Mahabharata* might have been fought sometime in 1100 B.C. and the epic, consequently must have been composed near that century. The story continued to be larded with more facts and by the 5th century A.D it acquired its present form". The date of Kalidasa had been a controversial issue yet after analyzing several theories "the first century B.C. theory now stands on a firm footing ..."[2] It gives evidence that the real happenings of the story have taken place in the Vedic age, for women and occupied an honourable position, considered in no way inferior to men. They took part in all religious functions and ceremonies. There were *brahmavadinis* "who have the rite of initiation into vedic learning (upanayana), feed the fire, study the Veda and obtain alms in their own house".[3]

Marriage was not compulsory for girls but unmarried girls were debarred from taking part in the Vedic *yagnas*. Women were free to choose their husbands and *swayamvaras* were held for princesses. *Gandharva vivah* was permitted. A woman could seek extramarital sex for conceiving a child in case the husband was incapable of giving her one. Woman was given prominence not only in the society but also in the Pantheon of Gods.

During the decline of the Vedic ages the social code maker Manu appeared on the horizon. It was during 800-500 B.C. that Manu laid down the guidelines and by putting definitive restrictive conditions reduced woman to a state of abject dependency throughout her lifetime. The social laws of Manu had made a strong impact on Kalidasa's thinking while writing his drama *Abhijnana Shakuntalam*.

Shakuntala (who is the adopted daughter of Sage Kanva) lives in the penance forests under the rule of King Dushyanta. She is an embodiment of heavenly beauty which she has inherited from her mother Menaka (the heavenly nymph who deviated Rishi Vishwamitra from his meditation and married him). King Dushyanta meets her for the first time in Kanva's hermitage and falls in love with her at first sight. When he comes to know her real paventage he finds her suitable to marry. Besides her external beauty her heart and soul are equally beautiful. As her life is influenced by higher ascetic forces. She is free from "coquettish trappings" and "insensible to the influence of passion till she saw the King" (Kale ixix). She does not reveal the strange feeling of love for him to her friends till she is forced by them to reveal. "So far she presents an illustration of the Aryan female modesty. When encountered by her lover, she is again the same picture of womanly modesty, peculiar to Hindu women. Though troubled by the arrows of cupid she shows a full sense of female honour. In their love when Dushyanta tries to come near her, she forbids him and utters:

> King of Puru's race, keep to decorum; smitten with love, I am not master of myself so that I can dispose of my person as I like
>
> (Act III, 21, 113)[4].

Shakuntala is unaware of the social codes, so she refuses to do the *Gandharva Vivah.* Ultimately Dushyanta convinces her by saying:

> O timid one, away with your fear of the elders. On knowing this, the revered patriarch, who knows the holy law, will not find fault with this. Moreover, Many daughter of royal sages are heard as married by the Gandharva form of marriage, and were approved by their father
>
> (Act III, 21; 14).

The statement of Dushyanta is a proof of the *Gandharva Vivah* as an accepted social code in the Vedic age. The same is followed by Shakuntala. This kind of marriage with no witness or proof becomes a curse for her life. She cannot forsee the stark realities of this marriage because of her innocence and tender age. Due to her blind love for Dushyanta she is unable to realize her responsibility to Rishi Kanva and gets tied in the nuptial knot. It results in her pregnancy which is realized after Dushyanta's departure from the hernitage. Kalidasa had been affected by

Manu's social codes, that is why he had presented that love marriage could bring adverse affects. "In *Manusmriti* 3/21 it is written that there are eight kinds of marriages – Brahma (related to the eternal spirit), Deva (related to the gods), Aarsha (related to sages), Prajapatya (realted to kings), Asura (related to demons), Gandharva (related to Gandharva community – a love marriage), Rakshas (related to demons and evil spirits) and Paisach (related to Satan). Of these eight, Manu approves the first four and considers others as inferior".[5] Regarding Kalidasa's attitude towards love marriage Kale commits, "It also appears from the same play that he was against love marriages, through always actuated with the most generous sentiments towards the fair sex" (Kale xxii).

After the departure of Dushyanta, Shakuntala is lost in his lovely memories when *Rishi* Durvasa arrives in the hermitage. In her absentmindedness she fails to notice him and does not welcome him. It raises his anger and he curses her:

> That person, thinking of whom, with a mind regardless of anything else, you notice not me, a treasure of penance, come here—he will not remember you though reminded (by you), just an intoxicated man does not (remember) the talk made before (ie. while drink)
>
> (Act IV, 1, 123)

Shakuntala still does not listen to his curse and she is lost in Dushyanta's memories. Her two friends Priyamvada and Anasuya listen to her and request Durvasa to forgive her. As a result he retracts his curse. After the arrival of *Rishi* Kanva the fact of Shankuntala's *Gandharva Vivah* is disclosed to him by divine words. He gives his acceptance to it as both Shakuntala and Dushyanta are worthy to marry each other. As Shakuntala is pregnant Kanva decides to send her to Dushyanta. During her departure she is blessed by everyone. She is given a customary farewell by the ascetics and the trees and animals of the penance grove. The teaching given to Shakuntala by Kanva at the time of her departure fully suits the Aryan modesty. He says:

> You, then, on going from here and joining your husband's household serve your elders, and act the part of a loving friend towards co-wives; though wronged do not act in are factory way towards your husband, in a fit of anger, be extremely polite towards your dependents, and not elated with pride in prosperity. Thus do young ladies attain the station (dignity) of a house wife; those of an opposite character are a curse to their family
>
> (Act IV, 18, 143)

The speech of Kanva gives indication of polygamy practised in the Aryan society. It embodies *Pativrata Dharma* that is a faith and a distinctive feature of Indian culture and tradition.

In the *Vashishtha Smriti*, 17/5 it is said, "one who has a son is entitled to enter all regions of the universe, one who has a grandson is entitled to eternity and one who has a great grandson is entitled to eternity to the abode of Surya" (Bhalla 312). It gives evidence of the importance of having a son in the Vedic age. Manu in *Manusmriti* 9/10 harps on the same when he says:

> पुंनाम्नो नरकाधस्मात त्रायते पितरं सुत:
> तस्मात्पुत्र इति प्रोक्ते: स्वयमेव स्वयंभुव:

He means to say that one who has a son can be protected from going to hell.

Kanva in order to console Shakuntala at the time of her departure says to her:

> Why are you so afraid, my child? Placed in the honourable position of the wife of a husband of noble birth, engrossed every moment in his affairs momentous by reason of his greatness, and having given birth to a son, the purifier (of his race), as the East gives birth to the holy sun, you my child, will not mind the grief of separation from me.
>
> (Act IV, 19, 155)

It means that having a son will be an asset for Shakuntala.

Shakuntala proceeds to the king's court escorted by the ascetics Saradvata, Sangarava and Gautami. Sangarava makes his motive clear with the message of *Rishi* Kanva:

> By mutual agreement, Your Honour married this daughter of mine, that of you both was approved of me, pleased. For you are known to us as the foremost of the worth, and Shakuntala is a virtue incarnate. It is after a long time that the creator bringing together a bride and a bridegroom of equal merit has not incurred censure. So let her, who is now quick with child, be accepted for for participation in religious observances
>
> (Act V, 15, 175)

Shakuntala is curious to know the answer of the king. The king remarks in wonder, "What is this being proposed to me?" His speech appears like fire to Shakuntala and the ascetics. Sangarva utters, "How possibly this? Your highness is surely fully conversant with the ways of the world. People suspect a woman, with her husband living, to be otherwise even though chaste, when exclusively residing in her Kinsmen's family. Hence (it is that) a young woman is desired by her relatives to be with her husband, whether she is loved by him or not" (Act V, 17,177). His speech reminds us of Manu in *Manusmriti* "that a girl, a young woman, or even an old woman was to do nothing independently, even in her own house. In childhood, they must be subject to their fathers, in youth to their husbands, and when in death to their sons. In short, women must never be independent".[6]

Even after removing Shakuntala's veil the king is unable to recognize her as his wife. He utters, "...I do not really remember having espoused this lady. How then shall I receive her bearing visible signs of pregnancy, suspecting my relation towards her to be that of a Kshetrin (i.e. nominal husband)?" (Act V, 20, 179). Shakuntala's honour is burnt at the stake in the court of Dushyanta. This is the question of her honour, chastity, identity and aspirations to be an honourable wife of the person whom she had loved with her whole soul. She utters to herself, "My lord has a doubt about the very marriage. Where can now be my lofty aspiration?[11] (Act V, 20,179) She tries to show him the reminder (the ring that was given to her by Dushyanta as his token of love) but it is lost as it had fallen in the river during worship.

Vindicating her honour as an individual she checks herself by addressing him as "My dear" and utters aloud, "Where marriage is doubted, this is not the proper form (of address). O descendant of Puru, it is indeed, becoming in you, having at first in that manner deceived this person, naturally simpleminded, after a formal agreement in the hermitage, thus to disown her now!" (ACT V, 21, 181). Still she does not lose her hope and tries to remind him several instances of time spent together by them. The king under the effect of the curse again satirises her by saying, "Intuitive cunning of the womanhood is seen in females other than human. What then in the case of those that possess power of understanding? Then female cuckoos, indeed cause their offspring to be reared by other birds, before flying into the sky" (ACT V, 22, 187). Shakuntala utters in anger "Who else will act as you, putting on the garb of virtue and resembling a well covered over with grass"? Shakuntala accuses him as a cheater "Who has honey on his tongue but poison in his heart" (Act V, 24, 189). The ascetics proceed to leave Shakuntala alone in her critical condition by saying, "For authority over a wife is admitted to be all reaching" (Act V, 26, 191). Now Shakuntala is a repudiated wife who can neither approach her parents nor her husband because of the narrow and and rigid social codes of the society. Sangarva's comment on Shakuntala's situation is evident:

> If thou art as the King says, what can the father with thee that art a disgrace to his family? But if thou believest the conduct to be irreproachable even servitude in the husband's family is proper for thee
>
> (Act V, 27, 193)

Even Sangarva wrathfully considers her as a wanton lady. She does not find anyone to support or accept her in that situation. None can provide shelter to her. Ultimately she calls mother earth, "O venerable earth, open a grave for me" (Act V, 29, 197). Her plight is similar to the archetypal model Sita who ultimately called mother earth to give her space after her repudiation by Lord

Rama. Mother earth is considered her real mother, so she takes Sita back. Similarly Shakuntala's real mother Menaka (a supernatural power) intervenes in the human world by taking her daughter Shakuntala with her. After this incidence the fisherman who was accused of theft of royal ring is brought to the king's court. After watching the ring the reality is in front of him and he recalls his marriage with Shakuntala. He feels repentant and "passes the night sleeplessly rolling about in the bed" (Act VI, 5, 211).

King Dushyant has been asked for help by Indra in the battle with the *asuras.* While coming back he stops near the mountain *Hemkuta* where the holy Sage Kashyap resides. While waiting to meet him he beholds a child "dragging away from its mother a lion's cub" (Act VII, 4, 267). The child appears to him his own image. While talking with the female ascetics who are attending to the child he comes to know that he is not a hermit's son but a descendant of Puru. Then the female ascetics tell him the story of his birth to the king. Gradually he comes to know that the child's mother is Shakuntala. When he goes to meet her he beholds her "wearing a pair of dusky garments, with face emaciated by her observance of vows, having her hair tied up once for all and pure conduct, has been practicing one long vow of separation from me, extremely cruel" (Act VII, 21, 279). Though repudiated by her husband yet Shakuntala does not forget her *Pativrata Dharma* and continues to lead an ascetic life. When Dushyant accepts her as his wife, she still thinks that her repudiation by him is the result of "an evil deed done" by her "in a past life obstructing virtue"... (Act VII, 24, 281). Her speech is symbolic of her submissive nature and her belief in the theory of *Punarjanma.*

After the reconciliation of their marital relations Dushyant and Shakuntala approach Maricha and Aditi (parents of Indra) to offer reverence, and oblige. In return they are blessed with several blessings. The interaction between the king and Maricha regarding the curse of Durvasa tends Shakuntala to think, "It's a lucky thing that my husband did not repudiate me without cause. I do not, however, remember myself to have been cursed or rather the curse, though incurred, was not known by me in the absent mindedness due to separation" (Act VII, 31, 291). Her thought reflects her love and *Pativrata Dharma* towards her husband, thus confering her as an archetypal stereotype of a submissive women.

An exhaustive study of Shakuntala's character results in a single idea that she is a pure woman, physically, emotionally, spiritually and intellectually. Kale writes regarding her beauty, "There was nothing artificial in her beauty; it was essentially natural, and free from coquettish trappings of which she had no conception. This proves the handsomeness for her external person, but heart was equally beautiful. She was a lovely young maiden, the soul of womanly modesty, and altogether sensible to the influence of passion till she saw the king. Her life therefore, was one of feminine purity of mind and womanly virtues greatly to the general surroundings a midst which she lived which characterized her nature throughout her life"... (Kale ixix).

At the time of her repudiation by the king in his court she is anguished. His remarks indicate her as an unchaste woman. It's a test of her identity, respect and her remarks are conducive to the situation. She knows her truth and chastity, and values them greatly, so she calls mother earth to open a grave for her in utter dejection. She follows the command of Sangarva and does not return back to Kanva. It is an evidence of her obedience and at the same time her self-respect. After her repudiation, in Maricha's ashrama, she leads a life of self- restraint, i.e., of an ascetic. She shows the strength of character in bringing up her son without his father. She has married according to the standards of Vedic age and has been faithful to her husband all her life.

She is an embodiment of a complete pure woman according to Aryan standards of modesty.

If the characters of Sita, Sati and Parvati are examined carefully they embody the strong woman characters who are not a simple woman tied to *Pativrata Dharma*. In the character of Sita her asceticism during her living in *Ashoka Vatika* and her success in passing the tests of chastity prove her to be a strong woman. "Rama, sometimes caught by his own sense of duty and sometimes caught by his own sense of duty and sometimes by his own weakness or ego, pales by comparison to her integrity, tenacity and chastity by which she upholds feminine norms" (Qtd. in Young 12). Sati observes a strong fast in order to unite with Shiva. On account of her asceticism she achieves Shiva as her husband. In another incarnation Sati (Parvati) by her ascetic powers forces Shiva to marry her. These myths suggest that "Women's asceticism can be extremely powerful and exert control over even the most powerful male Yogi" (Qtd in Young). Similarly Shakuntala gets back her husband by the power of her asceticism.

If Shakuntala is judged on the parameters of *Victorian standards of morality*[7] (the time period of Queen Victoria in England) then she is a pure woman. According to Victorian notions a Victorian woman could be either "the sexually passive and angelic wife, sister and, or the mother or she is the sexually charged and demonic mad woman in the attic.[8] Shakuntala belongs to the category of sexually passive, angelic wife and mother. She has always shown a self-control on her sexuality. Before repudiation she is engaged in her husband's memories. After repudiation she leads an ascetic life, so she is not a "wanton lady" as Sangarva has remarked to her by commenting wrathfully at the time of her repudiation by Dushyanta. Frazer has commented regarding her character. "Gentler more winning in her grace, more youthful than Gretchen or Juliet, she (Shakuntala) has a deeper note, a more human charm, than either. Eastern, subtle, evasive throbbing with love, veiled with reserve, there yet grows within her a passionate and seething love for the king, which she tries to stifle but from when she can find no peace" (Qtd in Kale ixix).

## References


1. Dr. Dhananjay Verma ed. *English Language and Indian Culture.* 2nd ed. Bhopal: M.P.Hindi Granth Academy, 2001, 62.
2. M.R. Kale Introduction. *The Abhijnana*Shakuntala*m of Kalidasa.* 10th ed. Delhi: Motilal Banarsidas Publishers, 1969, Hereafter cited as Kale.
3. Katherine K.Young. "Women and Hinduism" ed. Arvind Sharma. *Women in Indian Religions,* New Delhi: Oxford University Press, 2002, 7.
4. M.R. Kale Trans. Kalidasa's *Abhijnana*Shakuntala*m*, op. cit. All the quotations of AbhijnanaShakuntalam in the research paper are the translations done by M.R. Kale and quoted with Act and stanza number.
5. Prem P. Bhalla *Hindu Rites, Rituals, Customs and Traditions*, Pustak Mahal: Delhi, 2005, 98.
6. Manu 5. 147–148; CF Manu 9.2–3.
7. The time period of 1850–1900 in England when Queen Victoria ruled. Its corner stones are morality and respectability in character.
8. Kimberley Reynolds and Nicola Humble, *Victorian Heroines Representations of Feminity* in *Nineteenth century Literature and Art,* New York: New York University Press, 1993, 2.

# 11

# The Coquettes and the Winners of the Hearts: Women Characters in Sri Aurobindo's Dramas

— Aju Mukhopadhyay

Sri Aurobindo wrote five complete dramas besides five incomplete ones and two fragments of dramas carried from his student days. He began writing poems during his school days in England and then trying his hand in writing some dramas in verse.

His dramas are based on ancient histories spread among many countries. Besides the core issue they are largely the work of imagination. Full of conflict and contrast, full of suspense and romance, the guiding principles of such works are love. Fate flows like undercurrents in the lives of the dramatic personae, as in those days in countries referred.

Besides Andromeda and Rodogune, the two strong and revolting heroines, the other women characters, specially heroines in Sri Aurobindo's dramas, are soft-hearted but witty and sometimes coquettish nymphs, playing tricks. Not only do they attract their men but come out victorious against all odds at the end of the comedies.

Influenced by Hellenic myth and Greek history, with contents culled from ancient Greece, *Perseus the Deliverer* and *Rodogune*, the comedy and the tragedy, are enacted in Syrian background.

In *Perseus the Deliverer* Sri Aurobindo introduced the element of undaunted feminine spirit with sympathy for the humanity in Andromeda who risked her life to rescue the poor human victims from the jaws of the sea-monsters. Andromeda is the symbol of woman's revolt against oppression and suppression by men in those days, long before the time of Henrik Ibsen's *Dolls House*, against age-old superstition of human sacrifice at the alter of the Dark Vital God, connecting us to the main issue in Tagore's drama, *Visarjan* or *Sacrifice*. Finally, as a symbol of the triumph of love against evil she is rescued by her lover Perseus, propped by the divine blessing of Goddess Athene as he was the son of Zeus, at the end of her prolonged struggle against men and superstition.

Rodogune, the captive princess of Persia and the heroine of Sri Aurobindo's only tragic drama, *Rodogune*, remains steady against all odds to marry the man of her choice, Antiochus, the elder of the two brothers to claim the throne. And after the death of Antiochus she falls dead at his feet.

Sri Aurobindo could be a remarkable dramatist and fiction writer too apart from poet but he could not entirely engage himself in such creative works; he was either a secret revolutionary leader or a political leader in the open field, either a professor, journalist, social thinker or a philosopher doing yoga; in between his constant efforts to create literature, translate or edit them at different periods of his life. In a stormy life before Pondicherry, shifting from place to place, he often lost track of his own works. Many of his works were either seized by police or were lost otherwise. Some of them were found later after he had passed away. Many remained incomplete. Let us now discuss about the coquettish and soft hearted lover women characters in Sri Aurobindo's dramas.

## The Viziers of Bassora: A Coquettish Slave Rises to be Queen

Adapting the story from the *Tales of the Arabian Nights* told by

Shahrazad in six nights to the king, making him spellbound, forgetting to kill the teller for her stories which continued altogether for thousand and one nights, Sri Aurobindo made the story further interesting by bringing in all sorts of changes in it, twisting and turning it with fine dramatic taste. He loved this creation as he specially mentioned it in his introduction to the *Collected Poems and Plays* in 1942.

### The Drama begins at Bassora

Nureddene the hero of the drama though leads a haphazard life, eventually comes home and almost becomes homesick as he finds such a beauty as his father bought for the king, whose name is sweeter than her person perhaps, Anice-Aljalice. Enough of kisses has been mentioned as allusion to their love making. Doonya, the niece of the vizier, adds fire to the fuel as she too like Anice is a merry-making and fun-loving girl with a joyous personality. The happy boy to his mother says:

> Well, mother,
> Here I am back, your errant gadabout,
> Your vagabond scapegrace, tired of truancy (595)

And he continues, as his mother asks him not to be so wild as she fears that he will squander everything as his parents close their eyes:

> All your patrimony/You'll waste-and then? (397)
> I shall go forth, a daring errant-knight,
> To my true country out in Faeryland....
> And o'er romantic regions quite unknown (597-98)

Adding with zeal as natural for such a person in his situation:

> Preach Islam, sword in hand; sell bales of spice
> From Bassora to Java and Japan;
> Then on through undiscovered islands, seas
> And oceans yet unnamed; yes, everywhere
> Catch danger by the throat where I can find him (598)

But in fact he settles at home during nights, meeting Anice-Aljalice and making love with the help of her women slaves. Even Harkoos the Ethiopian eunuch and slave helps and jokes. The father was very annoyed but seeing the position, as his wife Ameena explains, gives indulgence and agrees to his son marrying her as a wife with condition never to resell her.

Anice-Aljalice adds sweet to her lover's approaching zeal by confirming her love:

> Closer than kisses, closer than delight,
> Close only as love whom sorrow and delight
> Cannot diminish, nor long absence change
> Nor daily prodigality of joy
> Expend immortal love. (609)

While going forth to Roum, Nureddene's father Sawy says to his wife:

> 'Tis likely that the boy,
> Left here in sole command, will waste his wealth....(p. 621)

He divides his property between his wife and son. He departs and the romance continues in full force between the two. The romance spreads among Ajebe, the nephew of Almuene, and his two slave girls. In ActThree we find the situation becoming grave. Alzayni the king says that hot exchange and high defiance have passed between the Caliph and the Romans. "Europe and Asia are at grips once more." (665)

In their world of romance Nureddene loses all his wealth. Deserted by friends and surrounded by creditors, he sells his slaves and furniture. Almuene, the crooked hearted vizier, ever an enemy of Sawy and Nureddene, advises his nephew and others to coax and rob him but even without them Nureddene, by extravagance ruins himself. When at last Nureddene goes for auction to sell his dear wife, as the slave herself proposes it out of sheer love for him, the evil hearted Almuene rejoices at it:

> Ah, it is true! All things come round at last
> With the full wheel of Fate; it is my hour.
> Fareed shall have her. She shall be well handled
> To plague her lover's heart before he dies. (659)

He intervenes but Nureddene, as advised, decides not to sell her to his enemy and takes her back, thrashing and injuring the advancing enemy as he tries to forcibly take the slave, Anice-Aljalice. Humiliated, he goes to the king and fabricating the story complaints bitterly against Sawy and Nureddene. The infuriated king orders the capture of Nureddene and Anice-Aljalice with the intention of executing Nureddene. With the help of Murad, the Turk Captain and husband of Doonya, and Ajebe, who even helps with purse, both of them flee to Bagdad by the ship that is ready to sail.

## Romance at Caliph's Garden

Reaching Bagdad, knowing none, they take shelter in the Caliph's magnificent garden. All romance vanished in Act 3 is revived here in Act 4. It comes back with much of wit, joy and beauty, winning over all authority and ill wishes.

They are overwhelmed observing the violet, dark blue and burning sulphur colours of the flowers and lemons like balls of gold, delightful cherries and pink-budded orange-blossoms; the rare glints of fruits- "plums almost as smooth / As your damask cheek" (672), says Nureddene to Aljalice.

The superintendent of the garden, Shaikh Ibrahim, approaches them from behind with a palmstick in hand to beat as trespassers but gets melted, passionately charmed after beholding their beauty, especially of the girl, Anice-Aljalice. Remaining open-mouthed for some time he answers her thus,

"Glory to Allah who made you! Glory to the angel who brought you down on earth! Glory to myself who am permitted to look upon you! I give glory to Allah for your beauty, O people of Paradise!" (674)

He tells them that the garden and the pavilion belong to him and that he does not accept the Caliphate of any other on earth. The scene ends with Ibrahim's hymn adoring Anice:

> Allah! Allah! She is a gazelle that springeth. Allah! Allah! the swan in my lake waddleth less perfectly. She is as a willow when the wind swayeth it. Allah! Allah! (676)

When next the guests ask for food and wine, the garden keeper gives a discourse full of wit and humour suggesting irony, bringing in the Allah with a glint of satire:

"I take refuge with Allah. Wine! For sixteen years I have not touched the evil thing. When I was young indeed!... But 'tis forbidden. What saith Ibn Batata? That wine worketh transmogrification. And Ibrahim Alhashhash bin Fuzfuz bin Bierbiloon al Sandilani of Bassora, he rateth wine sorely and averreth that the red glint of it is the shine of the red fires of Hell, its sweetness kisseth damnation and the coolness of it in the throat causeth bifurcation. Ay, verily, the great Alhashhash." (678)

That Ibrahim is the epitome of hypocrisy is repeatedly confirmed by all including the Caliph as he meets him. Observing him at the beginning Nureddene utters, "He is very gem of hypocrites." (679)

Observing his pavilion all alight, Haroun AL Rasheed with his friend and vizier proceeds to enquire who has done it without his knowledge even disbelieving the plausible explanation given by Jaafar the vizier. Reaching the spot they hear Shaik Ibrahim's voice accompanied by the play of lute:

> Chink-a-chunk-a-chink!
> We will kiss and drink,
> And be merry, O very very merry.
> For your eyes are bright
> Even by candle light
> And your lips as red as the red round cherry. (689)

Then into the tower of the pavilion they enter and seeing the young couple; lady playing the lute with Ibrahim singing, Haroun comments:

> The aged hypocrite! Who are this pair
> Of heavenly faces? Was there then such beauty
> In my Bagdad, yet Haroun's eyes defrauded
> Of seeing it? (689)

When they see Anice sings playing the lute Haroun wishes to meet them. As his vizier is afraid that the guests will find it difficult to talk to him if they know him, he decides to meet them disguised as a fisherman as he finds Kareem, a fisherman, catching fish in the garden's water body. He meets him and exchanges dress with him and then with fish in hand enters the pavilion and talks to them as a fisherman, causing no doubt that he is so. Ibrahim is so drunk that he misses him as a fisherman and talks frankly and loosely with him.

When Kareem (Haroun in disguise) refers to Caliph, Ibrahim asks, "Who talks of the Caliph? Dost thou speak of the Caliph Haroun or the Caliph Ibrahim?" (696). On hearing that he speaks of Haourn, he ejaculates:

> Oh, Haroun? He is fit only to be a gardener, a poor witless fellow without brains to dress himself with.... A very profligate tyrant, this Haroun! He has debauched half the women in Bagdad and will debauch the other half.... A very pestilence of a tyrant! (696)

The irony and hypocrisy of his utterances are manifest here. When Anice provokes him further asking if he wishes to be the Caliph, he replies, "Yes, my jewel, and thou shalt be my Zobeidah. And we will tipple, beauty, we will tipple." (696-697)

After a while the drunkard asserts that there is no voice in Bagdad like his and sings:

> When I was a young man,
> I'd a very good plan;

Every maid that I met,
In my lap I would set,
What mattered her age or her colour?
But now I am old
And the girls they grow cold
And my heartstrings, they ache
At the faces they make,
And my dancing is turned into dolour.

( 698)

This has been compared to the clown's closing song in Shakespeare's *Twelfth Night:*

When that I was a little tiny boy,
With hey, ho, the wind and the rain
A foolish thing was but a toy....
But when I came unto my beds,
With hey, ho, the wind and the rain,
With toss-pots still had drunken heads,
For the rain it raineth everyday.
A great while ago the world begun...
But that's all one, our play is done....

(William Shakespeare. *"Twelfth Night": The Complete Works.* London; Collins. 376)

Shaikh then praises himself, telling "A very sweet song!" (698), repeating from Shelley, "Our sweetest songs are those that tell of saddest thought." (Shelley, *Selected Poetry*. London; The Penguin Poetry Library. 185). Gradually the fisherman learns the story of the couple fleeing to Bagdad. Realising the unjust act of the vizier and the king at Bassora and as he was already moved by their appearance, the Caliph in the guise of a fisherman writes a firman declaring Nureddene as the future king of Bassora and calling the king and his vizier to Bagdad.

**Bassora Again**

When Nureddene is going to be executed by the king and the vizier there, Jaffar arrives and arrests both of them as prisoners of Caliph. He hails Nureddene, greeting him as the Sultan of

Bassora and offers him a slave girl as the Caliph's gift. And she happens to be Anice-Aljalice. Murad informs IBN Sway, the good vizier, that his wife Ameena and niece Doonya are safe under his care.

Finally arrives Haroun AL Rasheed, the great Caliph and addressing all he says:

> Noble Alfazzal, sit. Sit all of you.
> This is the thing that does my heart most good
> To watch these kind and happy looks and know
> Myself for cause. Therefore, I sit enthroned,
> Allah's Vicegerent, to put down all evil
> And pluck the virtuous out of danger's hand. (733)

To the king he says that he shall have judgment but that his vizier is guilty of open crime. He wishes the young king to decide his fate but Nureddene declines to pass any judgment so the Caliph orders him to be executed then and there. He is taken by the guards.

The Caliph concludes seeing all happy addressing them thus-

> Fair children worthy of each other's love
> And beauty!....
> Farewell.
> I go to Roman wars. With you the peace!
> IBN Sawy,
> Peace with thee, just and mighty Caliph, peace. (735)- Curtain

The Caliph in *Viziers of Bassora* has been compared with the Duke of Shakespeare's *Measure for Measure*—both being representatives of the Divine:

> Allah's Vicegerent", as claims the Caliph.
> Eric: A Passionate Beauty Succumbs to her Love

Neither Syria, India nor Greece, Eric takes us to ancient Norway. Based on the heroic age of the Norwegian history when different small kingdoms or earldoms fought with each other for supremacy without paying any heed to national unity, Eric emerged the most powerful king after the death of Olaf, even defying the claim of his son, Swegn. Though by the power of his sword and by the choice of the people he became the king, Swegn did not accept him and there loomed large chances of war and his losing the kingdom. By his immense military power and intelligence, specially by the power of love, he brings about a unity in Norway and finally becomes the sovereign king. In all such plays of Sri Aurobindo, Fate plays its inevitable role. And here love is the alchemy, the unifying agent, with its romantic touch in the life of the hero and the heroine the drama begins with Eric on the stage:

> I have found the way to join,-
> The warrior's sword, builder of unity;
> But where's the way to solder? (477)

He calls the gods, Thor and Odin, to help him. Instead of their answer he hears song from outside in the street:

> Love is the hoop of the gods
> Hearts to combine. (477)

Eric feels that it is God's answer:

> Is that your answer? Freya, Mother of Heaven,
> And the song continues—
> When love desires Love,
> Then Love is born; (478)

## The King Falls in Love with the Illusive Girl

When Eric understands that they who sing are dancing girls, he calls them inside.

Aslaug, the beautiful dame and Hertha, her companion, enter the palace. When the king asks who was singing, Aslaug answers, "My lips at least were used." And when she is asked by whom, she replies:

> By Fate.
> For she alone is prompter on our stage...
> She builds, she breaks,
> She thrones, she slays, as needed for her harmony. (479)

He comprehends that the two are not just dancing girls but some noble ladies who have come for some purpose, in the guise of dancing girls. Even guessing that she might be a spy from the enemy camp as he succeeded the late king by power of sword and election and as she has already spoken of "Olaf Thorleikson who ruled Norway once,/Swegn was his heir" (p.481), Eric invites Aslaug whom he has already fallen in love with, to live with him:

> Will you remain with me,
> Forgetting Gothberg and your golden gains?
> Since I have been the fount of your distress,
> Make me the source of your great plenty too. (481)

Fact is, Aslaug is the energetic sister of Swegn, the revolting son of Olaf and Hertha is the wife of Swegn. They have come secretly to murder the king to bring the Olaf family again to the throne. But the purpose of the two ladies seems to differ even within their main aim. While Aslaug is determined to do the thing, Hertha wishes to use her brain to bring about a harmonious end. She asks Aslaug:

> Are you not afraid,
> You who see Fate even in a sparrow's flight,
> When Odin is for him? (p.484)
> Aslaug answers,
> But Fate alone decides, when all is said,
> Not Thor, not Odin. I will try my Fate. (484)

Noticing the king looks at her, Hertha asks Aslaug, "did you see/ The eyes of Eric on you?" (p.486). Denying it Aslaug, while in conversation, challenges the king, "All Norway has not sold itself thy slave?" (489)

Eric retorts, "If Norway has not sold itself my slave,/Thou hast. Remember what thou art- or claimst to be." (p. 490)

> Aslaug realizes her position and utters to herself,
> He is subtle, terrible. I see the thing
> He drives at and admire unwillingly
> The mighty tyrant. (490)

It is a shadowy world of love and sword, patriotism, revenge and passion. The king understands the purpose of her coming and can subdue her by force but love does not permit and the lady, who could kill him at an opportune moment, really falters. She does not relent to the king's wish to disclose her identity, maintaining that she is a dancing girl.

Eric then throws a costly necklace and asks her to wear which Aslaug refuses telling that that is not the way to woo a woman's heart. The king goes out advising her to ponder over the matter seriously and not to show courage outrageously, to confess her treason.

As he goes out Aslaug, already hurt by the love-arrow, wears the necklace. And enters Hertha to address her thus:

> Sister of Swegn,
> There are new lustres in thy face and eyes.
> What said he to thee? (495)

Aslaug understands that she has become the captive of the king but her proud heart does not accept it, she feels the pull of love in her heart but does not relent to it. During a diatribe between the two, the king becomes stern and tells her:

> This earthly heaven
> In which thou liv'st shall not be thine at all;
> It was not shaped to bear thy joy but mine
> And only made for my immense desire.
> This hast thou understood?

Aslaug becomes pale and admits that a woman's heart sinks in such absolute surrender. Eric, realizing the situation born out of his own arrogance mixed with passion, comes and touches her to console with love and says:

> O thou unparalleled enchanting frame
> For housing of a strong immortal guest!...
> For if life's barriers twixt our souls were broken
> Men would be free and our earth paradise
> And the gods live neglected. (500)

And after a while she yields but do not agree for a rendezvous the same night, as demands Eric. After some more dialogues Eric says:

> I give thee time once more; misuse it not.
> Beware, provoke not the fierce god too much;
> Have dread of his flame round thee. (500)

Eric goes out and breaking into a laugh Aslaug monologuise:

> I have not thrown the dagger from my heart....
> It was a moment's wave; for it has passed
> And the high purpose in my soul lives on
> Unconquerably intending to fulfil. (502)

While talking to Hertha she has all praise for Eric and admits that "O he is far too great, too beautiful / For a dagger's penetration." Yet to Eric she yields not while suffering from utter dilemma all along. Eric says:

> "Yes, though thy eyes defy me,
> Thy colour changes and thy limbs betray thee.
> All is not lionlike and masculine there
> Within. (506)

He makes an advance and holds her tight. Though obstructed, he kisses her. Aslaug falters, "O gods! I love! O loose me!"

Eric requests her:

Sweetly, O Aslaug, to thy doom consent,
The doom to love, the death of hatred. Draw
No useless curtaining of shamed refusal...
Between us let there be
A noble daylight. (p.506)

Aslaug:

O Eric, King, usurper, conquerer!
O robber of men's hearts and kingdoms! O
Thou only monarch!
After he goes out Aslaug speaks to herself:
Can the world change within a moment? Can
Hate suddenly be love? Love is not here.
I have the dagger still within my heart.
O he is terrible and fair and swift!
He is not mortal. (p.511)

To Hertha she says, "Hertha, I strike tonight." (512).

After she goes out Hertha, who does not finally want a murder but peace through conciliation counsels the king to be cautious, divulging all their secrets, telling him finally who they are as he suspected some such thing.

## She Promises but Fails to Kill Her Lover

And the fatal night arrives when Eric calls Aslaug who comes, perforce. He bids her to sit beside him, nearer his heart and tells her to do what she feels with her free hands before he grasps them firmly. Earlier he wished and now she volunteers to dance with a dagger which she has in the meantime touched many times for her purpose. But she falters, feels unnerved to dance.

Aslaug:

O gods, I did not know myself till now...
I am in love
With chains and servitude and my heart desires,

Fluttering, like a wild bird within its cage,
A tyrant's harshness. (527)

Now Eric reveals his plan to march the next morning to fight with Swegn and to bring him living or dead and asks her to dance as promised.

Aslaug says that fate still drives her, even the call of Eric is fate's call to kill him. She says, as if to herself:

But he suspects, he knows. Yet will I strike,
Yet will I tread down my rebellious heart,
And when 'tis done, I'll strike myself and finish
With grief and shame and love. (.528)

Then Eric asks for the chain (Necklace) he gave and she goes out to bring it, saying:

The necklace? I will bring it.
Rubies of passion! Blood-drops still of death! (528)

Now the shrewd king feels that love has robbed her power to strike, only in her stubborn thought it survives. He feigns to sleep.

As she comes back he is found asleep. It is the golden chance to knife him. "Now I could slay him! But he will open his eyes/Appalling with the beauty of his gaze." (529)

She soliloquises:
But death
Now intervenes and claims thee at my hands-
And this alone he leaves to me, to slay thee
And die with thee, our only wedlock. Death! (529)

She says but at the last stage of her mighty effort lifts her dagger twice and twice lowers, then flings it on the ground, falling on her knees at Eric's feet. "Yes, with shame and grief and love/Thou art my Fate and I am in the grasp", she succumbs. This situation with Aslaug's "Now I could slay him!" has been compared by a critic to Hamlet's:

> Now might I do it pat, now 'a is a-praying;
> And now I'll do't- and so 'a goes to heaven

While Eric is sleeping as it seemed to Aslaug, Claudius kneels and prays. Hamlet does not kill him because he thought, "he is fit and seasoned for his passage?" No, he would do the work then but when the victim would be engaged in vile acts or drunk asleep. (*Hamlet.* William Shakespeare. *The Complete Works.* London; The English Language Book Society and Collins. 1964. 1053-54)

Eric claims her complete surrender and Aslaug does it with love. Eric says:

> Aslaug, the world's sole woman! Thou cam'st here
> To save for us our hidden hopes of joy
> Parted by old confusion. Some day surely
> The world too shall be saved from death by Love. (534)

This is typically Aurobindonian. This reminds us of Savitri's assertion before the Yama. In her debate with Yama, Savitri in Sri Aurobindo's epic poem, *Savitri* warns the Lord of Death this way:

> My will is greater than thy law, O Death;
> My love is stronger than the bonds of Fate...
> Love is man's lien on the absolute.
> (*Savitri.* Sri Aurobindo. Pondicherry; Sri Aurobindo Birth Centenary Library. 1972. V. 29. 633)

This love is a key point here which unlocks the door, opens the seal of Fate and Death. Earlier it was the reign of Odin or Woden, the Chief God of the Germanic people, and Thor, the Scandinavian Thunder God. In ancient lands such gods represented the war and strife which led the kingdoms. Sri Aurobindo's introduction of Freya, the God of Love and Compassion, turns the older world of revenge and enmity to world of love and sympathy. The night ends and Eric goes out for the purpose he declared before, reminding Aslaug that his ring on her hand with circle of ancient Norwegian rites is actually Freya's ring which means for one who wears it would adorn the throne of Norway. It would carry her through all perils to bind her to the joy of the king and the Norwegians.

## The King Wins the Heart of All

Towards the end ounselor that his sister has already been Eric's wife; to save his face and the face of the family Swegn finally yields to Eric and seeks for boon. Eric offers him four prisons; Olaf's house, the palace, king's court and at the Head of his army. Swegn then observes that his sister wears the ring of the king, they are married. Swegn is overwhelmed by the tactic and magnanimity of the king. He gladly says to Eric, "Thou has dealt with me as a King,/Then as a brother, Thou adorn'st thy throne." (558)

Finally the hero and the heroine summarize the whole drama:

> Eric—
> The gods have spoken since and shown their hand.
> They shut our eyes and drive us, but at last
> Our souls remember when the act is done.
>
> Aslaug—
> That it was fated. New for us, O beloved,
> The world begins again, who since the stars were formed
> Playing the game of games by Odin's will
> Have met and parted, parted, met again
> For ever. (559)

While Aslaug has profound faith on fate, Eric more believes in soul, God and heart.

In any way, they arrive at the conclusion as if everything was so arranged as to help them arrive at the place assigned to them beforehand. Though from the ancient history of another country not too often traversed by us, the story has some fundamental value and by imagination and intricate weaving of incidents the dramatist made it a comprehensive whole, very interesting and effective as a drama of action. It is said that the drama is very stage worthy and was successful when staged. Written between 912and1913, it carries Sri Aurobindo's seal of action made of love and understanding.

## Vasavadutta, a Nymph who Cooperates to be Carried Away and Married

Like *Eric* it is a dramatic romance, a comedy. But unlike *Eric* it is based on Indian soil. It is the last of Sri Aurobindo's completed drama, written in October 1915. Here love triumphs against the regal power. It is a very sweet love story where hero and heroine win against all odds by the force of love. It is taken from Somadeva's Sanskrit store house of stories, *Kathasaritasagara*, a favourite source of Indian romance and drama. Iyengar adds that the dramatist "Took a hint or two from Bhasa's dramatic version of the legend, *Pratijna Yougandharayana*. (*Sri Aurobindo-a biography and a history*. K. R. S. Iyengar. Pondicherry; SAICE. 1985. 137)

As usual, the dramatist made suitable changes to fit the whole into his dramatic theme. The action of the romance took place a hundred years after the *Mahabharata* war when the kingdoms of India were temporarily broken up under three main powers: Magadha in the East, Avunthie in the West and Cowsambie in the centre. Chunda Mahasegn of Avunthie subdued the southern kings.

The background of the story is that Avunthie has suffered a setback as it was defeated to Cowsambie after Vuthsa, its young king, was invested with regal power. It has been a rude shock to the king of Avunthie who always has the ambition of ruling the whole of India, making other kings his vassals. Though they were not subdued immediately, Vuthsa and his kingdom gave a warning shock and at the same time Cowsambie wishes to serve another blow to Avunthie to subdue the empire; it was a position of rivalry which the author signified as the prevalence of "armed peace between the two empires".

A rivalry between kings is won over by the love of the king's son and daughters; the impending tragedy turns to comedy. Whatever the source that inspired the poet, he seems to have followed a philosophy that guided his path throughout, that it is the God's will which finally triumphs, decides things on earth, even as the humans act to achieve their own errand.

## Both the Rival Kings Plan for Abduction of the Other's Child

Mahasegn, the king of Avunthie, counsels his son Gapalaca to bring Vuthsa as captive to Ujjayinie, the capital of the kingdom, where he plans to marry him to his daughter, Vasavadutta so that he finds her a jailor of his heart to be shut up in a prison of joy, thus becoming hers and the king's vassal. The king knows that to physical force he would not yield but would be a prisoner to a feminine charm. He orders:

> Gopalaca, I banish thee, my child,
> Return not with my violent will undone. (214)

Yougundharayan, the father of the young king Vuthsa, reveals his dream to him:

> One day perhaps thou shalt join war with wedlock
> And pluck out from her guarded nest by force
> The wonder of Avunthie, Vasavadutta. (219)

Thus both the fathers, the king and the de facto king, wishes their children to get married to help achieve their ends. A paragon of beauty, Vasavadutta is considered to be a jewel of any empire on earth. Neither her father wants to give up the idea of using her for his purpose, nor Cowsambie's guardian wishes to give up the opportunity to get her married to his son by snatching her by force from the enemy house as it is chivalrous to so get the coveted girl from another kingdom to marry in one's own palace. The desires are prompted by their rival ambitions.

A winning warrior, Vuthsa is very young with passion for nature and music. When Gopalaca approaches for his friendship, visiting his kingdom as a spy of his father, which the old and cunning Yougundharayan perceives and warns his son. But Vuthsa, as if without caring a bit of any warning, steps into the snare of the spy and follows him with entire trust. While so following the scion of the enemy kingdom he leaves a word to his friends to be conveyed to his father that he, the sovereign king, desires not any war, that he keeps the strength to come back on his own:

> Whatever seeks me from Fate, man or god,
> Leave all between me and the strength that seeks,
> War shall not sound without thy prince's leave.
> Vuthsa will rescue Vuthsa (239)

In the forest he throws his sword and surrenders to his new-found friend, Gopalacalying down amsng the trees. And Gopalaca says, "Thyself thou hast given wholly into my hands." Agreeing, Vuthsa says, "Yes, take me, brother." (pp. 240-41) Vuthsa's behaviour seems to be unusual, at the same time it seems that he has a super sense how to act in a given situation. Gopalaca takes him captive helped by the army to the king.

The king tells his daughter Vasavadutta before she meets Vuthsa:

> I mean that he shall be
> Thy husband, Vasavadutta, and thy slave.
> By thee he must become, who now resists,
> My vassal even as other monarchs are....
> Thou wilt not put thy own ambitions first,
> Nor justify a blind and clamorous heart. (252-53)

Vasavadutta replies, "My duty to my country and my sire/Shall rule me" (253). When her father confirms that women are guided by their heart and senses but she has a mind, she replies:

> Father, this is my pride,
> That thou ennoblest me to be an engine
> Of they great fortunes; that alone I am. (253)

With dialogues full of irony, the dramatist proceeds to unveil the Fate or God's plan against the human prideful scheme.

When Mahasegn squeezes Vuthsa with wry warning to make him his daughter's servent to be guarded by her handmaidens, Vuthsa readily agrees welcoming it "with a proud aspiring mind". In answer to king's order and question, "Thou smilest, boy?" he pronounces such things that the king does not comprehend:

> I smiled to see how strong and arrogant minds
> Dream themselves masters of the things they do. (260)

## Both the Lovers Fail to Keep Their Words

He is taken to the chamber of Vasavadutta to be introduced to her as her slave. By a further surrender he accepts his fate. In conversation with her he says:

> The deepest things are those thought seizes not;
> Our spirits live their hidden meaning out. (266)

She does not understand the purport of the words immediately but her heart feels at the first sight of him that it is beyond her to refuse him or to make him her servant. After sometime we hear her monologue:

> O joy, if he and all were only mine.
> O greatness to be queen of him and earth.
> I grow a rebel to my father's house. (278)

When her mother asks if she has done what her father wanted, to neglect her husband, she loses herself:

> Have I a father or a house? O none,
> O none, O none exists but only he. (280)

In a few days we find them engrossed with each other's thoughts. They talk and clasp and kiss.

> Vuthsa:
>
> If we could thus remain through many ages,
> Nor Time grow weary ever of such bliss,
> O Vasavadutta!
>
> Vasavadutta:
>
> I have loved thee always
> Even when I knew it not. Was't not the love
> Secret between us, drew thee here by force,
> Vuthsa? (287)

Munjoolica, the captive Princess of Sourashtra, who serves Vasavadutta, takes a revenge from the beginning and even by pushing the two lovers close together, by keeping them locked in the same room over night. Her other maids too help the earnest love mature between the two. Enamoured, Vasavadutta passionately exhorts:

> Wife, mother, sister, lover, playmate, friend,
> Queen, comrade, ounselor I will be to thee.
> Self shall not chill my heart with wedded strife,
> Nor age nor custom pale my fire of love.
> I have that strength in me, the strength to love of gods. (292)

## The Nymph Agrees to be Carried Away

Not only Vasavadutta, her brother Gopalaca, the obedient son of Mahasegn, also loves Vuthsa, so loving is his nature. Gopalaca's brother Vicurna revolts against his father in favour of Vuthsa. Ungarica is always in favour of her daughter getting married to Vuthsa honourably which means that she be forcibly taken by the young king of Cowsambie, a chivalrous act according to Arya practice. She foresees it. Munjoolica joins the force of Vuthsa becoming his charioteer with arms in hand for she too is aggrieved against the king. Finally, on a moonlit night when the dignitaries are invited to a party in a pleasure grove on purpose and eventually get drunk, Vuthsa abducts Vasavadutta helped by her two brothers, fiercely chased by the captain of the army of Ujjayinie. The scene is quite adventurous with prospect of two armies almost clashing as the armed force of Cowsambie led by the father of Vuthsa approaches the border and even enters the enemy kingdom. Realising the situation out of control, Mahasegn, the king of Avunthie exclaims, "Do all my house, my blood / Revolt against me?" (314)

> Gopalaca comments,
> But as a hero with a hero's child
> Has Vuthsa seized the girl. We planned a snare,
> He by a noble violence answers us....
> Let there be love 'twixt Vuthsa's house and us. (pp.314-15)

The king, finding no other way comes to compromise. He tells his son to follow them to Cowsambie with all gifts and dowry for the marriage: Full of suspense, twist and turn, the events take shape unexpectedly towards the desired end. K.R. S. Iyengar writes, "Mahasegn's moves and Yougundharayan's counter-moves are but frills in the background and the romantic action, with its psychological subtlety and dramatic intensity, is alone the life and soul of the play." (Iyengar. 141)

## Work Cited

Sri Aurobindo. *The Viziers of Bassora: Collected Plays.* Pondicherry; Sri Aurobindo Birth Centenary Library: Sri Aurobindo Ashram. 1971. V.7. pp. 563-735.

Sri Aurobindo. *Eric. Collected Plays.* Pondicherry; S.A.B.C.L. Sri Aurobindo Ashram. V. 6. pp. 471-559.

Sri Aurobindo. *Vasavadutta. Collected Plays.* Pondicherry; S.A.B.C.L. Sri Aurobindo Ashram. V. 6. pp. 203-329.

# 12

# Altercation of Ideologies and Topography of Identities: The Agency of Women Subjectivity in Mahasweta Devi's *Mother of 1084*

— **Ankur Konar**

On the note of an adherent sociology, Amartya Sen, by putting a debacle of transformation, observes: "Our shared humanity gets savagely challenged when the manifold *divisions* in the world are unified into one allegedly dominant system of *classification* – in terms of religion, or community, or culture, or nation, or civilization" (Sen xiii, my emphasis). Not only in the writings of Sen, but also in the writings of other modern social theorists as well, the process of divisional distinction has often been described to have disintegrational trope of segregational impulse and impact.

Classificatory theory, working on the different identical levels of social networks, has its terrible effect in the "impasse situation" of Mahasweta Devi's writings because her "creative universe repeatedly dwells upon the impasse situation in which postcolonial Indian subaltern existence is stuck. A quagmire of corruption and exploitation has ensnared the lives of countless anonymous Indian faces who even fail to make two ends meet, let alone crave a niche of their own. Engulfed in the vicious cycle of penury and superstition, they have to dare just in order to love, let alone dream. And even if they try to break out of this trap, they win momentarily. Doom waits to engulf the last sparks of rebellion in this country where off-the-centre people, like beasts, live of each other" (Chakravorty 332). Most of the disturbing drastic dramas written by her, for example, *Mother of 1084*, *Bayen*, *Water*, *Aajir* and *Urvashi O'Johnny*, by casting a possibility of negotiation between socio-political, socio-economic, socio-psychological aura, portray the "articulation of class, caste and gender in the specific situations she depicts" (Sasie and Lalitha 235). Against the backdrop of patriarchal ideologies, Mahasweta's *Mother of 1084*, a play of political preferences to the patterns of polarization in predatory pre-cultural parallax, projects a daunting sense of scale and scope where the larger sense of fair and foul and Wasteland and Roseland are synonymous.[1]

Viewers and reviewers of this drama have always focused on how the hegemonic voyage of extreme contrasts has the cogent pertinent in our morally functional society. From this perspective, Dharwadker's reading of the play to have "an intimately human quality to the Naxalite movement in Bengal" does not sound an overstatement (279). The drama incidentally begins with the telephonic relatedness between police station and domestic dynamics and with subsequent organic separateness between parents and son. The voice ordered Sujata "to identify Brati" (683). Identification, be it social or individual, is a buzz word in the study of social interaction. Similarly, 'Cut off' of 'connection' (683) is the marker of sudden separateness, not between the speaker and listener, but between parents and child. The use of the word 'understand' (683) does have a Sassurean sign of individual as well as social fabrication and Sujata's inability to 'understand' is a clear obstacle to such interaction. Hence Sujata is isolated: "I am all alone" (684). Jyoti and Dibya may have "a clear understanding of what had happened" (683) but Sujata, as Tuli accuses, "won't understand" (687). In fact, the characters of this play lack proper acceptance of understanding. Since there is 'a relation' of Jyoti's "mother in law's in the police" (684), the process to connect the police station becomes easier for them. To connect or 'only connect' has an immense ideological implication in the characters' pedagogic principle and influential imposition.

Administrative figures like Soraj Pal legitimizes the identity games by putting proclamation of affective bonding of "Brati's character's relationship" (683) with others.

'Impersonal' (684) approach of the 'officer-in-charge' (685) and the description of the Dome as "one of the untouchables" (685) makes blurred the social gulf of superior and inferior, a haunted tale of social drifters. Even the crying voice laments for the disjointed fragmentation of this world and that world: "Bring him back to me. Let me hold him close to my breast for once, and I'll weep no more. My Somu" (685). By triggering mass and class, possession and obsession, separateness makes large the meaning of relatedness. Extraordinary interpolation of "inter-collegiate riffle-shooting" (703) is one such case of rigorous relatedness. Even much planned engagement is a referral to the upcoming bond of relationship, though on showy level. "Tuli's engagement" (686), through its continuous slippage and spillage of connection and disconnection, is a clear case of mixing relatedness with separateness. But surprisingly enough, when Tuli is going to enter into the brand new relationship through the sacrosanct custom of marriage, she is also negating the prenatal connection with her parent because she "didn't ask" (686) her mother Sujata on the day of their designed engagement. And this Tuli can easily put a cavil that "Nobody cares to come down for tea on time" (687). She even describes Bini's prayer as "All sham!" (687). She is spiritually isolated and devotionally rootless that Bini is not because even after bringing up in Britain she can "offer flowers and water to the gods in her prayer room" (687). On the contrary, Tuli has the contingent web of belief in her "future mother in law's guru" (687).

Obeying the 'Swami's decision' (685), Tuli, through her own inflated sensitivity and deflated connectivity, can arrange her ancillary engagement on that day that is the dead Brati's birthday. It is very natural that through different lens an altogether different direction will be revealed. As Tuli is busy with her own engagement she "does not feel" (688) the emotional engagement of her mother for her son who is also her own brother. Tuli, in this drama of ruthless discrimination, even accuses Sujata's nexus of being "too possessive about Brati" (689) and projects Sujata to be belonging to Brati's 'camp' (689).

Concomitant reflection of adherence brings an evocative zone of eschatology where Brati, even not being 'a drunkard' or a 'hardened fraud' (689) can easily be bracketed as an out and out guilty persona because of his, to use Steele's phrase, "vacuous alliance" (02) in the Naxalite movement which so-called 'civilized' people did not and does not support. Sujata may belong to the 'opposite camp' (689) but her inner humanism wishes: "Tuli, you'll be happy in life" (689) because the true essence of humanism, in a general sense, is connected to the dignity of man as rational being.[2]

Sujata's compendious statement ["When I visit her, I find Brati" (689)] can well be marked to be the sign of related association of Brati, Somu and Somu's mother: "He'd come and call out, Mashima, a cup of tea please, a glass of water! Sweet words" (691). In fact, it is after Brati's death, Sujata "begins a process of education and discovery through which she comes to understand oppression, resistance, and her son's true nature for the first time" (Dharwadker 279). Psychological topography of any individual internalizes that the relation to the past makes a sloppy separation from the present: "But I can't forget".[3] Due to government's suppression of the Naxalite movement, the young men, related and dedicated to this movement, become "homeless. All those families banished from the colony" (690). Through the residential segregationist grotto of isolation, many families have been banished because such families are the storehouse and powerhouse of disturbing and disobedient rebellions. Typical ideologies of such families can be questioned on the basis of child rearing: "With all the attention we paid to Somu, we never had time to look to her schooling" (690). Rigorous reading of the rhetorical *tour de force* hints us that male child is taken care of, not the female one. Female baby, as in Dattani's *Tara*, is separated from the proposed progress of the family - a clear case of powerful patriarchal parade.

In the revulsion against revolution, forces of separateness and relatedness have been controlled by the terror stricken manipulation of different *contrarium* ideologies: "There's no disturbance any more, no terror, no sirens, no gunshots, no screaming young men – no!" (689). Young men like Somu and Brati 'gifted' their 'life away' (690) and people like Soraj Pal ironically enough played the "heroic role in the suppression" (688) of their revolt. It is nothing but the altercation of ideologies, a monolithic polarization of opposites to construct the living sense of repressive ideologies. Rigorous refutation is a mere attempt to control sheer activities. Such mendacious politicization of ethics cannot ameliorate the social sufferings. Does the authoritative dimension of Soroj Pal has the right of 'authority'?[4] The oppressively dominant Soroj Pal may attain a partial and temporary triumph; his tantalizing logic in a terroristic abyss may bring a disciplinary debate regarding the manipulation of power through Ideological State Apparatus. The Naxalite movement by the young men was an attempt to resist the suppression made by the government; and young men like Somu, Laltu and Brati "died for it" (691) because they never considered civilization as an escaping mask. But a 'civilized' society paid a least attention to this dedicated revolt. Brati, even being from 'a rich home' (691), was part of this so called complex process of interpellation.[5] The subservient Anindya, a resultant reflection of damaging betrayal, is a gross villain in the cross-textual art of trust. By using his relatedness to the group of Somu, he "informed the police station" (691) – an incident (or, accident) that heightens the miasma of misunderstanding in the maverick multiplicity of monolithic movement. Anindya's meekness is very opposite to the apposite visionary project of Brati and others.

As Sujata has a sympathetic inference to the activities of Somu, Laltu and Brati, other members of her family "bully" (692) her a lot. Activities like "playing a game of ludo" (692), discussing about 'birthday' and a proposed promise of making "a little *payesh*" (693) on the birthday – all are emphasizing the bond of maternal transmission. The following conversation is a literary museamization of affectionate human relationship:

> BRATI Don't worry if I'm late.
> SUJATA Do you care if I worry or not?
> BRATI I'm off. (694)

Brati's desperate jump to grab the telephone captures his determined dedication in the movement ["He is obviously agitated" (693)]. Agile agitation is the marker of the gulf between success and determination in the subterranean duality of activity and passivity. *Ala* Bakhtin, language is the marker of separateness. Brati can be separated from the others for his use of standard language. As far as linguistic identity is concerned he is the outsiders to the locality of Somu. Preferentiality of unity during the threat from outside is a sure confirmation of what Shelley believed 'to quicken a new birth'. Somu's father had 'faith' (696) in the police department but he could not understand that it is state-sponsored violence that only can cast demonic force and corrosive power.[6] He got a premature death because he could not tolerate the prevalent confirmation injustice in society. Incidentally, as expected from Mahasweta Devi, this play is once again about the "human development" of "immediate physicality" in the entropic decay of stringent morality.[7]

The narrative voice sounds pathetic when the mother laments: "the day Brati died, it was his birthday" (697). Lamenting the loss when relationship is unbound puts the human beings in the convex against the concave. Desire and distance are the marker of social interaction: "Grief had brought Somu's mother and me *together* one day, time has *split us apart* again" (698, my emphasis). Even the thought of Sujata always unconsciously reflects the buffeting role of memory in imaginative activity: "I was with Brati the whole day" (707). Nandini and Sujata are different through tenses because the latter "live(s) with" the 'past' and the former "have to harness my present, and think of the future" (706). Subjective visionary experience through the 'demeaning' revolution has taught Nandini lessons, both of its transparency and uncertainty that ultimately casts the resultant reflection of her "impression of a tight secretiveness, a self-imprisonment" (698), a clear case of self-imposed 'othering':

> Yet another feature of Mahasweta Devi's writing is that she projects women as symbols of resilience and love. May be it is being a woman that enables her to recognize this power that emerges even when a woman is isolated, victimized or oppressed. In *Mother of 1084* in spite of her despair and emotional isolation from the rest of her family Sujata reveals a sensitivity and compassion which ironically only her "social outcast" son Brati recognized and appreciated.
>
> (Thankamma 87)

For Nandini, there can't be any 'end of history'; to her, history always meant struggle and it will always remain so. The statement reflects the verbal composition in a darkly conscious state of mind when she says:

> Failings, mistakes, deviations. I still wonder how we could afford not to know that with all that has happened since 1947, all human loyalties has dissolved by 1970. I wonder how we could be unaware that they could betray us to kill us ... But some day there will be people who'll say that behind all our apparent hatred lay a craving to love and to revere. (699)

Forced or imposed space of torture cannot bring palpable solace. Marginalization of disobedient subjects is a moratorium refuge to the hinterland of shelter; it is not the natural outcome. Self-nullifying piercing power of Nandini projects a cartographical map of dream and nightmare in the unchattered territory of self-conscious subjectivity. Mortification, though a menace to men, cannot touch the mounting sense of revolutionary zeal. Struggle gives meaning to life and frustration after failure is the part of this existential struggle.

Assortment of separateness and relatedness had their own impact in a same action "for the possibility of people joining the Party as friends only to betray us ultimately" (699). Disguise is a trick; and the 'rampant' (699) betrayal is an automatic outcome of that superimposed manipulation of the trick. For certain people, trick turns into treat. Lazy, hazy, crazy days of delight are 'dead forever' because Nandini is 'not the same person' (700); she is no longer living in the days of 'delight' (700). She is now dwelling in the dialectic display of 'forth world'[8] and consequently suffering from what Asish Nandy terms 'isomorphic oppression' (31). Nandini cannot believe in the 'end of history'[9] but eventually her own statement is a powerful presage of 'end of history':

> No. No. No. No. it was never quite, nothing's quite. Nothings changed ... Torture continues with greater sophistication and more secrecy, and yet you'ds say it's all quite? All quite? (705)

In such interrogatory stance of illocutionary force, struggle seems to be anachronism in the present society; shedding a globule of blood in this globe seems to be old wives' tale. Possibly, there is no prospect through the retrospect. Vis-à-vis such standpoint it would be relevant to mention Derek Layder's strong argument that has impressed me: "Since the tensions and dynamics between the forces of seperatedness and relatedness are such that individuals can never bring them into perfect alignment, then they are constantly embroiled in struggles to control the effects of one or the other. Social involvement brings with it the possibility of being controlled or in some way being overly influenced by others and yet a quest for aloneness or seperatedness underlines the issue of our routine dependence on others." (28)

Great men have always talked about their emotional, sympathetic rapport with the abasement and debasement in Bangladesh, but have always remained mute about the red rampage in West Bengal. Leading journals and periodicals have always apparently tried to glorify the problem of the movement makers, but in reality their intention was something other. As the political parties have always played their games by using the young movement makers as their toy, it "has come close to criminality in many parts of India and violence has become endemic to public life."[10] Naturally, the Naxalite message through the members' "range of vocabulary" (704) is diminished. Poet like unflappable Amit can only put a decent response of projecting "homage to Brati and his generation" (707) and can only indulge in the grape of joy. For these pseudo-intellectuals, Brati, to borrow Virginia Woolf's phrase for Shelley, is definitely "not one of us". Incidentally, 'Brati's laughter' (691) has the potentiality to mock the present stagnant society because laughter sometimes functions as a social corrective.[11] In fact, we "are so infiltrated by corrupt forces that we cannot imagine an alternative" (Steele 45). Like her all other dramas Mahasweta here too "tries to find solutions to problems";[12] but Nandini's message is a too small interstice to evoke a consent formation. Since manufacturing consent is more pertinent to ponder over the psyche of the characters living during interregnum, we need a flashing eye, a floating throat. Resolution should bring inclusion of a solution, but the conclusion tells us the permanence of an everlasting revolution.

## Notes and References

1. Vis-à-vis such thematic pattern of exclusiveness Paul Brian writes: "South Asian literature is a colorful kaleidoscope of fragmented views, colored by the perceptions of its authors, reflecting myriad realities – and fantasies." (*Modern South Asian Literature in English*. London: Greenwood P, 2003, p 06. Print.)
2. See Crossley, Nick. "Humanism and anti-Humanism." *Key Concepts in Critical Social Theory*. London: Sage, 2005, pp 121-8. Print.
3. It is the web of continuous memory that projects the picture how "hearts (are) burning like bodies on fire" (690). It would be relevant to mention Marianne Hirsch who differentiates between Morrison's notion of 'rememory' (in *Beloved*) as 'a memory that communicated through bodily

symptoms becomes a form of repetition and reenactment" and 'postmemory' as "one that works through indirection and multiple mediation" ("Marked by Memory: Feminist Reflections on Trauma and Transmission." *Extremities: Trauma, Testimony, and Community*, Urbana: Urbana U of Illinois P, 2002, p 74. Print.)

4. Micheal D. Bristol writes: "Authority ... is identified with the power to influence and to disseminate thought and opinion as well as feeling. When this power approaches from without, in the form of an official mandate or sacred writ, it is likely to be coercive and deadening in its effects. Authority in this sense is actualized by means of discourse enjoying obedience to a person, an institution or an ideological formation in final and definite form" (*Carnival and Theatre: Plebian Culture and the Structure of Authority in Renaissance England.* New York and London: Methun, 1985, pp 21-2. Print.)
5. Let me quote some bright lines from *Rethinking Youth* to give the sense of virile vanguard from the young men of our country: "Young people grow up in incredibly varied circumstances, with different priorities and perspectives." (01) and "In many countries, the experience and meaning of youth is also changing as young people actively construct their own group identities." (01) and "Young people are growing up in a world in which local and national identities are being reaffirmed, fiercely guarded and shaped." (02) and "Young people are important because they reflect the results of political struggles over the priority given to the public over the private." (05) (J Wyn and R White, Sage, 1992. Print.)
6. In recent time Mahasweta Devi, in an annual general meeting of West Bengal Police Association (WBPA), warned that injustice to police will pave the way for mutiny as the political parties are now making the policemen scapegoats. (Reported in *The Statesman*, Dated 25th November, 2010. Kolkata: p 06, Print.)
7. Mahasweta Devi, Quoted. Samik Bandyopadhyaya. "Introduction." *Five Plays*. Calcutta: Seagull, 1986, pp vii-viii. Print.
8. The concept of 'forth world' has been initiated by George Manuel and Micheal Posluns in their *The Forth World: An Indian Reality* (New York: Free P, 1974. Print). This much debated term hints those persons who were once colonized but now have became much more marginalized in their own country which was once ideologically their own.
9. The phrase 'end of history' was first used by Cournot in 1861 to mark the full stop to the historical dynamic with the perfection of civil society. Arnold Gehlen, Heidegger and Vattimo have also exploited this phrase in their philosophical discourse. In recent times, Francis Fukuyama, after publication of the much appealing book *The End of History and the Last Man* in 1992, has almost monopolized the phrase.

10. Ashis Nandy in conversation with Ramin Jahanbegloo in *Talking India* (New Delhi: Oxford UP, 2006, p 46. Print.).
11. In *Laughter: An Essay on the Meaning of the Comic* (1900), Bergson indicates that laughter functions as a social corrective (Cited in *Routledge Encyclopedia*, p 735). Compare Benare's sarcastic laughter at the end of Tendulkar's *Silence! The Court Is In Session.*
12. Venugopal, N. "In Wright Earnest." *Indian Express*, 13th October. 1991, p 02, Print.

## Works Cited

Chakravorty, Shreya. "Possibility of Negation: Postcolonial Impasse in Mahasweta Devi." Bakshi, Kaustav et al. (eds). *Anxieties, Influences and After: Critical Response to Postcolonialism and Neocolonialism.* Delhi and Kolkata: Worldview, 2009, pp 322-33, Print.

Dharwadker, A B. *Theatres of Independence: Drama, Theory, and Urban Performance in India since 1947.* New Delhi: Oxford UP, 2005. Print.

Layder, Derek. *Modern Social Theory: Key Concepts and New Directions.* London: UCL Press, 1997. Print.

Nandy, Ashis. *The Intimate Enemy: Loss and Recovery of Self under Colonialism.* New Delhi: Oxford UP, 1983. Print.

Sasie, Tharu and K Lalitha. *Women Writing in India*, V II. New York: Feminist P, 1993. Print.

Sen, Amartya. *Identity and Violence: The Illusion of Destiny.* London: Penguin, 2006. Print.

Steele, Meili. *Theorizing Textual Subjects: Agency and Oppression.* Cambridge: Cambridge UP, 1997. Print.

Thjankamma, Catherine. "Women that Patriarchy Created: the Plays of Vijay Tendulkar, Mahesh Dattani and Mahasweta Devi." Madge, V M (Ed). *Vijay Tendulkar's Plays: An Anthology of Recent Criticism.* Delhi: Pencraft, 2009, pp 80-7. Print.

# 13

## *The Vultures*: A Vestige of Venomous Vengeance

—Ulka S. Wadekar

The human being is an integral part of society. There are various facets of human behaviour and attitude. A value of human life is always at the centre in socio-political system. Drama is an art form that materializes complex experiences of life. Change, development and transformation are natural processes but sometimes along with human development; psychological perversion also get rooted and forms a chain of violence, torture and harassment.

Vijay Tendulkar is an established name in the world of literature. *The Vultures* is a play of inhuman violence, greed, drunkenness, avarice and ruthlessness. Originally written in Marathi, *The Vultures* is a two-act play that presents the vulturine attitude and reality of unmitigated violence. Women are always at the centre of his plays. Through this play Tendulkar displays the psyche of people interested in power obtained by betrayal, selfish, greedy leaders and indulged in exploitation of people on whom physical and mental slavery has been forcibly inflicted. To prove it the dramatist has effectively used the dramatic devices like dialogues, comment and presentation. Actually it is a satirical drama that brings about a piercing sharp glimpse of reality.

The story of the play takes place in the family of Pappa Hari Pitale and his brother Sakharam. Both of them jointly worked in a construction firm called 'The Hari Sakharam Company'. The story is built on the cruel relationship among Pappa, his two sons, namely, Ramakant and Umakant, his daughter Manik and a tender love relationship between Rama, Ramakant's wife and Rajaninath, Pappa's illegitimate son. The vulture in Pappa Hari Pitale gets awake and he maliciously wrests the company from his brother by betrayal and false law suits. As a result Sakharam becomes a pauper and finds himself on the street. He could not tolerate the thought of his own brother deceiving him. It is a sudden shock to his mind. He becomes frustrated and to overcome his distress he starts drinking. Unfortunately Pappa's success and satisfaction did not last long. His sons and daughter made a similar conspiracy against him and drove him out of the house. Thus human relations are staked for the sake of greed, selfishness, power and immorality. Though married to Ramakant, Rama has an illicit relation with Rajaninath. She used Rajaninath just to douse her fire of physical pleasure and to quench the thirst of motherhood. Finally she gets pregnant from Rajaninath.

The layout of the story is characteristic. It has more remarkable experiences of blistering and bitter reality, captivating and brilliant constructive technique, stimulating atmosphere but it fails to offer any relief to the readers. The unbridled upsurge of violence that has manifested in the familial relationship shows social and moral discontent. Power hungry people who enjoys the sensibility have no sensibility in making others life a hell. In a changing socio-political scenario, morality has been replaced by cunningness and violence. Arundhati Bannerjee added in the Appendix of the volume Tendulkar's Collected Plays: "The play (*The Vultures*) is a ruthless dissection of human nature revealing its inherent tendencies to violence, avarice, selfishness, sensuality and sheer wickedness.... The decadence and degeneration of human individual's belonging to a middle class milieu is exposed through the interactions among the members of the family."

Some psychological elements play a vital role in themakinf of the inner self of the major characters of the play. Pappa's sons

Umakant, and Ramakant and his daughter Manik inherited viciousness and cruelty from him. Rajaninath, the illegitimate son of Hari Pitale plays a role of chorus and through his songs he narrated the past and present of the family. He remembers the day of Ramakant's marriage when Rama was:

> ...like a doe
> An innocent doe untouched.
> As loving as the earth. (203)

She was brought to the home of vultures where there is no place for relations and humanity.

> But it was no home,
> Not a home, but a hole in a tree
> Where vultures lived in a shape of men (204)

In her house Rama does not get any attention and love from the members of the family. Her husband also never pays any heed to her desires. The greed for power and wealth is so high that he cannot find anything wrong in his misdeeds. He becomes addicted to liquor. The liquor in turn made him impotent. He neglects and tortures Rama. Rama has a great desire of bearing a child. According to her, it is a right of every woman to become a mother.

> But only she knew
> One longing
> Only one...
> Threw of her chains in her need.
> The need to well with fruit

because

> Each womb-bearing woman's right
> By birth (205)

Rama can be considered as a perfection of womanhood but all her hopes, desires are darkened by the neglect of her husband.

But with the help of courage, patience, perseverance and integrity she decides to revolt. She selects her brother-in-law Rajaninath to fulfill her desire of becoming a mother. Rajaninath also finds consolation in her company.

Other female character Manik is also suffers neglect. Her greedy and selfish father does not love her. Her brothers treat her inhumanly. Her brothers are as cruel, selfish and greedy as their father. Like their father they also have a habit of drinking and smoking. They also follow the same path of their father and quarrel violently to get the largest share of their father's property. Having grown in such wild and beastly atmosphere, Manik feels insecure and to overcome the feeling of insecurity she makes friend with different men. She also develops a habit of drinking and smoking.

The feudalistic behaviour of males in the patriarchal organization is always to overpower women. They presume that women are object of utilization, physical and mental torture and by doing so they are proving their manliness and valour. They purposefully forget that women tolerates the blisters and burns of life. Thus the fear of rejection and hatred cause Manik to develop love relationship with the Raja of Hondur. She became pregnant. When her brothers come to know about her pregnancy, they decided to take benefit of the situation and make money from it. Both Ramakant and Umakant behave like a vulture having no sensible mind and heart. They do not want to think of their only sister fame and feelings. Ramakant demanded:

> She's is pregnant if you want her fixed, put down the money. Cash down
> Twenty thousand, what?, More, if you like. Otherwise
> Bloody publicity! Uproar in the bloody newspapers! (236)

Unfortunately they cannot grab the handsome income from the Raja as he died due to the shock of blackmail and a fear of defamation. His death makes the two brothers more ruthless and violent. They ruthlessly kick on her belly and the child is aborted. The vulture in them is so violent that they cannot hesitate to kill their sister's child. Manik screams with suffering and loss. The feeling of hatred and anger grows in her mind and she wants to avenge her brothers. She is brutal by nature and her brothers' attitude added more fuel to her brutality. To take revenge, she finds a soft and innocent victim in form of Rama.

Rama, who gets inclined towards Rajaninath, finds physical and emotional support. She finds that Rajaninath can fulfill her desire of becoming mother. When Rajaninath refuses to develop such relations she becomes frustrated. She expresses her desire by saying that she is born to become a mother.

> This soil's rich. Its hungry. But the seed won't take root.
> If the Seed's soaked in poison. If it's weak, feeble, lifeless,
> Devoid of virtue – then why blame the soil? (241)

So she stepped out of the boundaries of tradition and gets conceived from Rajaninath. It is important to note here that the brutal Ramakant starts taking care of his wife after learning the news of her pregnancy. On the other hand his sister Manik assumes it a great opportunity to take revenge. With the same anger and bestiality she kicks Rama and ultimately succeeds in aborting her child. Due to the vulture residing in Manik's inner self, she does not hesitate to empty Rama's womb. Rama's scream grabs attention of both Ramakant and Rajaninath. Ramakant becomes bewildered with the loss of child. When he comes to know that the child was not his own, he starts drinking more and more. In a rage he hits Umakant.

Manik and Pappa want to take revenge of Ramakant and ask Rajninath to join them in their crime. Thus the house of the vultures disintegrates. Both the brothers use abuses for their father and compared him to a mangy dog. But the old man's soul is hardened by past deeds and crimes.

A sudden appearance of Sakharam, Pappa's brother brings a twist in the story. Betrayed by his own brother Sakharam becomes insensible. He worked honestly for the upbringing and success of their company. So he demands his share of money from Pappa. Both Ramakant and Umakant get shocked by the demand and a seed of suspicion against their father arouse in them. They think that their father still has money. So they drive away Sakharam. Ramakant, Umakant and Manik make Pappa drink more so that he could reveal the truth about money. It is necessary to mention here that Pappa who adopted the heinous means like treachery and violence to ruin his brother; now faces the same consequences. He gets the same treatment from his sons and thus his cruelty is being repaid by them. All boundaries of violence and cruelty are surpassed when trio beats him ruthlessly. It is a scene of violence which is inflicted on father by children. Pappa gets seriously injured. Unable to tolerate further assault, he confides to them that he has deposited seven thousand rupees in Punjab Bank. Thus it is the greed for money that decides the fate of characters. A pathetic and desperate confession of Pappa shows his defeat against the will of his sons.

> Theirs is no more you devils: There isn't
> That's all there is, really. Please don't
> Kill me: I am your father, you pimps:
> Your father (230)

Throughout his life Pappa yearns for money. His greed and passion for money converts him into a cruel personality. Thus although he is humiliated and assaulted by his sons just for some amount of money, he denied to part with it. His refusal enragsses the children. So they try to kill him. In order to save his own life Pappa runs away from the house. This situation can be considered as one of the most vicious and venomous act of the sons. Rajaninath sings the incidence of Pappa's escape as:

> The oldest vulture,
> That stubborn ghost
> With death in his desires,
> Hiding his ugly maw,
> Trailing a wing,
> Departed from a hollow of a tree
> Where he lived (232)

Scene I of the Act two reveal that the two vultures namely Ramakant and Umakant are ready to take one more bite of human flesh. Here the victim is their only sister Manik. To grab the share of her wealth both of them hatched a plan. Umakant tries to kill her by choking her neck when Ramakant suggests:

> Don't bloody let her go, Umya: Drag the bloody money out: Look, How she's wriggling: Squash her bloody neck: Twist it. (235)

They try to break Manik's leg to prevent her from meeting her lovers further. Even they do not show a slight hesitation in aborting Manik's child. Another victim of similar circumstance is Rama whose child is aborted by Manik.

*The Vultures* represents a moral and psychological degradation of a middle class family. According to N.S. Dharan:

> *The Vultures* is indeed the most violent of Tendulkar's plays. It reminds one of Webster's "The Duchess of Malfi". It is replete with violent imagery, consisting of blood, eeriness and mad raving. Both Hari Pitale and Manik thirst for revenge. Both succeed in their mission. While Pappa succeeds in driving Ramakant to streets, Manik succeeds in causing Rama's abortion. The dialogue is composed of words which seem appropriate in the mouths of the characters who utter them. On the whole, the play is, no doubt, naturalistic in its portrayal of domestic violence caused by greed.[2]

Through *The Vultures*, Tendulkar is succeeded in treating various beastly attitudes in human behaviour. In this drama, the element of violence is more prominent in various forms like power struggle, greed for money, feudalistic mentality. Helplessness of women characters, loss of hope and indignity in society are effectively presented through exact language and dialogue. The house in which the characters are placed to act is actually symbolized as a hollow of a tree where the people are deprived of their rights, exploited by all means, trampled one another's emotions and frenzied with power, greed, violence and sexual pleasure. Having a good knowledge of phraseology, the dramatist, used the language that keeps a grip on plot, theme and characters and exposes the reality. Thus the story is a story of anger, violence, and greed for money, resentment, revenge, depression, and brutality. It shows an inhuman strength of system of exploitation.

## Works Cited

Benerjee, Arundhati. Appendix I. *Collected Plays in Translation.* New Delhi: Oxford University Press, 2008

Dharan N.S. "*The Vultures:* A Drama of Domestic Violence" in *The Plays of Vijay Tendulkar*, New Delhi: Creative Books, 1999

# 14

# Female Status, Their Roles and the Psychological Situation as Depicted in the Plays of Vijay Tendulkar

— Sapna Chaturvedi and Seeme Mahmood

In Indian society women were treated generally as maids or slaves as if they had no will or desire of their own. The pre-Independence period women in India were just restricted to household work. They were more of a puppet in the hands of their husbands, sort of to produce kids and look after them cook food in the house, etc. They were never given any freedom to do anything on their own nor were they allowed out of the house unless they went with their husbands. The position of women in society has changed markedly in the last 20 years.

Society is changing a lot in terms of acceptance of the many roles of women as professionals, as bread-earners in families and as independent thinking individuals. Women have proved themselves as equals in many professions as well as proved themselves even better suited than men in others. The situation for the changing role of women is improving fast. But on the other hand, female foeticide, dowry deaths and domestic abuse provide a macabre background of primitive barbarism; it is because the system is so complex with interplaying factors such as sex, gender, class, caste, ethnicity, and race that it encircles women within its control of exploitation, discrimination and oppression. It is the cycle that needs to be understood by women themselves and by those who are working to support women's struggles in society. In the contemporary scenario there are many Indian writers who, through their writings, have been successful in projecting the existing social inequality and demonstrate the status of women. Eminent writers like Arundhati Roy, Jhumpa Lahiri, Shashi Deshpande, Anita Desai, Girish Karnad, Mahesh Dattani etc.

As everybody knows, Vijay Dhondopant Tendulkar is undeniably a greatest living Indian playwright, screen and television writer, literary essayist, political journalist, and social commentator of the twentieth century. He is known for as a versatile and prolific Marathi writer. Tendulkar played a vital role in the modernization of India. As a writer he has excelled in many departments of literature: essays, short stories, criticism, screenplay writing and drama. In the beginning he appeared as a controversial writer, but his works showed him as an honest artist. His honesty and skill won him reputation and recognition. His works have highlighted a new concept to the perennially profound issues confronting man in the metaphysical, cultural, social, economical, emotional, intellectual and political spheres. There are many works which has been translated and performed in various languages but his prominent contribution in both English as well as Marathi works. Tendulkar presented the modern changed time which is very complex: the difficulties, conflicts, dilemma and sufferings of the modern man. His conception in his drama: treating violence as a human natural trait and the best thing about his plays is dealt with themes that unravel the exploitation of power and latent violence in human relationships which is focused on caste, gender, individual isolation, love, sexuality, marriage and double standard view of society. His wide and rich literature examines the effects of development on women and he has clearly exposed that in many areas of the country the rights of women are infringed and women are exploited emotionally, socially, and physically. Women play a central role in Tendulkar's plays. His female characters are mainly from the lower and middle classes:

housewives, teachers, mistresses, daughters, film extras, slaves, and servants. These women bring not just variety of social station but also a broad range of emotions into the plays:

> from the unbelievably gullible to the clever, from the malleable to the stubborn, from the conservative to the rebellious, from the self-sacrificing to the grasping. [6]

Explore the dramatic representation of male dominance in many different ways in Tendulkar's *Silence! the Court is in Session*. The play is a powerful satire on the shallow conventions and the shameful hypocrisy of the middle-class male-dominated society and also the deplorable legal system found in contemporary society. By using the techniques of dramatic irony and satire effectively the playwright portrays how a young woman (Miss. Leela Benare) suffers a lot and undergoes deep mental agony when she is betrayed by the other members of the group. Tendulkar has depicted the difficulty of a young woman, who is a victim of the male dominated society. A amateur group of actors, who perform plays in around the city as the occasion demands.The actual play was scheduled to be staged in the night. But as they have plenty of time for the regular play, they plan to stage a mock trial and also found it as an opportunity to dig up Leela's past life. Miss Leela Benare is an actress in an amateur drama group and a central figure of the play is made the accused. Benare is an educated, independent, frank, bold woman about thirty-four years old. She worked as a school teacher. During the first half of the mock trail play, Benare is able to outsmart them. She is not caught in their net. Her voice is not throttled. But the later half of the play witnesses a mock trial of Benare that is actually a trial of the whole female race in this country. It shows our hypocrisy, our double standards regarding men and women. The charges of infanticide and unmarried motherhood are leveled against her. She is charged with leading a licentious life. It is proved against her that she fell in love with her own maternal uncle when she was hardly fourteen and tried to commit suicide when she could not marry him. As a mature women then she fell in love with Prof Damle, a married man with children and became pregnant by him.

In the beginning of her exploitation begins with her uncle who had exploited her sexually in her teen age. To top the torture, even her own mother fails to understand and support her. But Benare shows guts, she starts her life all over again, studies and finally settles into a teaching job. As a teacher, she comes in contact with Prof. Damle whom she considers quite intelligent, and academically bright. Though married, the Professor exploits her sexually and naturally refuses to marry her. Tendulkar's Benare is unmarried, sexually exploited and has to abort her pregnancy to maintain the facade of honour. In the course of rehearsal, the play thus reveals the moral hypocrisy, the sadistic tendencies, the hostility and the verbal violence of the male-dominated society against women. As a sensitive and committed writer Tendulkar perceives the harsh realities of contemporary society and depicts them artistically without preconceived notions. Neither Mr. Kashikar nor the other members of the troupe find fault with Profs Damle who, despite having a wife and five children, has willfully acted against the sacred institution of marriage by indulging in an extramarital affair. Leela fell in love with Prof. Damle as a young woman in spite of her previous failure in a love with her maternal uncle.

Prof. Damle, who also wanted to satisfy his bodily thirst, she was pregnant without marriage and this was a reason that she was discharged from her school. Infact, she has been loyal to her profession. She declares in the final act that she has always kept her professional life away from her personal life. She has justified her role of being a teacher. In spite of all this, the school management has holded an enquiry. Benare questions the propriety of her management trying to mix up her life with her profession. She feels that they should judge her only as a teacher for she has put her whole life into it. She has worn herself to shadow in that job. She has never hurt anyone except her own self. Here Vijay Tendulkar has created a satire on the unjust male dominating society and on the working of Court.

Man has all the rights to be sinful in the society. All the rights to are reserved specially for him. On the other hand, a woman must be deserted, ignored, thrown away and should be punished for her sins. Mrs. Kashikar is middle aged, married, a house wife and disapproving of childless. Even she does not help the helpless Ms. Benare in the court in spite of being a woman. She thinks that it is woman because of being a man and husband. She does not oppose her insults and still seen. She does not hesitate to say that these young unmarried girls get everything without marrying. Benare, on the other hand was a progressive contemporary woman. She breaks down during the mock-trail because the story of the character in the play she is performing at the mock-trail is identical to her own. She was psychologically tortured but was still starving to search for her existence.

Arundhati Banerjee, an observer, maintains that the accusation brought against Benare at the beginning of the trial turns into the verdict in last because contemporary Indian Society, with its roots grounded firmly in reactionary ideas, cannot allow the birth of a child out of wedlock. This very, reversal in the attitude of the authorities expresses the basic hypocrisy and double standards on which our society is founded. In the course of court proceedings, Miss Benare's private life is exposed and publicly dissected revealing that she is a woman of loose character.

All the characters drawn by Tendulkar except Ms. Benare represents the male dominated Indian society. Benare is accused of cheap conduct, of wooing men, of fulfilling her bodily needs and so on and so forth. But the intellectual, Prof, Damle who is equally a part of the bad conduct, is not at all held responsible. Man has all the rights to be sinful in the society. He can be harsh, notorious and innocent too. All the rights are reserved specially for him. On the other hand, a woman must be deserted, abandoned, ignored, thrown away and should be tainted for her sins. There is no escape for her in our society. She must be brutally destroyed for her actions both physically and mentally.

The characters of Mr. and Mrs. Kashikar, Ponkshe, Rokde, Sukhatme represents hypocrisy and inferior complex. Tendulkar digs the inner self of all the characters in the plays, how they present themselves and what they actually are. He has identified the role of society in shaping and determining their identities. *Silence! The Court is in Session* brings into focus the psychological torture that is forced onto a young and independent woman, Leela Benare, who dared to defy the patriarchal authority and institutic , thus bringing upon herself the societal violence that destroys her at the end.

Tendulkar's *Sakharam Binder,* carries out pathetic position of women in the male-dominated Indian world. He shows the terrible and harsh reality of man and woman in Sakharam Binder. Sakharam explores with great objectivity the complication in human nature two necessary component of which are sex and violence. The main character, Sakharam Binder, a bookbinder, takes in a succession of women who have been thrown out of their homes by their husbands. He offers them food, shelter and living essentials in exchange for domestic services and companionship. Brahmin by birth, Sakhârâm, is a man devoid of ethics and morality, and opposes the outdated social codes and conventional marriage systems as he doesn't believe in wedlock society. He accordingly uses the society for his own pleasure. He justifies all his acts through claims of modern, unconventional thinking, and comes up with hollow arguments meant in fact to enslave women.

## Relationship between Sakharam and Lakshmi

The play opens with seventh woman, Lakshmi following Sakharam to his door. When she comes, he informs this dainty, suffering woman of the rules of the house, and of his requirements. Lakshmi is very religious and moral, she turned him into religious, made him to have a bath daily but it didn't affect anymore on his personal nature. Poor Lakshmi gets her head smashed against the wall. She endures all things because she is woman while he tortures because he is a man. Sakharam treats her like a slave and uses her for different purposes. She is a loyal, hardworking and docile woman unable to keep Sakharam happy for long, although she is adept at household work. Her husband has tortured her as she fails to conceive a child by him. Now, for her, Sakharam is her husband. She tries her best to fulfill his every need despite the fact that he even fails to understand her expectations and exploits her physically as well as psychologically. Sakharam's defence of his sexual needs makes him insensitive to the violence inflicted by him on the body and mind of the women in his life. He has the traits of a sadist; he inflicts immense agony on Laxmi. When she gets her foot burnt on coals, he shows no sympathy and, instead, asks her to laugh in order to arouse himself. Laxmi bears Sakharam's cruelties calmly and silently for one whole year. One day he beat her so horribly that she couldn't bear his tyranny and finally, she gets exasperated and can take it no more.

When he came to know that she is not enduring all this, he decided to send her to her nephew.Sakharam treats the women in his life like dirt. Although he makes them work like a slave yet he likes to believe he is their saviour. The elements like culture; history, religion, and society around him are responsible to make him so. He was born in Brahmin society but his parents failed to civilize him. His father would beat him terribly so he ran away from his house when he was eleven years old. Being a man he had some physical desirers and was impossible to live except fulfilling them. As he was against to social system, he disliked to have any wives so he began to bring abandoned women to do household duties and share his bed. After turning Laxmi out, he brings home, Champa. She has been treated very badly by her husband, ever since she was married at a tender age. She runs away from her husband, because her husband, Fauzdar Sindhe, becomes more of an animal than a man to her. He treats her like a beast, and gratifies his sadism and sexual needs in unnatural ways. Champa is not a submissive woman who would take things lying down. She stands for her rights at times and protests when an injustice is done to her. She is not helpless like Laxmi. She uses her sexuality as a weapon to protect herself and to get things done.

Laxmi, on the other hand, is a more complex person. She apparently has unlimited capacity to suffer violence, but she still retains her innocence. She can converse with various creatures, from an ant to a crow. She befriends them and talks to them for hours. And she even gets a scolding from Sakharam for speaking to and laughing with an ant. He thinks it to be a sign of lunacy in her. But for Laxmi this is a soothing experience and it keeps her going in the face of physical and mental torture that she endures regularly. Laxmi has infinite courage and capacity for hard labour. She works from morning to night in Sakharam's house and tries to satisfy his insatiable sexual appetite as well. But she is unable to take it for long. She then goes to her nephew, who has recently married. The couple throws her out of their house on charges of stealth, as they feel that she is a nuisance to their privacy. So Laxmi once again returns to Sakharam as she has nowhere else to go, but only to receive a fresh round of beating as a welcome. Laxmi envies Champa for her influence over Sakharam. But she does not want to be like her. She detests her because she believes that the patriarchal tradition in vogue for ages is sacred though it causes immense suffering to women.

Champa protects Laxmi from Sakharam who wants to turn Laxmi out as he considers her an obstruction in his privacy. But Champa sees in Laxmi a relief from the household chores in which Laxmi says she is adept. Laxmi stays under Champa's wing for a while and she knows that it is only Champa who can challenge Sakharam's decision. But as soon as she knows about Champa's affair with Dawood, she starts hating her for cheating on Sakharam. Laxmi accepts Sakharam almost as a husband and, therefore, submits herself to him willingly; Champa, on the other hand, accepts him merely as her man in sheer helplessness. She has no alternative but to share bed with him, but, for that, she has to reluctantly help herself with an alcoholic drink also. Nevertheless, in one corner of her mind, she feels that all men are equally bad. Laxmi, who outwardly appears to be generous and kind-hearted, turns out inwardly to be vicious or violent.

On Champa's murder, she shows more presence of mind than Sakharam. Champa's character exhibits woman's torture at different levels. She suffers at the hands of her mother, her husband, her male-companion, and, at the end, her female-companion also. Appearance is totally deceptive so far as Laxmi's character is concerned. Throughout the play, she appears meek and polite, but at its end, she incites wrath in Sakharam, which goads him on to killing Champa. Both Champa and Laxmi, have their share of suffering sexual, physical, and psychological at the instance of Sakharam, for he gives them shelter and they just receive it in their helplessness. In the drama, it is found that how man is responsible to destroy a lovely relationship between man and woman. Although Sakharam is the protagonist of the play, the action of the play revolves round the character of Laxmi. The drama explores the plight of women in all helplessness along with the depiction of complexity of human nature.

Tendulkar's 'Kamala', written in the naturalistic mode, like in his previous plays. The play is inspired by a real-life incident - the Indian Express exposé by Ashwin Sarin, who actually bought a girl from a rural flesh market and presented her at a press conference. By using this incident as a launching pad, Tendulkar grapples with the issues of morality and hypocrisy. The female body as object of male sexual fantasy and desire is theatrically psresented by Tendulkar. His women are essentially the marginalized objects in the interlocking system of sexual politics and power politics. The play exposes the story of an unfortunate woman sold away in the flesh market and a so-called happy housewife married to a daring journalist, both having a revelation of finding themselves on the common platform of sexual slavery in this male dominated world. The male character of the play is a self-seeking journalist, Jai Singh Jadhav, who treats the woman he has purchased from the flesh market as an object that can buy him a promotion in his job and a reputation in his professional life. Jadhav wishes to present Kamala at a surprise press conference as a genuine proof that such flesh-trade still happens in modern democratic India. He is one of those modern individuals, who pursue their goal unquestioningly, with a single-track mind. Jadhav is never bothered of what will happen to Kamala after exhibiting her at the press conference. Kamala is introduced to Jadhav's family as a commodity. His wife Sarita is educated, helps a lot in his 'business' with proper care. She opines that Kamala should be given a decent dress, but she is denied when Jadhav suggests that she should look natural so that the press conference would get its hype. It is evident that Sarita as a wife of Jadhav has to live only as the shadow of her husband for. Sarita was extremely sensitive to her husband's needs. Without any hesitation she takes notes of all phone calls, gives every satisfaction to her husband, carries out all his instructions and behaves just like a puppet. Though educated and able to live independent life, her doubtless acceptance of male authority turned her into a slave, a bonded laborer. This indicates her ignorance and lack of self knowledge. Kamala's entry in the household reveals to Sarita the selfish hypocrisy of her husband and the insignificance of her own existence in Jaisingh's life. Kamala, an uneducated woman, unconsciously lit the flame that enlightened the life of Sarita. She says to Sarita: How much did he buy you for?

And after that Kamala proposes that she will do all housework while Sarita will look after accounts and such sophisticated things. She adds that cache of them will share their master's bed half a month each. Somehow, Sarita painfully and shockingly realizes that she too, like Kamala, functions as a mere pawn in Jadhav's game of chess. Kamala to Jadhav is only an object that helps him win instant fame while Sarita is also an object to be paraded as a wife at parties, to enhance his status as a successful journalist. This question compelled her to think of her own self and she reviled the truth. She says:

> ....I was asleep, I was unconscious even when I was awake. Kamala woke me up... Kamala showed me everything. I saw the man I thought my partner was the master of a slave. I have no rights at all in this house...slaves don't have rights, do Kakasaheb?...Dance to their master's whim. Laugh, when he says laugh. Cry, when he says, cry...when he says lie on the bed –they (She's twisted in pain).

Sarita realized that she was used merely as an object of sexual satisfaction, of social companionship and of domestic comfort. She finds herself treated as a slave. On realizing that she holds no value in her husband's busy and materialistic lifestyle, she takes a re-birth. And finally a new Sarita emerges. She discards her submissive attitude and decides to convene a Press Conference where she would expose to the whole world the real Jaisingh Jadhav. She is determined to put forth her husband as a great advocate of freedom. She would tell how he bought the slave Kamala and used her for his own selfish ends. Sarita, who was asleep to her reality, was awakened by Kamala. She has come face to face with her domestic slavery. The feminine ideology, which pities women in direct encounter with chauvinistic male opposes, finds its complete expression. The character of Sarita consists of a great variety and depth in comparison to her male counterparts. She reacts against social injustices and the subservient position of women in the institution of marriage.

Tendulkar uses the play also to dwell on the characteristic suffering of the Indian middle class woman made to suffer by selfish, malicious and hypocritical male chauvinists. The man-woman relationship is also deftly touched upon in the complex relationship between Jadhav and his wife, Sarita. Kamala is a femalecentered play in the sense that it is built on the metamorphosis of Sarita emerging from being a docile wife to an assertive, mature and strong woman in the end.

Domestic violence and abuse can happen to anyone, regardless of size, gender, or strength, yet the problem is often overlooked, excused, or denied. Tendulkar's *Kanyadaan* is another example of women subordination. As the title *Kanyadaan* is an irony. It spells out the contradiction between the play's statement and the scriptural meaning of the word, the giving away of the daughter to someone as a philanthropic 'gift' where the right of ownership is passed on from the girl's (*kanya*) father to her husband. The play deals with the theme of marriage, thus suggests a daughter's sacrifice, which Nath performs in the name of the norms of civilized humanity. The problem and the consequences of the marriage Vijay Tendulkar shows is self-created. In *Kanyadaan,* the protagonist, Jyoti, is an educated, Brahmin girl who comes from a politically and socially active family. Her father, Nath Devlalikar and her mother Seva, both are socialists and work hard for dalits for a long time. Her brother Jayaprakash is a M.Sc. student. Theirs is an urban middle class family.

Brought up in such a progressive minded family Jyoti decides to marry Arun Athavale, a dalit youth from a village whom she had known only for two months. Seva is shocked to know it but Nath is relaxed and happy inside because he wants to remove the class-system which is his dream. He consents Jyoti to get married with Arun, whom she knew for the last two months. Her father encourages her in the belief that the marriage would set a progressive example. Jyoti stands in awe of her idealistic father and tries to follow him in letter and spirit. Motivated more by the ideals of a caste-free society and dalit upliftment than by passionate love, she wishes to marry Arun and so announces her decision to her family. She admits that she does not even know him well. It is the liberal ideas that the father teaches to his daughter that give her the courage and will to break the caste-based marriage tradition as she goes on to marry the man, Arun. Even she is horrified by doubts and not sure about marrying him but her idealistic training helps her reach a decision. Although she soon realizes that her decision might be wrong and that Arun may not be the kind of person she thought him to be, it is now difficult for her to reconsider her decision. A conflict between ideals and reality thus makes her indecisive. Her doubts show clearly in her dialogues:

> I don't know much about him. The little I know about him is through his poems. He asked me, I said yes, quite spontaneously. To tell you the truth, I have been learning something of him only since then. Not only getting to know him, but also getting to know about him. And sometimes he shows such a different side, that it strikes me, I don't know him at all. At times I feel I can trust him, but the very next instant I am left miles behind him. I ask myself – this thing that I want to do, is it the right thing... ? [9]

As the play moves on, the lights turn on her subjectivity as she tries to negotiate between ideals and reality. Both Seva and Jayaprakash try to persuade her to reconsider her decision. But Jyoti would hate to go back on her decision and is supported and assured by Nath to go ahead. Nath sees a streak of his own idealism and will for social reform in Jyoti's decision and is pleased. He thinks that educated and socially aware girls like her ought to make such bold experiments to break the caste barriers. But her mother Sewa and brother Jayaprakash were not keen about the marriage at all. After marriage, Jyoti becomes the victim of domestic violence at the hands of Arun who himself had developed violent and aggressive tendencies after years of political and social oppression suffered by him. Seva warns Jyoti for her hasty decision. Although she is self-righteous enough to say that she is not opposed to inter-caste marriages. In fact Sewa's anxiety is perfectly natural and genuine since cultural deformities foster the problem of identity crisis and become the cause of marital disharmony. Sewa here seems more rational and pragmatic than Nath and Jyoti. After getting married to him, she soon realizes that the devil and the poet-lover are one and the same person. Arun, who makes his devoted wife his punching bag, beating her everyday, getting drunk to his eyeballs, taunting her Brahmin antecedents, living off her earnings and in short, using her as his object of hate against the entire hierarchy of caste that has humiliated, oppressed, insulted and tortured his dalit forefathers. Her silent response and quiet tolerance of this all-pervasive violence angers him into further violence, creating a vicious circle for both the violator and the victim. Both Nath and Seva are worried about Jyoti. Her brother, Jayaprakash feels that Jyoti is herself responsible for her situation as it was her decision to marry Arun.

Arun apologizes to Jyoti as he had beaten her and expresses his helplessness to behave like civilized people and blames it on his upbringing. He tries to explain away his personal misconduct with the help of the suffering endured by his caste, but does not have the strength to change his behavior. Tendulkar, in this way, exposes here the not so uncommon reality of Indian homes, supposed to be united by bonds of love but concealing widespread violence. Jyoti is influenced, by the discourse of reformist idealism and social equality fed to her by Nath since her childhood. She reveres her father and craves his approval in all the decisions she takes. Her actions are guided by the discourse in which her father believes and which he wants her to subscribe to. So she once again submits to Arun's requests and goes with him. And she is once again subjected to intense violence and economic exploitation. Arun is an idler and spends Jyoti's money on alcohol and beats her mercilessly even when she is pregnant. Arun invites his father-in-law at the launch of his autobiography, in which he is dealing with the theme of oppression and miserable condition of the lower class. But the irony is that Arun himself exploits Jyoti and lives as a parasite on her. Though Jyoti is pregnant, he makes her work at home. Seva remarks at this point:

> I will say that in this excellent book whatever the author has said about injustice and exploitation is hypocrisy of the first order. Because this man himself exploits my daughter. Like a shameless parasite, he lives on my daughter's blood and on top of that he gets drunk and bashes her up. Constantly he taunts her about her caste and about her parents, heaping foul abuse on them for being highborn. [10]

Nath hates to go as a chief guest, but is forced to accept because refusal to grace the occasion might bring more violence upon his beloved daughter. Nath gives a hypocrite speech by praising Arun's autobiography against his will, but Jyoti does not tolerate this and she leaves home for forever. Jyoti is her daddy's baby, sweet and sugary, obedient and subservient in the beginning, then with time, slowly learning to imbibe her victimization with tolerance. Though she is quick to learn the error of the choice she has made, she is determined to live on with her husband. It is her way of avenging her father who gave her away perhaps the minute she was born, to his preaching's—impractical, grandiose and self-adulatory and to imbibe the seeing the world as it is.

The concept of "kanyadaan" is taken from mainstream Hindu rituals ideology. It suggests the patriarchal arrangement of giving the daughter as a gift. This is a play situated in the confines of patriarchal institutional arrangements. There is a displacement from the title to the thematic of the play—a shift from gender and patriarchy to caste.

From the above discussion, it is proven Tendulkar has thus been able to portray the sordid reality of everyday life. He has been candid enough with the issues which epitomizes the precarious conditions of a woman's life in India. If his plays raise curiosity about violence, at the end of the plays, the audience comes out with a deep feeling and understanding of the realities at stake.

Tendulakar plays like *'Silence! The court is in Session*; *Sakharam Binder*; *Kamla*; and *Kanyadaan*; focuses on love, sex, marriage, violence and moral values prevalent in Indian society. He makes ample use of irony, satire, pathos and mock element. All women characters of Tendulkar's plays represent the Indian woman who has long been under suppression and cruel domination of man, but emerging as a new woman in modern times. The roles Tendulkar's female protagonists' plays overshadow those played by the men figuring in them. It is Leela

Benare in *Silence*!, Laxmi in *Sakharam Binder*, Sarita in *Kamla*, and Jyoti in *Knayadaan*, who play the leading roles, which present a world apparently, dominated by male chauvinists. As a poignant reality is that till today women in India are exploited, oppressed and dominated by men in varied forms. Be it physical, mental or psychological violence, the psyche of Indian male largely, yet considers women as slaves whose chief duty is to serve him and lead a life as per his whims and fancies. Tendulkar successfully gives the readers a clear insight into the lives of his individual characters and evokes empathy for them all, as they seem to be victims of their own trappings. Her portrayal of women characters range from the socially depraved characters who are so close to the real life. Tendulkar's strengths are evident and there is tenderness and realism in his depiction of the central character he focused upon.

## Works Cited

Gokhle, Shanta, "Tendulkar on his Own Terms," in Geeta Rajan and Shoma Choudhry (eds), *Vijay Tendulkar* New-Delhi: Katha, 2001, p. 81.

Saxena, Sumit, "A Conversation with Sir Vijay Tendulkar, 'Passion for Cinema, 20 December, 2006. http://passionforcinema.com/a-conversation-with-sir-vijay-tendulkar 10: Web cited,http://shodhganga.inflibnet.ac.in/bitstream/10603/2092/8/08_chapter%202.pdf, p.p. 120

Tendulkar, Vijay, *Silence! The Court is in Session, Five Plays*, Oxford University Press, Bombay, 1992.The five plays translated in this book are: *Kamala, Silence! The Court is in Session, Sakharam Binder, The Vultures*, and *Encounter in Umbugland.*

______, *Five Plays*, Oxford University Press, Bombay, 1992, P.34

______, *Kanyadaan*. Trans. Gowri Ramnarayan. *Collected Plays in Translation*. New Delhi: Oxford University Press, 2001. Print.

Web cited, http://shodhganga.inflibnet.ac.in/bitstream/10603/2092/8/08_chapter%202.pdf, p.p. 11

# 15

# Women in Asif Currimbhoy's Socio-Realistic Plays

— Kamlakar K. Askar

Although the place of woman in society has differed from culture to culture and from age to age, yet one fact common to almost all societies is that women have never been considered equal to men. The ideal of nation is often imaged as a woman, and the ideology of nationalism often invests the nation's core identity upon an idealized, patriarchal image of ideal womanhood. When this happens, women are reduced to the status of refugee, asylum seeker, with no nation. It is only theoretically that woman is extolled as goddess in Indian society.

Rabindranath Tagore's feelings for women are romantic and idealistic. He says: "They came to me as the seasons come to the earth, with varied urgings of flowers and fruitfulness; they brought to my life, the inspiration of love and beauty, invocation of the power that lies dormant until touched by womanly grace" (Tagore, 677). What we see in actual practice is not in sync with this romantic exaltation. Women in literature, through the centuries, have been based upon the mythic models from the *Ramayana* and the *Puranas*: Sita—the silent sufferer, the archetype of Indian womanhood; the Earth-Mother, forbearance personified; Savitri—the devotion and dedication incarnate, woman as mother and protector, woman as inspirer and cherisher, woman as the motivating primal force—"Shakti" protecting good and destroying evil, or woman as charmer or lurer. Womanhood in all its variety is equated with selflessness, powerlessness, chastity, docility, virtuosity etc.—that are quite antagonistic to 'me-ness', autonomy and self-definition. Women and modernity came to be regarded as antithetical entities, with the result that the goal of national emancipation involved a betrayal of all prospect of progressive change for women.

Most human societies are male-dominated, and so woman is grudgingly given a secondary status, that is, when she is not positively subjected to inhuman tyranny. Simone de Beauvoir is of the view that the history of humanity is a history of systematic attempt to silence the female. She states, "One is not born, but rather becomes a woman. It is civilization as a whole that produces this creature...which is described as feminine" (295). During colonial rule in India, there was an awareness of the need of improvement in women's condition, and the idea to impart education to women was revived. However, the plight of women is not different from that of marginals in the contemporary Indian society. Moreover, the striking development of religious nationalism in the postcolonial era—which in certain respects has even defined the postcolonial era—has actually placed women in a situation comparable to that in which they found themselves during colonialism. Our economy and society are still extremely biased against women. "No one knows what a woman suffers...How much she has to bear, silently and without protest, the abuse and the condemnation" (Anand 39). To begin with, we are still largely a feudal and patriarchal society. In many parts of our country, there is a commodification of women; they are often treated as if they were a piece of property. In India, especially the northern parts, the sex ratio is most skewed because families often snuff out the lives of girl children before or immediately they are born.

Women are viewed as an economic liability despite their contribution in several ways to our society and economy. They are doubly suppressed in the society. "It is said that man's cruelty towards man is exceeded only by man's cruelty to woman" (Menninger 149). This is particularly true in our country, where constitution provides equal rights to men and women. Time was when woman was a prey to such social evils as *purdah,* female infanticide, child marriage, dowry system, enforced widowhood, domestic violence and denial of education. Though these evils have now been removed—only partially after sixty years of Independence—owing to the constant efforts of several reformers and other socio-economic and political factors, woman is still continued to be treated, by and large, as an inferior creature, a pleasure giving commodity or child bearing machine. She is made to act the part of an unpaid domestic servant with a marginally superior status. She is put to a killing physical and mental torture by a demanding husband or ruthless and nagging in-laws. That the status of Indian women is among the world's worst is endorsed when a woman like Kamala Das narrates the tragedy of her life in *My Story* which is her personal protest against the marginalization and suppression of women in this male-ordained society. Phoolan Devi, a low caste *dasyu sundary*, victim of a *Thakur's* gang rape (the worst of many abuses she had suffered) was a dramatic and highly visible political symbol of the political assertion of subaltern women and the oppressed lower caste in postcolonial India. As a popular hero, she became the first woman to join the symbolic iconography of champions of the poor and oppressed. Robert J.C. Young ranks her with Che Guevara, Franz Fanon and Sub-commandant Marcos. In many states, after the bulk of energy had been dedicated to achieving national sovereignty, at independence women's political objectives had to be reasserted and a second liberation struggle begun. For this reason, postcolonial politics has often more in common with women's than men's struggles of the colonial era, with a politics of egalitarianism that supports diversity rather than cultural uniformity demanded for nationalism. A new theatrical renaissance was marked by the publication of G.B. Shaw's *Widower's Houses* (1892) under the combined influences of

Henrik Ibsen on the one hand, and the economic outlook of Karl Marx on the other. As a result, the New Women came to be projected in literary world, challenging male authority and attempting to remake the world created by men.

Asif Currimbhoy, "the first authentic voice of Indian theatre in English", in his plays of social realism—*Inquilab, The Miracle Seed, The Doldrummers, The Dissident MLA* and *The Hungry Ones*—offers a space for the new woman, who while retaining all the grace of manner and feminine charm, has thrown off all the silliness, hysterical feebleness of sex and improved herself so as to be in everyway the best companion for man. He portrayed women as mother, wife, daughter, daughters-in-law, etc. His women are from the rural and the urban, the privileged and the underprivileged strata of society. They are traditional and modern in their views and attitudes to life. They are result of postcolonial feminism. Postcolonialism ushered in to claim "the right of all people on this earth to the same material and cultural well being" (Young 2). As a political phenomenon and practice postcolonial feminism aims at the emancipation and empowerment of women in every walk of life. Currimbhoy, pleads for freedom of individual, especially for the cause of women who raise the burning topic of the day that is the women's place in society, their freedom from domination, suppression and exploitation. P.B. Reddy rightly says: "Though his primary characters are generally men, Currimbhoy endows his women characters with strength and power" (147). He believes that the extent of social progress is best measured by the extent of women's freedom.

The play *Inquilab* presents three women—Suprea, Sarala and Prof. Datta's wife—who stand worth considering for the purpose of the article. Suprea, the only daughter of the widower landlord, Jain, is an educated young, beautiful, innocent and modest girl, deeply in love with Amar who is possessed by his dream of egalitarian society. "It's dangerous. It leaves....no room....for other things" (Currimbhoy 1971, 25) like love in his life. Suprea exhorts Amar not to ruin his life by joining the violent mission, that is, the Naxalite movement, but to spare his life to be shared by her. She has a strong urge to live as Amar's wife, and lead a happy family life. But her love for Amar fails to get proper response owing to his commitment to social cause. Her love for life stands jarring with Amar's wrath against the corrupt system and his resultant pessimism, as she says: "Yes, even moths propagate before they die, and in so doing, learn to love life. Indeed, find it beautiful too..." (58).

Naturally, Suprea is truly human in her hatred for violence in life, social or individual. To her, an individual is of utmost importance, whosoever he or she is. She has capacity to empathize with people, their weal and woes. When the Naxal revolt becomes bloody and violent, gutting down lives of many innocent people – women, policemen, children, she suffers acute pain at heart. She disapproves of Amar's justification for violence, saying: "they're human beings...with flesh and blood like you and I" (58). She desperately struggles, all alone, to save life of her father from the clutches of Naxalite violence. But alas, all goes in vain. She is horribly bereaved of her father, her only shelter in life. Still somehow, she gathers courage, and rises from the tragedy to live life further. Now, Amar is the only hope in her life. She just asks Amar as to why he failed to save her father's life. But, she does not have any grudge against him for that, nor does she harbour any passion to take revenge on those who killed her father. On the contrary, she urges Amar to come out of the vortex of violence in life, and to prove his loyalty to his self, his inner conscience, his duty to nearest and dearest, instead of his loyalty to his hardcore revolutionaries. Hers is the heart kind and human, where Amar seeks solace, venting out his pent up feelings in his moments of mental upheaval and dilemma, aimlessness and frustration.

That the end of the play is marked by Suprea's voice, calling out "Amar" "Amar", which is symbolic of the call to "come back" to the "life of love and harmony" giving up violence in life, for any cause, social or individual. Suprea's is the character that stands for love and affection, harmony and understanding in society which is wounded by the sanguinary Naxal revolt. Suprea, being an epitome of humanity, love and beauty, aptly reminds one of Malini in Tagore's play *Sanyasi* (*Prakitir Pratishodh*). Like Malini, Suprea too shows to the humanity the path of love in the midst of darkness of violence. She is meant to be new revelation – "forgive, whatever the crime! Killing doesn't mend anything." Like Tagore's Malini, Suprea is portrayed by Currimbhoy "to throw this challenge at us as the Buddha did, as Christ did" (B.R. Agrawal 131). "We may not be able to rise to her heights, but the playwright did not intend to drag her somehow to our level. In Suprea, Currimbhoy has presented his ideal concept of womanhood as 'Shakti' the living symbol of divine energy whose inner shrine is in subconscious depth of human nature and outer manifestations in sweetness of service, simplicity, of self dedication and silent heroism of daily sacrifice. Suprea's is a minor character, "but she becomes pivotal in terms of the dramatist's thesis" (Reddy 147).

Sarala is Shomik'wife; she has a caring attitude to her full-fledged poor family. We recognize her as a simple, devoted house-wife, taking care of her peasant husband, children and her old, feeble in-laws. But, she is very anxious and worried about her husband, Shomik and his secret, dangerous, cruel activities, taking place in the dark of night, in the name of socioeconomic justice and equality, and for the well being of his family too, as he justifies. But she is not convinced; what she wants in life is all to live a happy and peaceful family life, though in poverty and diligence. That is why, she opposes and urges Shomik: "I don't want you to be their leader. I want you to protect this house, bring safety for yourself... and your children" (33). Sarala is very much aware of the ulterior motif of Naxalite mission, undertaken by Shomik. So, she is relentlessly at discord with Shomik who very often snubs her, swollen with his male chauvinism and stirred by his deep sense of dignity and self respect: "You don't know, ignorant woman, you don't know anything outside of this house. ...you want me to be a dog.... Or like those animals ploughing these fields...!" (33). Shomik claims himself to be the only potent leader of the peasants who reposed their faith in him. Therefore, he looks upon himself to be the champion of the peasants' cause. Liberation, self-respect, revenge and power are the passions that rules over Shomik's mind. But, Sarala sticks to her guns strongly insisting: "In what way have we been harmed?" (34). Sarala is worried about her husband and children. She does not want Shomik to lead the whole nation into a violent revolution. But Shomik is adamant in his violent mission. He deserts home leaving behind Sarala, all alone, to take care of her family. Thus, Sarala's dream of a happy family is ruined by Shomik who, blinded by his mission, ruthlessly neglects her feeling and anxiety. She stands out as the victim of Shomik's over-ambitious nature, all given to the cause of Naxalism.

Currimbhoy's mother character, Prof. Datta's wife is a woman who stands for family and religiosity. She has lost her elder son and husband in the Naxal vendetta. She is always seen worshiping the statue of Durga, in the hope of her lost son, Ahmed to come back. She is a simple, sensitive woman, only to be accounted as a "primitive superstitious woman" (63) by her husband. It is very difficult for her to sustain the shock of her son whom she has lost for the cause of Naxal movement. It is a cruel irony that Ahmed is none other than her lost son about whom she remains in dark forever. It is the universal mother within her that comes up when she says:

> Do you know...what it means...to have child torn out from your womb! The cry of the mother that is at once a relief and despair too. For the child that is born is the child that is lost. (20)

So, it is quite natural, if she never believes that her son is dead, as Prof. Datta does. Through her, Currimbhoy presents the Earth Mother with magnanimity in her maternal love. It seems that Currimbhoy, like Tagore, takes mother and son relationship as a significant aspect of man-woman relationship. Currimbhoy deals with conviction that a mother, by nursing a child in her womb, makes the greatest sacrifice and deserves the dues of it. But Currimbhoy's mother character manifests the truth that the bond of affection determined by birth is not the end of maternal affection. He probes into the mother's psyche and unravels the crisscross movements of their impulses and instincts. As regards sorrows of bereavement of son, Prof. Datta's wife has parallels with Kunti in Tagore's play *Karna and Kunti*. Kunti, suppressing all her maternal instincts and sentiments, deserts her son Karna to avoid social calumny, whereas Prof. Datta's wife is deserted by her son, Ahmed to fight socioeconomic injustice in society. What she utters casually but out of faith and purity of her heart is significant to understand her love for life and her optimism, looking for a change, a good for all, in the face of Naxalite violence:

> I wait. The monsoon end. Puja's here. Autumn comes. I still smell the fresh wet earth, longing for planting of the new seed... for it's all barren! The new harvest, the new green. The food for survival, turning of the new generation. It needs to be planted with care. For the earth is fresh and fertile. Only the seed must be strong...like the growth of new revolt! (27).

It seems that the women—Suprea, Sarala and Prof. Datta's wife—are good wives and good mothers. They are full of basic human feelings: love, affection and sacrifice. They are simple and positively traditional, standing for family at any cost. Though they are not part of the violent Naxalite revolt, they are not free from and unaffected by its devastating consequences. They have lost their sons and husbands, their kith and kin. Their dreams of happy family have come to be shattered, not for their own fault but for their male's attitude to snub them. Ultimately, they are victims of the defective social system, wherein their emotions and feelings are hardly responded to, where males are always sternly monopolistic to rule the socioeconomic and political affairs of society where women seem to be solely confined to home and hearth.

The play, *The Dissident MLA* has just two women—Shanti and Sonal—who are condemned to live a wretched life in this phallocentric society. Shanti, being wife of Manubhai, an MLA belongs to the rich upper class society. She is a simple house-wife who is condemned to crave for love and emotional fulfillment as a woman. She does not live, but just drags her married life, as she has to. Hers is the life, the marriage of two conflicting minds, abusing each other, as if not made for each other. All she has for her husband is nothing but hatred and revenge, as she vents out to her son Ramesh:

> He smelt of bad breath every time he kissed me… and the rest was worse. Grow up and disgrace him, son…. He'll try to shine through you, my noble beautiful boy. But…you…down…him! He sucked the life out of me. Don't let him escape! (Currimbhoy 1974, 9).

It is not without cause that at the very outset of the play, we see Shanti burning with full hatred and anger for her husband. She is very much aware of the fact that her husband, Manubhai is a dishonest and corrupt MLA, which she does not like at all. Like Tagore's spirited Sumitra in play *The King and the Queen,* Shanti, aware of demands of society, walks out of home, mobilizes the women's protest against her husband who is lost in his pleasures, neglects his subjects. In her open revolt against her husband, Shanti may be equated with Ibsen's Nora who is modern in the sense that she readily abjures her traditional role of a puppet wife and a doll-mother for the sake of gaining self-liberation, individuality and independence. So, she is naturally exceedingly possessive of her young son, her only hope in life. She does not live her life, but braves it wailing in frustration, humiliation, exploitation and neglect. So, she has grown into a peevish and repulsive woman. Except being a woman, her character in itself does not account for the plight of her life which is a gruesome perdition. She appears to be a victim of her husband, Manubhai's nasty male chauvinism. He is merely scornful of her not only as a wife but as a female too, as is evident from his approach:

> Don't listen to her, my man-son. Woman's frustration, woman's talk. Their brains ooze down into falling flesh, and then it's nothing but carping, carping, carping...Mine? This? Falling flesh? (9).

Obviously, she is made to be underestimated as a woman even by her son, as opposed to masculine strength and virility. Her marriage with Manubhai is nothing but a fiasco. It robbed her of her original self, her beauty, her mental peace and sweet pleasures in life, and it reduced her to an object only to be used in a selfish way. She is no more what she was before marriage. She can't help, but articulates her wretchedness and wrath:

> Oh, what a wreck he'll be then. And who clears the muck then, do you know? Me! Me! That's what I've been doing for the last twenty four years. Shanti... never gave me that. Ask him what I was like when he married me. Like a *gulab*. See me now: he's right: I'm repulsive. He closed his mind. I couldn't reach him. (10)

In spirit, Shanti's married life is not different from that of Nora in Ibsen's play *A Doll's House*. She says:

> But our house has never been anything but a play-room. I have been your doll-wife, just as at home I was Daddy's doll child. And the children in turn have been my dolls. I thought it was fun when you came and played with me, just as they thought it was fun when I played with them. That's been our marriage (Act iii).

It holds a key to the status of women in society. It is a satire on marriage as an institution becoming a mockery without equal rights to the partners. Here Currimbhoy appears to be on the line of Ibsen, as a social propagandist pleading for the better status of women as partners in marriage. Shanti does not have any say in any family matter or other decisions. She does not have freedom even to mull her son's future. She is divested of her right to prevent her son from going or from being led astray in life. She can give birth to a child, but can't claim any right as a mother over her son. She is pierced at heart to know that Ramesh, her only son, young and innocent, her only ray of hope in life, is being relentlessly used as a puppet by his father in the game of his petty politics to do what he Manubhai cannot do himself, just making a devil of him Ramesh. When Manubhai provokes Ramesh who is reluctant to tonsure the Home Minister's head and to blacken his face to be paraded on donkey with eunuchs dancing around him in the city, a mother in Shanti comes up to demur and protect her son from being dehumanized. But, what she gets in turn is untold humiliation at the hands of her husband who calls her "bitch", threatens to ... smash her teeth. She is treated like anything, as if she is meant for humiliation and disregard. She is totally alienated and isolated from her husband, and suffers the pangs of isolation in life. It is a height of humiliation as her husband speaks of the feelings in an aside he has for her, "I never made love to you, woman. I only had you... (25). Shanti is the victim of her husband's infidelity and adultery. Manubhai secretly gets off with Sonal, a young, sexy woman working in his house. Naturally, Shanti's married life with Manubhai is totally ruined. Shanti's life is an eternal longing for sexual, mental and emotional fulfillment which she never gets from her husband.

It appears that a female in Shanti is not cared for, whereas male in Manubhai gets pampered in the company of other women like Sonal. It shows, when a married man indulges in sexual promiscuity, the woman at home is immediately put to injustice and negligence, just as Shanti is. Shanti's is a flawless character. We do not find any defect in her character which will account for the accursed life she leads. Ultimately, Shanti is victim of her husband's nasty male ego, who in turn is product of the male dominated society where woman is not treated at par with man. Consequently, Shanti has to drag 'life' which is not worth-living at all. Shanti's life is an embodiment of a woman's married life sans *esprit de corps*. Male domination has had some very unfortunate effects. It reminds one of Bertrand Russell who feels: "It made the most intimate of human relations that of marriage, one of master and slave, instead of one between equal partners" (158). In truth, Currimbhoy, in this play, tries to probe the true basis of man-woman relationship in one of its most intimate forms, namely, marriage. The play does not concern with feminism as much as it concerns with those ethical and spiritual factors without which marriage remains a mere "living together" as pointed out by Nora in the third Act of the play *A Doll's House* after her disillusionment with her husband, Torvald Helmer.

Sonal, a working woman at Manubhai's house is a simple, young and attractive woman, rescued from the Rescue Home by Kantibhai and entrusted to Manubhai to take care of. Of course she is a defenseless, lonely woman in society. She is more sinned against than sinning. Prior to her stay in Rescue Home, Sonal was exploited by one drunkard, "lecher and scoundrel". And during her stay in Rescue Home, she was frequently molested and sexually exploited by the attendant and many elite politicians. Her experiences in Rescue Home remained very painful. The women like Sonal are not safe either at home or at a Rescue Home which is a brothel in disguise in the so-called civilized society where women social workers act as vamps in disguise to procure women to the perverted elite class and politicians in society. The Rescue Home is in no way different from the notorious Juvenile House figured in the famous novel *Q & A: Slumdog Millionaire* (2009).

As regards her sexual exploitation and oppression by the hypocritical, middle class male dominated society, Sonal's character reminds one of Leena Benare in Vijay Tedulakar's play *Silence! The Court Is in Session*, which exposes the vulnerability of women in postcolonial Indian society. It is an irony in Sonal's life that she is rescued from Rescue Home, and is brought to Manubhai's shelter, all for her well-being. But she is once again made to gratify Manubhai's lust regularly. It is different that Sonal has consent to, and enjoys illicit sexual relationship with Manubhai who feels nothing for Sonal's woeful, desolate life, past or present. That is why we see him "giggling and slapping his thighs in sheer fun and exuberance of her frankness" (20) as she discloses her piercing ordeal at Rescue Home. The voluptuous, sexual beauty, full of youth, Sonal is an aphrodisiac substance to Manubhai. Certainly, Sonal's presence in Manubhai's life contributes to miseries of Shanti's marital life. It is not without significance when Sonal and Manubhai are in amorous mood and "braying of mule, outside" is heard, Manubhai tells Sonal: "Sounded like my wife. (Then realizes what he has said, and laughs out aloud.) Sounds like my wife... Did you hear that? I said it sounded like my wife" (21). His demeanour is suggestive of Shanti's insignificance in her husband's life. Soanal's having sex with Manuhai makes him articulate: "can't wait...can't wait..." (30), whereas Shanti's urge for sex reminds him of Kantibhai's "practice of abstinence" (32). This contrast shows when the male promiscuity pounces on a female, it is just the woman who is ruined, be it Sonal or Shanti. Though both are separate victims of life and society as well, their victimizations are symbiotically related.

A charge of depravity may be leveled against Sonal. But viewed from a female point of view and as victim of life and hypocritical male dominated society, she is innocent and human too. Otherwise, she would not have gone to old Kantibhai who is on fast unto death, and that too leaving behind Manubhai who sincerely pursues her not to go. Manubhai has begun to feel something for Sonal who is now inclined to Kantibhai for whom she has fatherly feelings and deep sense of gratitude. What she feels for Kantibhai signifies her goodness of heart. And Sonal leaves Manubhai for Kantibhai whose health is critical.

The one-Act play *The Hungry Ones* presents a single woman protagonist, called Razia who is a dominating force from the beginning to the end of the play. She is a Bengali Muslim woman. Razia, along with her inamorato, Ramesh who is a Bengali Hindu man, forms an inter-religious couple. Theirs is a marriage of true minds. Razia loves her man from the depth of her heart, and extends her helping hand to his 'hungry acts' by twirling the bitting drum on the streets. Razia too is a victim both of life and society. She lives with Ramesh in a tattered hovel. Her life is fraught with penury, beggary, pain and suffering which she braves without any grudge. As she lives with a Hindu man, she has been disowned by her parental family, and the dread of her violent, vindictive brothers looms large over the couple's life.

Razia is vehemently religious, a staunch Muslim in her practice of doling out charity food to beggars in the month of Ramzan, despite her own beggerish life. She is truly a stoic in her suffering from hunger, pain and privation in life. The American hippies, Sam and Al are intrigued to see her incredible strength to suffer, taking it as something mysterious. So is her voice: "…the hunger that goes with fasting, Sam… learn this now, stranger…" (Currimbhoy 1977, 24). It appears that she is used to hunger and pain in her life which she looks upon as a religious aspect of her life. However, the Muslim religious part of her never comes to jar with that of Ramesh who is a hidebound Hindu. Ramesh is in no way less than Razia in his Hindu religious practice in life. He grows literally superstitious in his Yogic meditation. So is his articulation: "the hunger that goes with meditation and Yoga, Al…learn this now, stranger…" (28).

As preached by his guru, Ramesh looks upon Yogic meditation as a panacea to all the evils, pains and hardships in life. And in his blind pursuit of Yogic meditation, the female in Razia is smothered and neglected by him, reminding one of Anita Desai's *Cry, The Peacock* wherein Maya has been completely neglected by her husband Gautama because he has been influenced by the philosophy of non-attachment in the *Bhagavad Gita* and practised it absurdly in his relationship with his wife. A night scene in the hovel bears testimony to Razia's plight:

> Back to the house, in their room, Razia is sitting on bed ana watching with concern, Ramesh sitting bared to the waist, with black Hindu thread… across his neck and shoulder…breathing

> through all the hours of darkness and night, while Razia watches wide-eyed.... (30)

Meanwhile, Al breaks in, and attempts, though through no desire or ill will, to molest and rape Razia who raises stifling scream, raises bed sheet to cover her nudity, but Ramesh continues to meditate undisturbed, impassive like stone. This is how, chastity of Razia and both of female and a woman within her is subordinated to, and it is not valued at all by the Hindu man, Ramesh given to his religious Yogic meditation. Thus, she is torn between two equally strong impulses – the religious impulse and the impulse of womanhood. And Razia has nothing to say, but to scream against the outrageous event in her life. Still, her love for Ramesh does not wane at all. Razia is still full of humility and pardon for Al. She asks Sam to forgive Al for his misbehaviour. Hers is the forgiving approach towards the American duo, Sam and Al whom she provides shelter and relief, when they are hungry. She accepts food from Sam and Al, only when she is convinced that Sam and Al have worked for the food. Latter on, she treats them as her brothers. Lastly, Razia meets with a tragedy in her life, as her love, Ramesh is killed in violence, and she is once again condemned to live life all alone in hunger, pain and privation, with nobody to wipe her tears in life. Sam and Al leave for America. Thus, Razia is the rose, but being indigent and neglected, is crushed by life and society as well.

The one-Act play, *The Miracle Seed* has Malti, the woman character portrayed in a very realistic manner as the quintessence of women's lives in rural India. They are in no way less than men in their struggle for survival, especially when there are situations of natural disasters like draught. Ram, a draught affected Maharashtrian farmer, could survive two successive draughts in his life. Where did he get his essential strength and forbearance from? Of course, it is none other but his wife, Malti who is pregnant, and whose first child Savitry, while in womb, has already been the victim of draught sixteen years ago. Savitry is malnourished and she stammers. And it is her second child in womb that braves the draught. So, it is her overwhelming angst for the child in the womb that she reveals to her husband, "I meant my condition. My thoughts, depressions... they shape..." (Currimbhoy 1973,13).

When she sees, her husband is in depressed, hapless conditions, she smothers her own cares and anxieties, and always comes forward to replenish Ram with essential moral courage and fortitude to face miseries of draught, saying, "Don't worry, my husband ... I won't loose this child. I'll never... And it will grow strong like you. I promise" (13). Although pregnant, she does work hard. She draws water from the well. She does not get enough food to eat; still she has no grudge or anger against anybody. Unlike Ram, she does not grow peevish while living. She takes care of her husband, daughter, her old father-in-law, sometimes that too at the cost of her life. She is affectionate towards Laxman who is an orphan. Unlike Ram, she does not look down upon Laxman as a "rogue" or "a crooked city slicker". Her affection is selfless and indiscriminate. On the contrary, she tries to clear Ram's doubts about Laxman's goodness. She says, "All city people aren't crooks. And your nephew certainly isn't" (19). It shows that Malti is simple and free from prejudices and complexes in life. Moreover, she is a woman with a rational and objective approach to life, which we find lacking in Ram. When she sees the cow dying of famine, she apprehends the exigencies of the hour, and nods Laxman to dispose of the cow at a slaughter house. She turns dry, all to take care of her family which Ram cannot do owing to his emotional attachment to the cow.

Unlike Ram, Malti does not think that working at road repairing or breaking stones is a "convicts' job" or an affront to one's sense of dignity and self esteem, if it is to feed one and his family. That is why, she tells Ram, it is "better than waiting for the rains and doing nothing" (35). Clearly, it is her loyalty to or an urge for life that overpowers her other sensibilities in life.

Despite miseries of her life which is an inexorable saga of agony and privations, her faith in god never dwindles. We always see her worshipping the idol of god, Ganpati, whereas the time comes when Ram 'spits on it.' Juxtaposed with Ram, it appears that she is the woman of perfect mental and emotional balance and patience which she never loses withstanding the test of time. It is worth noticing that Malti does not cherish unreachable or romantic dreams in life. In her views she is quite down to earth. If Laxman's "miracle seed" happens to bring about a miracle and result in a golden harvest to reap, Malti hopes for nothing, but "Never to be in want again.... All I want...is not to have to worry and worry...from year to year...about the terrible draught" (21). She does not want bracelets and things that Ram could never afford.

Lastly, though it is Laxman's 'miracle seed' that shows a miracle of growing into healthy plants in the face of draught, that rejuvenates Ram and his family with gusto of optimism enough to stay back and not to migrate to the city, one cannot neglect Malti's diligence, her presence of mind, her hope and faith in life which make Laxman's seed capable of showing miracle. It is Malti who invested Laxman's seed with the power of Miracle. It was Malti who saved well-water drawn by her for daily house use, and gave it to the seeds, so that it could grow. And nobody knows about it till Malti discloses it herself. This act of Malti proves that behind success of every man there is a woman like Malti who eventually stands out as 'the paragon of womanhood', proving a good mother, a good wife, and a good human being.

In her binding influence on Ram to survive the ordeal of drought, Malti reminds one of Kamala Markandaya's Rukmani in *Nectar in a Seive*. Like Rukmani, she too seems to be the legendry archetype of an ideal housewife. She reveals an unconquerable spirit in the face of suffering and misery caused by drought and ensuing poverty. It seems that Currimbhoy wants to establish the principle that when a binding influence that Malti has on her husband, Ram, is lacking, real community and ideal family life would be impossible and the evil inherent in social order would become manifest at home, as Kamala Markandaya does in her novel.

*The Doldrummers,* "a powerful and highly moving play, exploring human relationships" (Reddy, 61) presents the two women protagonists, Rita and Liza who realistically epitomize the physical and the mental life of the modern, urban unmarried young girls living in shacks of Juhu Beach in the suburbs of metropolitan city of Mumbai.

Rita is a young thing, fully physical and very much in love with her jobless boy friend, called Tony who is good for nothing. She controls the whole plot and thus, emerges stronger and more memorable than Tony and Joe. Alienated and uprooted, Rita initially earns her livelihood by stitching dresses, and maintains a positive approach to life. She is optimistic when she says, "You can be better than you are, you could be swinging on a star" (Currimbhoy:1992, 24). She provides Tony with free boarding and lodging at her shack, hoping in return that Tony will love her, and will be her support in life. "She's nature's own child, sweet and loving. Her heart is pure. She lives only for Tony, and there is nothing that she would not do for him. She worships him "like God, Almighty" (53). But it is an irony of her life that Tony gets addicted to his fixation for nice, costly presents which he receives from his another girl friend, Liza, despite Rita's strong objection to it. Rita knows that Liza intends to attract Tony towards her by offering the nice costly gifts to him who, as a result, gets drifted to Liza.

When ungrateful and reckless Tony secretly receives a gold-plated watch-strap as a "token of friendship" from Liza, and as it becomes known to all, his reckless angry defense—"Why should Rita mind it? What right has she to mind! After all, I'm not married to her!" (16)—testifies to the fact that Rita is the victim of her 'live-in relationship' with Tony who does not even feel that he exploits her like anything. She suffers an excruciating mental crisis when she is induced by Joe, Tony's friend, to bring about a change in herself to earn more in order to gratify Tony's insatiable lust for the nice, costly presents, enabling him to lead a fashionable, rich life which is the weakness of his character.

As Rita cannot live without Tony, Joe advises Rita to receive costly presents from other rich men in society—which is nothing but taking recourse to whoring —so that she could keep up Tony's love for her. Eventually, Rita, being at her wit's end, stoops to whoring, anticipating that Tony will pay heed to her, and will come forward to prevent her from being a slut. But Tony continues to be cold and passive. He does not bother even to know how Rita could afford to offer him costly gifts. He just keeps on enjoying his life full of pomp and show at the cost of Rita.

Lastly, it is Joe who manages to awaken Tony to the type of change that Rita has undergone to quench his lust for costly gifts, but it serves no purpose. Rita begs hoarsely to Tony to kill the Fat and Bald Man, Tony's ex-boss, who has just sexually exploited Rita at her shack, promising in return the work for Tony who stands drunk as witness to this bizarre incident, but does nothing. On the contrary, he accepts money from his Ex-boss, and lets him go. Rita is shocked to witness the height of insensitivity and apathy of Tony for whom she has now become "the goose that lays the golden eggs" (61).

Here Rita's life is worse than Tendulkar's eponymous heroine of his play *Kamala* which is a denunciation of the success-oriented male-dominated society where women are often victims or stepping stones in men's self-advancement. Rita is utterly frustrated and disillusioned; she has now become cynical. To her 'self-sacrifice', 'Love', 'Hope', 'Faith', have no significance in life; hers is the conviction: "These are mere words. Prove it all to me" (62). Overwhelmed by the feelings of frustration and loneliness, she declines to indulge in perverted and immoral life all for the sake of money

Taking disadvantage of the miserable and helpless conditions in Rita's life, Joe too like other men offers himself as a party, offering in exchange a diamond ring as a present. And Rita surrenders herself mechanically to Joe. She comes out fully as a prostitute when she says:

> It's open house now. Lay your money on the table, Joe. It does not have to be a present anymore, and it need not come from a friend either. Tony won't mind.... (63)

Now, Rita is no longer what she was. She behaves hysterically like a schizophrenic. She becomes pregnant from Joe, and wishes to become mother of his child, hoping that Joe will accept her along with her child, despite the advice of Liza to get the pregnancy dissolved. But the wheel of fortune is yet to have its full round in her life. Joe suddenly leaves her to her own lot in such miserable condition. And Tony, ignorant of Rita's pregnancy, slaps her around for no reason in the state of drunkenness. However, Rita urges Tony to make a fresh start, and to live a normal life once again. But Tony, always inebriated, gives negative response, and treats her with apathy, humiliation and harassment. He presents before Rita, his more-drunk idiotic looking friend, completely plastered, with a chain-like lasso tied around his neck like a dog. What Tony says at this juncture is terribly humiliating and torturing to Rita:

> Listen to the dog whine. He's got no tongue, but he can still whine. I got me a substitute now, I'm not Tony anymore. I'm Joe. This here is Tony. He'll serve you well; I've even taught him to play the guitar. And he is the hottest thing in the bed. He does not much. He doesn't even feel much. He is almost like a portable, do-it-yourself-kit. He'll take my place well, and I'll be gone far, far away. (85)

Rita's lovelorn emotional world and her strong will to live a normal family life with Tony is superbly presented through the episode of a couple of teenage schoolboys that serves as an 'objective co-relative' to probe into Rita's mental and emotional world. The two schoolboys are standing at a distance from the shack of sex worker who is none other than Rita. The two teenage boys are there with an intention to have a sex experience for the first time in their lives. But one of the two remembers his beloved, called Jean with whom he identifies the call-girl before him. Not only that he feels that going to the pros is to show infidelity to his beloved who will, as a result, be deceived and hurt, if it comes to be discovered by her. And he tells his friend, "But I don't want her to get over it. I just don't want to hurt her" (81). This conversation between the two teenage boys is overheard by Rita who feels euphoric to see the innocence, pure love and loyalty of the boy for his beloved. Rita, being overwhelmed with joy and emotions, fantasizes herself to be Jean, the boy's beloved, and starts dancing and singing. But the very next movement, she realizes what she has dreamt is a mere fantasy, and it can never be a fact in her life which is accursed with infidelity, hatred and everything that is inimical to love and affection. Hence, K.R.S. Iyengar is very apt when he says: "The play is but a vivid portraiture of certain segments of everyday actuality."

Rita, being tortured with humiliation, frustration, depression and disillusionment in life, attempts to drown herself in the sea. But when she realizes that Tony, who cannot swim in his efforts to save her life, is drowning in the sea, she comes back from the deep sea water, and saves Tony's life. So, it appears that Rita is pre-destined neither to live for herself, nor to die for herself. Rita is a very wise and reasonable woman. She thinks that you can't love someone you don't love. The news of Joe's sudden and mysterious death comes up as a big jolt to Rita as she is taking care of Joe's child in her womb. It is her pierced soul and her sense of being devastated that makes her moan: "Perhaps... it never happened... and perhaps we never existed" (92). It occurs that Rita's also is the character more sinned against than sinning arousing pity and sympathy. Hers is the life that fully testifies to Joe's realistic comment on plight of women in the male dominated society, reminding one of Kamala Das's views about man-woman relationship: "Man always pins a woman 'neath him. Like a butterfly, with beautiful wings, spread out and pinned. For a woman, it's crucifixion" (35).

Liza is a technicolour doll; everything about her is painted. She is a woman of carefree, candid and straight forward nature, always living in the present. As compared with Rita, Liza is less sentimental and more rational and practical in her approach to life. Truly "a representative of modern society," (K.A Agarwal 91) she does not see anything wrong in receiving costly gifts from her many rich male friends, and keeping relations with them to any extent. It is a matter of pride for her, when she says, "I've got too many admirers. More than I can handle" (22). The costly bracelets and necklace received from her rich male friends as presents make her "feel gay and secure" (22) in life. It is the material pleasure of life that appeals her most even at the cost of moral and spiritual ethics in life. She is always prepared to shower costly gifts like gold-plated watchstrap and rich, fancy shirts on Tony just to attract him to herself, whereas she knows that her friend, Rita who has live-in relationship with Tony, is highly possessive of him. Therefore, Liza is one of the factors along with Joe responsible for Rita's estrangement with Tony, exposing her to further miseries in life.

Like Rita, Liza also pines for true love and affection in her life, though she claims herself to be a girl of many male admirers and friends. Liza, though a spinster, has a good experience of sex life. When Rita betrays about her own pregnancy, Liza speaks out of her own experience in life, expressing her implicit fear of conception: "I've known, it happened to me time and again… Not having a baby, of course, but, being mistaken" (75). Moreover, she talks of her own physical relations with a doctor friend who does not miss to assure her of safety from an unwanted pregnancy. Liza approaches Rita very sympathetically and humanly, and tries to understand her as a woman, when she comes to know that Rita is pregnant, and there is none to take care of her, Liza advises Rita of a practical solution to get the pregnancy dissolved, and not to take any risk arising therefrom. Rita is highly impressed by Joe's philosophical nature, but Liza shows her good sense of judgment when she says, "He's like one of those comedy actors in a Shakespearean play… a crazy hipster with hallucinations" (78).

Unlike Rita, Liza is not confused in her life. She hardly believes in good of others, and always thinks down to the ground. But like Rita, Liza too is frustrated and disappointed in life. "They are too close to reality to live the life of imagination, and whose idealism turned to cynicism" (Bower X). As a result, she finds her own modus operandi to be happy with herself, as she says, "I love living with myself" (78). She tells Rita that the male society is most inhuman against women. Therefore, the women should also change their behaviour, and be harsh and reasonable.

When a policeman approaches Liza with a view to inquire about the incident of Joe's death, she being a bit schizophrenic, grows unnecessarily eloquent and bold only to misgive, mistake and misunderstand the situation, without giving a chance to policeman to speak, discloses to him about the previous day's incident of Rita's attempt to drown herself in the sea, and thereby makes show of her so-called knowledge of detective novels and fashionable life style as well – all being out of place. But when Liza is told by the policeman that Joe is dead, she, along with Rita, feels deep sorrow over Joe's death.

Both Rita and Liza are involved in their struggle for existence. No doubt they are the creatures of the society in which they live; they are conditioned by the social matrix. However, their views and attitudes to life are also the crucial factors to shape the life they live. They make many wrong choices which are in tune with their philosophical beliefs and personal ethics. As a result, their life is miserable. It seems, it is their way of life along with social milieu that the playwright wants to emphasize. Their way of life is an eye-opener to the young people that they should be honest in their lives. For, easy pleasures are always the cause of ruins of their lives. Though Liza indulges in promiscuity in her life, she is not without human qualities. She, along with Currimbhoy's other women characters, deserves to be treated with sympathy. Hence, the play may be taken as "a protest against the indecency and immorality to which a prudish and complacent society gives birth" (Reddy 61).

To conclude, Gayatri Spivak in her discourse *Can the Subaltern Speak?* analyses the question of female subaltern, whom she describes as doubly marginalized subjects in postcolonial discourse:

> Within the effected itinerary of the Subaltern subjects, the track of sexual difference is doubly affected... It is rather that, both as object of colonialist historiography and subject of insurgency, the ideological construction of gender keeps the male dominant. If in the context of colonial production, the subaltern has no history and cannot speak, the female as female is even more deeply in shadow (28).

Thus the women - Malti, Rita, Liza, Shanti, Sonal, Razia, Sarala, Suprea, Prof. Datta's wife – all testify to the veracity of Gayatri Spivak's said view. The female is condemned to live in 'the valley of humiliation', exploitation, discrimination and deprivation in the society which includes the male dominated patriarchal society along with its social, economic, cultural and political evils. It is well evident, how the women in Currimbhoy's socio-realistic plays are starved of love and emotional fulfilment in their lives; how they are victims of sexual abuse and exploitation. They suffer from incompatibility of married life. They are not unaffected from the existing harrowing socioeconomic and political conditions in the contemporary society. Malti, Razia, Suprea, Sarala, Prof. Datta's wife are directly or indirectly victimized by the existing socio-economic conditions in the society. They are immediate, soft targets of poverty, social unrest, violence and bloodshed. They stand bereaved of their husbands, sons, fathers, rendered homeless and defenseless, again to be abused and exploited like Rita, Shanti, Sonal, Nafesa by the given archetype male dominated society. A woman like Shanti bolsters up courage to revolt against her tyrannical husband, Manubhai, but in vain. The plight of Sonal, Shanti and Rita reminds one of Ammu's life in Arundhati Roy's *The God of Small Things* as they fall a prey to the sexual abuse and exploitation by the mismatched, drunkard husbands or partners or other males. To them life is meaningless, for, "they had nothing. No future. So they stick to small things" (Roy, 338). Here women are victims of the patriarchal, male dominated society. They are not treated at par with men, be it the social or familial affairs. They are the burning instances of 'Otherness' in India's postcolonial literature, which realistically holds mirror to the contemporary Indian society. So it appears, "Everything's coming apart in this country. Families, marriages – everything" (Adiga 215).

Women like Malti and Sarla represent the bulk of India's rustic women's lives in villages. They, not only singly but coupled with their men, are a force to reckon with, and their power dominates the action of the play. They are a source of inspiration in their struggle to keep their families alive in the face of society which is horrifyingly threatened by social evils like poverty, Nature's vagaries, socioeconomic injustice and violence. They, endowed with the human qualities of love, affection and optimism, are the prime moving force in the institution of family. Despite the fact, they are constantly snubbed by the male dominance and arrogance. Females like Razia, Rita, Liza and Sonal are the product of the poor down-trodden strata of Indian urban society. They are the victims of life and society as well. They are sexually abused and exploited. They are so devastated in their lives that they behave like schizophrenic. They have no roots in society. Helplessness and hopelessness is their lot. Shanti who is an MLA's wife and so a part of an affluent privileged class of the society, is in no way an exception to the general predicament of women from the poor marginalized class of Indian society, rural or urban. Shanti is victim of her husband's tyranny, humiliation, negligence and infidelity. She drags the life wherein she is denied what she is entitled to both as a wife and a woman. The Landlord's daughter, Suprea and Prof. Datta's wife though not suffer from any domestic violence or evils of male-dominated society, are caught in the vortex of revolt which is an outcome of dire socioeconomic disparity and injustice wildly prevalent in the postcolonial India. It is the women who are highly vulnerable and susceptible to any consequences as and when the families lose their men in violence and riots in society.

Obviously, the portrayal of women in Currimbhoy's socio-realistic plays manifests that the contemporary postcolonial Indian society, rural or urban, the privileged or underprivileged, has a long way to go to assure women of their safety and dignity in society. His women characters are the quintessence of goodness and humanity. Currimbhoy reveals that the place of women in society are like dolls—a doll being a thing in human shape without the hard-won, distinctively human attributes, in *A Doll's House*. Children make the dolls perform social roles over which the lifeless dolls have no control. Initially, she is confined in her father's home and made to do what he wants. She then goes directly to her husband where she is treated as a child. She is not allowed to be herself as she grows. It seems, they are destined to suffer. If destiny fails, their existentialist approach to life comes to the fore to plague them in life. Unlike Hardy, Currimbhoy's women characters suffer either for destiny or for character or sometimes both. And on this count, he is a realist, a step further. For no single theory is perfect to account for human life which is so complex in itself that it abounds in rich variety of theories and isms which are per se diametrically different.

Currimbhoy's sympathetic attitude towards women was an off-shoot of his passionate belief in human freedom. He was convinced that the women in society were denied rights and opportunities to grow like men. Currimbhoy's progressive and feminist outlook is very well revealed, especially in his portrayal of defiant and assertive women, probably the result of his personal thinking and the progressivist thinking of the West. It seems that he has drawn his women with a purpose to stress upon the spiritual powers of love, dignity and grace. With his firm conviction in women's innate divinity and spiritual power, Currimbhoy has delineated them as an incarnation of evolution of human love from the physical to the spiritual. They tend to be symbolic and allegorical and sometimes archetypal of humanity, love, beauty and nature's splendour and majesty of human spirit. He fills his dramatic canvas with a wide range of women characters drawn from the society around him, and makes them represent varied facets of human life. He is equally well-versed in delineating their maternal sentiments, heart-pangs and passions in love, socio-political assertions, masculine defiance, selfish motives and ego-clashes. Above all, they are firmly rooted in Indian ethos, revealing his deep and uncanny insight into feminine mind. Thus, Currimbhoy, the playwright emerges as the champion of feminism for the cause of women. Many of his women revolt against the sexiest image of woman in patriarchy and her consequent socioeconomic exploitation based on female biological essentialism. He strongly believes that a woman has a potential for action, a passion for liberation and a desire to assert herself.

## Works Cited

Agarwal, B. R. "Insight into Feminine Mind: Study of Tagore's Dramatic World", *Perspectives and Challenges in Indian English Dram,* ed. N. Tondon. New Delhi: Atlantic Publishers, 2006. Print.

Agarwal, K. A. *The Best Plays of Asif Currimbhoy*. Jaipur: Book Enclave, 2007. Print.

Adiga, Aravind. *The White Tiger*. New Delhi: Harper Collins & India Today Group, 2008. Print.

Anand, Mulk Raj. *The Big Heart.* New Delhi: Arnold Heinemann, 1945. Print.

Beauvoir, Simone de. *The Second Sex*, transl. and ed. H.M. Parshley. London: Penguin, 1974. Print.

Bower, Faubion. *Introduction* to Currimbhoy's Plays. New Delhi: Oxford & IBH, 1972. Print.

Currimbhoy, Asif. *Inquilab*. Calcutta: Writers Workshop Book, 1971. Print.

________. *The Miracle Seed.* Calcutta: Writers Workshop Book, 1973. Print.

________. *The Dissident MLA*. Calcutta: Writers Workshop Book, 1974. Print.

________. *The Hungry Ones*. Calcutta: Writers Workshop Book, 1977. Print.

________. *The Doldrummers*. Calcutta: Writers Workshop Bluebird Book, 1992. Print.

Ibsen, Henrik. *A Doll's House,* ed. G. Vaidyanathan. Agra: Educational Publishers, 2007. Print.

Iyengar, K. R. S. "The Dramatic Art of Asif Currimbhoy", *Indo-English Literature*, ed. K. K. Sharma. Ghaziabad: Vimal Prakashan, 1977. Print.

Menninger, Karl. "Love against Hate", quoted by Ashis Nandi in "Woman versus Womanliness: An Essay in Speculative Psychology", *Indian Woman: From Purdha to Modernity*, ed. B. R. Nanda. Delhi: Vikas Publishing House Pvt. Ltd., 1976. Print.

Reddy, P. B. *The Plays of Asif Currimbhoy*. Calcutta: Writers Workshop Book, 1985. Print.

Roy, Arundhati. *The God of Small Things*. New Delhi: India Ink, 1998. Print.

Spivak, Gayatri. *Can the Subaltern Speak? Post-colonial Studies Reader*. London: Routledge, 1985. Print.

Russell, Bertrand. "Ideas That Have Harmed Mankind", *Unpopular Essays*. New York: A Clarion Book, 1950. Print.

Tagore, Rabindranath. "Woman's Place in the World", *English Writings of Rabindranath Tagore,* ed. Sisir Kumar Das Vol. III. New Delhi: Sahitya Academy Ed., 1996. Print.

Young, Robert J. C. *Postcolonialism: A Very Short Introduction*. New York: Oxford Press, 2006. Print.

# 16

# Feminine Perspective in the Plays of Girish Karnad

— Ajit Kumar

Contemporary Indian drama, deviating from classical and European models, is experimental and innovative in terms of thematic and technical qualities. It is not an offspring of any specific tradition, and it has laid the foundation of a distinctive tradition in the history of world drama by reinvestigating history, legend, myth, religion and folklore with context to contemporary socio-political issues. A cumulative theatrical tradition evolved by Mohan Rakesh, Badal Sirkar, Vijay Tendulkar and Girish Karnad, prepared the background of contemporary Indian English theatre.

Girish Karnad in the capacity of writer, director and actor substantially contributed to enrich the tradition of Indian English theatre. His dramatic sensibility was moulded under the influence of touring Natak Companies and especially Yakshagana which was in those days not accepted as the purified art form. His well known plays are *Yayati* (1961), *Tughlaq* (1962), *Hayvadana* (1970), and *Nagamandala* (1972). He borrowed his plots from history, mythology and old legends but with intricate symbolism, he tried to establish their relevance in contemporary socio-political conditions.

Karnad's deep-rooted humanism allowed him to give voice to the silenced majority through his plays. His plays abound with subalterns, especially women and lower caste people subjected since ancient time by patriarchy or upper hierarchy of the society. He has not only exposed their subalternity but also fused energy in their lives so that they can speak; and shifted their position from "margin" to "centre". *Yayati, Tughlaq, Hayavadana, Naga-Mandala, Tale-Danda, The Fire and the Rain* etc. amply exemplify the above notion. Devayani, Sharmishtha and Chitralekha in *Yayati,* Kapil and Padmini in *Hayavadana,* Rani and Kurudavva in *Naga-Mandala,* lower caste people in *Tale-Danda,* tribals, Nitilai and Vishakha in *The Fire and the Rain* the Mahout in *Bali: The Sacrifice*, Chandrawati in *Flowers*, Malini in *Broken Images* and Rahabai in *Wedding Album* display subalternity of the class they represent. Karnad as a cultural administrator goes beyond this, and attempts to provide them their due space and defy the traditional hierarchies prevalent in Indian society. The paper endeavours to analyse Karnad's handling of the feminine issue and remedial measures suggested in his plays.

In the post-Independence Indian plays, Girish has brought a sea-change in the world of drama as he shocked the sensibility of the conservative audience by projecting the stark realities of life, relationship and existence. Seeking to present the modern society with its real worth, predicament, challenges, difficulties and complexities in true colours, his characters are drawn on the canvas of originality without any attempt to moralizing. Most of his plays are written in a naturalistic vein and reject the idealized portrayal of life while attaining complete accuracy in presenting life realistically. He has discussed and touched upon every aspect of life, not only the happy, and gleeful but also on human weaknesses, follies and foibles. His plays are neither moral, nor immoral in tone but may rather be seen as amoral. In a limited sense, he may be seen as a silent 'social activist' who covertly wishes to bring about a change in people's modes.

*Naga-Mandala* appears to be a battleground where ideological conflicts, power relations, and the struggle for identity have been dramatized effectively. In *Naga-Mandala* Rani, the female protagonist, and Kurudavva, the other female character, both are generic, represent the extreme physical torture and mental trauma, struggle for their identity as a woman, as a wife, and as a mother. Four Flames, Story, and the Man also reflect the sufferings and exploitations of women. Rani is treated in a slavish manner, imprisoned like a caged bird, neither she is allowed to talk to outsider nor outsider is allowed to do the same. Despite her chastity and fidelity, she is forced to face the Naga Ordeal. Appanna (Rani's husband), Naga (Cobra), Dog, Mongoose, Three Village Elders and the orthodox society have been used as the forces of subjection. Rani's acceptance of Naga as her own is a curt reply to the question of extra-marital relation in which only males are allowed to go freely, even after getting married, to concubine (as Appanna does) whereas the yardstick of morality is imposed upon women.

J.D. Soni judiciously comments that Karnad in the play tries to "fuse artistically dialectical relationship between tradition and modernity" (76). Prologue introduces Four Flames, which are animated, symbolic representations employed to report the sufferings of women. The tragic sufferings of women are extended to other female character, e.g., Kurudavva, who is an example of wisdom and philanthropy. Nobody in the society has eyes to see Rani's laceration at the hands of her philandering husband, but blind Kurudavva alone can see the truth. She extends motherly love and care to Appanna as well as to Rani. She is also the victim of orthodox society where the role of a woman is subservient and marginalized. Except her son Kappanna, there is none to look after her. Even the Village Elders treat her cruelly and unsympathetically while she has lost her only son. Karnad views:

> A distinctly woman's understanding of the reality around her, a lived counter point to the patriarchal structure of classical texts and institutions. The position of Rani in the story of *Naga-Mandala*, for instance, can be seen as a metaphor for the situation of a young girl in the bosom of a joint family where she sees her husband only in two unconnected roles—as a stranger during the

> day and as lover at night. Inevitably, the pattern of relationships she is forced to weave from these disjointed encounters must be something of a fiction. The empty house Rani is locked in could be the family she is married into
>
> (Introduction to *Three Plays: Naga Mandala, Hayavadana, Tughlaq* 17).

Karnad has always tried to present an ideological image of women and different phases of this society through her plays. Karnad shows in *Naga-Mandala* the double oppression of women in the society. It comes out to be a sociological study of Indian women; richly textured dramatic transmutation of two folk tales of Karnataka usually narrated by women while feeding children in the kitchen. It not only exposes the ugliness of a society where woman is considered "second sex", "other", "subject", "non-man"- women are taught in the process of being socialized, to internalize the reigning patriarchal ideology, e.g., male superiority; and so conditioned to derogate their own sex and to cooperate in their own subordination. Patriarchal dominance has prevented women from realizing their productive and creative possibility. The play also suggests remedial measures and slaps the orthodox society by an act of reconciliation between Rani and Naga. In fact, Karnad has always trusted in the equality based society, where men and women live happily and regard each other's needs.

*Hayavadana* is the next in Girish Karnad's writings where endeavour attempts of women are seen. Padmini is unlike of Rani of *Naga-Mandala.* She belongs to a family of leading merchant of Pavana Veethi of Dharampura. Though, in the play she enjoys commanding position, she is close to the spirit of Cleopatra of Shakespeare, succumbs to Dionysian tendency and indulges into cuckoldry. She camouflages love of Devadatta, his poetry gets new charm and vitality. She is so fascinating that Devadatta finds her "beyond my wildest dreams" (Karnad 14) and swears "if I ever get her as my wife, I will sacrifice my two arms to the goddess Kali, I'll sacrifice my head to Lord Rudra..."( Karnad, *Hayavadana* 14). Even Kapila finds "Yakshini, Shakuntala,

Urvashi, Indumati all rolled into one" ( Karnad, *Hayavadana* 16) and warns Devadatta, "She is not for the likes of you. What she needs is a man of steel" (Karnad, *Hayavadana* 19).

While talking to Padmini Kapila rightly says: "I know what you want, Padmini. Devadatta's clever head and Kapil's strong body"(Karnad, *Hayavadana* 38). Different images of women appear intelligent and mature. Devadatta and Kapila represent Apollonian and Dionysian tendencies respectively hence Padmini's hunger for Kapila is very outcome of her own nature. But in the temple of Kali, after Devadatta and Kapila's sacrifice, she is so much embarrassed to see the melodramatic scene and frightened to sense the sarcasm of people, anticipating people would blame her for both deaths. She instantly decides to kill herself. Transposition, no doubt, was a very frightening experience to her, yet she felt she had the best of both the man: "My Devadatta comes like a bridegroom with the ornament of a new body.... It's my duty to go with Devadatta. But, remember I'm going with your Kapil's body"(Karnad, *Hayavadana* 41), "fabulous body—fabulous brain" ( Karnad, *Hayavadana* 43) and "male smell" (Karnad, *Hayavadana* 43) express her nymphomaniac ecstasy and lust for sexual gratification. Even Doll I and Doll II comment on her psychic reactions—dreams, phantasies and reveries in which Kapila figures "climbing a tree!", "dived into a river" (Karnad, *Hayavadana* 50) symbolically let loose Padmini's suppressed sexual desire and hunger for Kapila. Soon she is disillusioned and finds herself, like Devadatta, Kapila and Hayavadana a victim of "mad dance of incompleteness" (Karnad, *Hayavadana* 57). Even after marriage, she can't resist herself and goes to the forest with her son and enjoys extramarital sexual relation with Kapila cuckolding her husband for four or five days.

In a duel Devadatta and Kapila exchange forgiveness and kill each other. Subsequently, Padmini finds herself nowhere. She suffers from alienation and perplexing situation erupts. She is abetted to perform *sati*—for the sake of the glory of her son or she couldn't live without Devadatta and Kapila: "Kali, Mother of all Nature, you must have your joke even now. Other women can die praying that they should get the same husband in all lives to come. You haven't left me even that little consolation" (Karnad, *Hayavadana* 63).

Padmini's practice of *sati,* comments Bhagavatta, "it would not be an exaggeration to say that no *pativrata* went the way Padmini did" (Karnad, *Hayavadana* 63). Female Chorus justifies Padmini's misdemeanor, "Why should love stick to the sap of a single body? When the stem is drunk with the thick yearning of the many-petalled, many-flowered lantana, why should it be tied down to the relation of a single flower?... I have neither regret nor shame" (Karnad, *Hayavadana* 64). Karnad attempts to give due space to women in human society where she is marginalized since time immemorial. Her plays present evolution of women and quest for better position in the world. *Hayavadana* has nicely been appreciated among the critics for Girish Karnad's efforts for the sublimity of women.

Sharmishtha, Swarnlata and Chitralekha in *Yayati* are generic; represent the subalternity of woman in masculinist society where she is identified as "other", "non-man", or "second sex" despite her high position in the society. Karnad doesn't adhere to traditional glorification of the son's 'self-sacrifice' rather raises question against this. Devayani, the Queen has to endure every sort of humiliation and becomes insane; Swarnlata is tortured by her husband's unfounded doubts of infidelity, insults and finally deserted; Sharmishtha is an easy prey of Yayati's filthy sexual gratification. Though Chitrlekha also faces similar conditions, she emerges as a new woman who boldly challenges the decision of Pooru and false rhetoric of Yayati. She doesn't allow Pooru to enter into her bedroom—who accepts the curse of his father for his moral transgression and becomes old, "I will not let my husband step back into my bedroom unless he returns a young man" (Karnad, *Yayati* 61) and frankly elaborates the reason of her marriage to Pooru: "I married him for his youth. For his potential to plant the seed of the Bharatas in my womb. He has lost that potency now. He doesn't possess any of the qualities for which I married him. But you do" (Karnad, *Yayati* 65-66). Yayati abuses her for these piercing words, "whore" ( Karnad, *Yayati* 66). She defies everything, i.e., kingdom and high reputation of Bharat dynasty and wants "room" for herself. She smiles defiantly and swallows the poison and dies. She prefers to die rather than yield before old conventions and assigned roles set for woman. Her death endorses new woman's quest for emancipation. Sharmishtha precisely explains the condition of women, "A woman dead (Chitrlekha), another gone mad (Devayani), and a third in danger of her life (Sharmishtha)" (68). Jealousy and racial conflict also weaken their lot. The play reinforces the centrality of women. John C. Hawley in *Contemporary Indian Writers in English* grants this view telling that "women have really suffered in the hands of men as they used women in all ways to have their comforts and royalty" (158). Later he says, "...however women have struggled and proved their existence in the society" (Hawley 219).

The discussion of the relationship between man and woman have been prescribed by man not by woman. Man who is ruled by the mastery-motive has imposed her limits on her. She accepts it because of "biosocial reasons" (Krishnamay 64-65). The play *Tale-Danda* endeavours to highlight the subjection, role, upsurge, and revolution of women living in poor area. Under Basavanna, a social reformer of the 12th century assembled a congregation of poets, mystics and social revolutionaries and philosophers form a new group, giving impetus to courageous questionings and social commitment. The abolition of caste, equality of sexes, rejection of idol worship, repudiation of Brahaminism, and of Sanskrit in favour of the mother tongue i.e. Kannad; were the main tenets of subaltern revolution. The resentment reaches its climax when Madhuvarsa, a Brahmin gives his daughter Kalavati in a marriage to an untouchable—Sheelvanta. This last act opposing caste hierarchy, not just in theory but in practice also, brought down upon the wrath of orthodox; the movement ended in terror and bloodshed. The playwright wants to suggest whenever such important issues are not considered seriously and solutions offered by these thinkers go unheeded, disastrous results would follow again. *Tale- Danda* draws its story from the life of Kannada saint Basavanna who resisted ideologically against the prevailing evils of caste hierarchy. And the historical context, deeply implanted in his mind, which proved catalyst to the plays of Karnad was predominated with, Karnad himself explains: "...tensions between the cultural past of the country and its colonial past, between the attractions of Western modes of thought and our own traditions, and finally between the various visions of the future that opened up once the common cause of the political freedom was achieved" (Introduction to *Three Plays: Naga-Mandala, Hayavadana, Tughlaq* 1). Drawing our attention to the genesis of the present, the play illuminates the endemic affliction of the caste and class politics infecting our body politic in the medieval period of history. It was the strong sense of history, which has nurtured in Karnad a dominant will for social justice, a sincere compassion for the socially oppressed and subaltern. Karnad's astute transformation of the metaphysical into the contemporary dimensions and history into trans-historical perspective is, not linked to the Western philosophical matrix, but, Vanashree Tripathi comments, "playwright's understanding of a long tradition of humanism in India...since the earliest periods" (25). So, his plays not only portray the struggle and idealism of women but social reformation of the patriarchal society too.

Ideal life which educated, wise and civilized people talk about has got a special position in his plays. One's caste is like one's home – meant for one's self and one's family. It is shaped to one's needs, one's comforts, and one's traditions. And that is why the Vedic tradition can absorb and accommodate all differences, from Kashmir to Kanya Kumari. And even those said to be its victims have embraced its logic of inequality. Sovidéva, the Prince wins the game of power politics exploiting the Hindu

Braminical sentiments; but subtly used to perpetuate Vedic traditions. With the coronation of Sovideva the triumph of the oppressor rings loud. Sanskrit chanting from ancient scriptures denotes the re-stabilization of caste order at least for the time being till another revolution. Diversity in cultural and social formation of this world is a strong subject of modern playwrights. Vishakha and Nittilai belong to two different socio-cultural backgrounds in *The Fire and the Rain.* Vishakha is the wife of Paravasu, a Brahmin, and daughter-in-law of Raibhya, a learned ascetic whereas Nittilai hails from a tribal community. Despite cultural polarities, both experience similar socio-psychological taboos and restrictions and feel bounded. For Nittilai, subjection is more intense—apart from patriarchy her inferior position in social hierarchy deteriorates her standing in the society. Though the play is based on C. Rajgopalachari's prose retelling of the *Mahabharata* especially the myth of Yavakri in Vana Parva, Karnad constructs a story of passion, loss, and sacrifice in the contexts of Vedic rituals, spiritual discipline, social and ethical differences between human agents, and interrelated forms of performance still close to their moments of origin, yet the treatment of feminine world, images of women, their subjection and changing status is not less remarkable.

Girish Karnad has shown the value of morality and idealism in the life of an Indian married woman. How she struggles to save her social status and the way she emerges is really a subject of praise for all the women. The meeting of Vishakha with her former lover Yavakri infuriates Raibhya who grabs her by her hair and start beating and kicking her. She is condemned as "whore" (Karnad, *Fire* 127) and "bitch" (Karnad, *Fire* 138) thereafter left to be handled by her husband. She is an easy prey to Raibhya's anger over his rejection as the Chief Priest by the king. He creates *Brahma Raksha* to kill Yavakri. Vishakha is bold and acknowledges her meeting with Yavakri before her husband candidly.

Nittilai, a tribal girl of 14 loves Arvasu, a brahmin of 18. Both work in a troupe. She is exposed to face the world and know how cruel and ruthless it can be. Only Andhak appreciates their love; the elders of Nittilai's tribe are anxious to interrogate Arvasu. Hers is a romantic love, a world of teenage phantasies ignorant from caste and cultural distinctions. On the contrary, Raibhya condemns her as "savage" (Karnad, Fire 126). When Arvasu fails to appear before Council of tribal Elders; they decreed, "Nitilai will marry another boy—of our own tribe" (Karnad, Fire 135). She is handed over to a tribal boy and married against her wishes. She has no say. Her protest touches climax when she runs away from her husband, family and everything for the sake of love. But, as an Indian married woman, she doesn't want to cuckold her husband. She transcends from petty sexual gratification and romantic love and develops pious relationship with Arvasu.

Karnad has great concern for the caste or gendered subalterns in his plays and he has brought them from margin to centre through his plays. His plays are the medium where through he raises socio-political and cultural problems prevalent in Indian society and calls upon us to discuss and evolve a common consensus rather than provide a readymade answer to the problem. Recently the country has given us some brilliant playwrights like Manjula Padmanabhan and Mahesh Dattani.

Manjula Padmanabhan was the first Indian to earn international fame with her Harvest, a futuristic play that deals with the exploitation of human body in twenty-first century. Padmanabhan projects a dehumanized, tefrrifying world in which mothers sell their sons for the price of rice. But her plays are intellectual and not suited for stage while Dattani is taken to be a true successor of Girish Karnad and responsible for the revolutionary progression of English drama, as a drama teaches, as a stage director, as a sociologist explaining various complexities of society.

Dattani Karnad emerges as a compelling playwright who projects the postcolonial dichotomy at various levels. He keeps women at the centre of his dramatic world and may be called avant-garde feminist. He was greatly influenced by Tennessee Williams, Arthur Miller and Giyratti playwright Madhurye. At one phase he says, "The playwright Madhu Rye influenced me a great deal in his portrayal of middle class Giyrati hypocrisises" (Lakshmi Subramanyam 13-14). His play '*Tara*' gives us a glimpse into the modern society which claims to be liberal and advanced into thought and action. It speaks about male chauvinism prevalent in the present society and brings about the stark reality of the woman playing second fiddle to man.

Homosexuality is the another significant subject matter chosen by Dattani. In '*Bravely Fought the Queen*' he highlights the absurdity of the situation in which woman is trapped by birth. The questions that haunt him are (a) Is homosexuality assertion of individuality? (b) Is it guided by some conviction? Does it lead to some meaningful goal ? (d) What is the utility of marriage to such people ? (e) Is it quest for some exclusive identity? *Seven Steps Round the Fire*, the most popular play, dwells on the theme of eunuchs, their identity, their constitution and their connotation.

In *Where There is a Will* Dattani Portrays complicated modern urban family where the old patriarchal code finds a formidable foe in the feminist ideas. His *Do the Needful* exposes the fact that the institute of marriage today has lost its sanctity and is nothing but a compromise to promote personal needs. His plays fulfil the postcolonial condition of writing. His cry of dichotomy is present in most of his plays. He says "Change does not happen overnight, we grow liberal after not because we want to, but have to". (Vandana Datta 157)

Thus, postcolonialism has taken up hitherto untouched issues like feminism and marginalization. The efficacy of postcolonial literature is far reaching and has awakened its readers and people to show their place and prestige among the comity of nations. According to Chandran, "Post-Colonial' literature is a form of cultural criticism and cultural critique; a mode of misidentifying whole societies from the sovereign codes of cultural organization, and an inherently dialectical intervention in the hegemonic production of cultural meaning"(238). The objective of postcolonial theatre is to focus the past and present social milieu including political situation, which often becomes the pivotal issue involving the colonial legacy and the retinue of its disturbing features. In literature, nationalism cannot be isolated from the imperial history, which produced the contemporary version of the nation.

As regards the portrayal of gender in postcolonial plays is they admit androgyny as merely a hypothetical category which can be dissolved into male or female when the biological markers of sex are known. A few plays gave accent on feminism interest in destabilizing gender binaries. They also demarcated areas of woman's subjugation under imperialism. karnad is a staunch follower of non-vedic tradition, presents social, cultural, moral, religious and political culture of vedic society. As a truth-teller, he exposes all evilsome aspects alongwith good points of then society. In his plays, woman's modesty became the subject matter and inter racial gender anathema became an analogue for the colonizers violation of the land, and also far related forms of economic and political exploitation.

## Works Cited

Abrams, M.H. *A Glossary of Literary Terms.* (Seventh Edition), Singapore: Thomason Asia Pvt. Ltd., 2003. Print

Burke, Rupalee. "India Then and Now: The Contemporary Relevance of Girish Karnad's *Tale-Danda" Studies in Indian Drama in English.* Eds. Prasad, Amar Nath and Saryug Yadav. Bareilly: Prakash Book Depot, 2003. Print

Chandran, S. Subhash. "'*Bali: The Sacrifice*' and Dionysian Life Assertion." *Girish Karnad's Plays: Performance and Critical Perspectives,* ed. Tutun Mukherjee. Delhi: Pencraft International, 2006. Print

Das, B.K. *Twentieth Century Literary Criticism.* (Fifth Edition), New Delhi: Atlantic Publishers and Distributors, Pvt. Ltd. 2007. Print

Devy, G.N. Ed. *Indian Literary Criticism.* Hyderabad: Orient Longman, Pvt. Ltd., 2007.

Dharwadker, Aparna Bhargava, ed. With an Introduction *Collected Plays*. Vol. One: *Tughlaq, Hayavadana, Bali: The Sacrifice, Naga-Mandala*. New Delhi: O.U.P., Fourth Impression, 2008. Print

_________. Ed. With an Introduction *Collected Plays*. Vol. Two: *Tale-Danda, The Fire and the Rain, The Dreams of Tipu Sultan, Two Monologues, Flowers, Broken Images*. New Delhi: O.U.P., 2005. Print

Hawley, John C.. *Contemporary Indian Writers in English*. Delhi: Foundation Books, 2005.Print

Gandhi, Leela. *Postcolonial Theory: A Critical Introduction* (Sixth Edition), New Delhi: OUP, 2005. Print

Jagamonarchari, A. "Karnad's *Hayavadana* and *Naga-Mandala*: A Study in Post Colonial Dialectics", *New Directions in Indian Drama*. Eds. Sudhaker Pandey & Freya Barua. New Delhi: Prestige, 1994. Print

Joshipura, Pranav. "*Tale-Danda:* A Problem Play" *Indian English Drama: Critical Perspectives*. Eds. Dondiya & Sunderan. New Delhi: Sarup & Sons, 2000. Print

Karnad, Girish. *Two Plays: Dream of Tipu Sultan, Bali: The Sacrifice*. New Delhi: O.U.P., Fourth Impression, 2005. Print

_________. "Inroduction" to *Three Plays: Naga-Mandala, Hayavadana, Tughlaq*. New Delhi: O.U.P., 2002. Print

_________. *Tale-Danada*. Delhi: Ravi Dayal, 1993. Print

_________. *Yayati*. New Delhi: O.U.P., 2008. Print

_________. *Hayavadana*. (Fourteenth Impression), Chennai: OUP,1998. Print

_________. *The Fire and the Rain*, New Delhi: Oxford University Press,1998. Print

_________. "Interview" *Flowering of Indian English Drama: Growth and Development*. Eds. Reddy, K. Venkata & R.K. Dhawan, New Delhi: Prestige, 2004. Print

Krishanamayi. "Redefinig the Insurgent Female Psyche in an Andrcentric Milieu" *The Indian Journal of English Studies*. Vol. XLI, 2003-04. Print

Lodge, David and Wood, Nigel. Eds. *Modern Criticism and Theory*. New Delhi: Dorling Kinderslay (India) Pvt. Ltd., 2007. Print

Mukherjee, Tutun, ed. *Girish Karnad's Plays: Performance and Critical Perspectives*. Delhi: Pencraft International, 2006. Print

Naik, M. K. *Littcrit*. Vol 23, Numbers1 & 2, June-Dec, 2001. Print

Nayar, Pramod K. *Literary Theory Today*. New Delhi: Prestige / Asia Book Club, 2002.

Somalata, Y. "Girish Karnad's *Tale-Danda:* Painful Rite of Passage" *Flowering of Indian English Drama: Growth and Development*. Eds. Reddey, Venkata K & R.K. Dhawan. New Delhi: Prestige, 2004. Print

Soni, J.D. " Girish Karnad's *Naga-Mandala*: An Experiment in Technique" *Indian Writing in the New Millenium.* Ed. Dhawan, R.K. New Delhi: Indian Association for English Studies, 2000. Print

Tripathi, Vanashree. *Three Plays of Girish Karnad: A Study in Poetics and Culture—Hayavadana, Tale-Danda, The Fire and the Rain.* New Delhi: Prestige Books, 2004. Print

# 17

# Girish Karnad's *Yayati:* A Play of Unheroic Filial Sacrifice

— Jaybhaye Vithal Khandujj

> When I first read Yayati, I was amazed.
> Those characters, those minds, so alive and true!
>
> —Vijay Tendulkar (*The Hindu*, 9 Feb.1998)

*Yayati* is Girish Karnad's first play originally written in Kannada at the age of 22. The play was written in1960, which marked the opening of 'The Modern Kannada Theatre' in Karnataka. The play *Yayati* was translated in English by Karnad in 2008. The important difference between the Kannada play *Yayati* and the English translated *Yayati* is the age and experience of the scholar-writer Karnad. He translated the play at the age of 69, as a mature artist, actor, critic and writer of literary and theatrical world. Another important thing about the play is that its first performance in Hindi was in the seventies with Amrish Puri in its eponymous role established, and directed by Satyadev Dubey. Apart from this, the play has been translated in various Indian languages and interesting for the armature actors in India.

The English play *Yayati* was translated by Karnad in stressful situation at the time of his first visit to London as a 'Rhodes Scholarship Fellow' of Oxford in 1960. He was the first fellow of the Karnad family to go abroad, so his family members were frightened about his settling in England after two years of his scholarship. Karnad felt that his family was emotionally blackmailing him and was asking him to sacrifice his career for their interest. Like Robinson Crusoe of Daniel Defoe, Karnad had to protest against his family for the fulfilment of his Eliotian and Yeatsian dreams. To escape from this stressful situation, he took to writing the play *Yayati*.

Karnad has taken the theme of the play from an ancient Indian mythology; but he was alienated from it. As he admits, "A greater surprise was the theme of the play, for it was taken from ancient Indian mythology from which I had believed myself alienated." The treatment of myth like Rabindranath Tagore is appropriate in the present situation. As Aparna Dharwadkar says, "*Yayati* establishes at the outset of Karnad's career that myth is not merely a narrative to be bent to present purposes, but a structure of meanings.....or the necessity of contemporary setting." (xiii-xxxvii)

For the plot of the play, Girish Karnad has used the myth of King Yayati from the Adi Parva in the *Mahabharata*. The story of the play is about the wives of King Yayati and his lust (not love) for them. His one beloved is the tribal princess known as Sharmishtha and Devyani, the daughter of Sage Shukracharya and the broken-hearted belle of Kacha, who live together as King Yayati's Queen and the royal maid slave. King Yayati falls in love with Sharmishtha and enraged Shukracharya curses him with decrepitude. As remedy, he is allowed to escape from the curse if any youth is ready to exchange his youth with his old age. King Yayati was disappointed by all his relatives, who don't accede to his. Finally the King turns to his youngest son Pooru, who agrees to do so out of his love for his father. After enjoying his youth for a thousand years, Yayati returns Pooru his youth and leaves for the forest.

Unlike Rabindranath Tagore's play *Chitra*, Karnad has treated the myth from the *Mahabharata* very skilfully in the play *Yayati*. But playwright Karnad has ignored the myth's traditional sacredness in order to preach the social ideals. The myth from the *Mahabharata* is the tale of racial tensions, female jealousy, the royal lust and existential escape. According to a critic R.T. Bedre, "Karnad deprives the filial sacrifice of Pooru of its traditional glory and an aura of idealism. In addition to the mythical characters of King Yayati, Sharmishtha, Devyani and Pooru, the playwright has added two new characters—Chitralekha, the newlywed wife of Pooru, and, Swarnlata the royal made." (18) The character of King Yayati from the Karnad's *Yayati* is more lecherous than the original mythical King Yayati from the *Mahabharata*. Karnad doesn't spare any opportunity to mark Yayati's lechery, and makes not only the other characters speak about his lechery but also King Yayati himself confeses his lust and fascination for women. This shows the beastly lust of a man (from any century) for women. King Yayati's wives, Sharmishtha and Devyani, both do not fail to "examine those eyes (of Yayati) and acknowledge the lust burning there" (Karnad, *Yayati,* 11). Even King Yayati proudly confesses his lust for the charm of a woman. He says, "I am no stranger to women" (16). His youth is only for the fulfilment of his lust (sex). He speaks to Sharmishtha, "I want people around me. Queens, ministers, armies, enemies, the populace. I love them all….I have to be young. I must have my youth." (Karnad, *Yayati* 43)

When Sage Shukracharya curse King Yayati, he is frightened by the thought of decrepitude, but falsely shows to be unmoved. But when he realizes the seriousness of the curse, he loses his patiente and begins to shout at Sharmishtha, Devyani, Shukracharya and Pooru. But he comes to know the curse will not have its effect on him if any young man agrees to take it upon himself and offers his youth to him in exchange; he is overjoyed like an innocent child. But Prince Pooru asks him a direct question about the acceptance of the King's curse. King Yayati answers the question with overconfidence that anybody could accept his kingdom. He tells Pooru, "Oh that! Surely that is not serious question. Surely there is no shortage of men who will come out to take their King's burden......They are trained to lay down their lives for me (46)". King Yayati thinks that anyone can accept his curse voluntarily for the sake of their King's youth. He offers them wealth and public respect as well as he even offers to return youth after few years. This attitude of King shows the man's lust for youth and sexual pleasure.

But after the declaration and offers by the king, no one accepts his offers or is ready to sacrifice his youth. Then King Yayati asks to his son Pooru, "What shall I do, Pooru? What am I to do?" He becomes mad with the curse of Shukracharya. Prince Pooru becomes serious about the condition of his father and he willingly accepts the curse of his lustful-mad father. Now Yayati becomes overjoyed to with his son Pooru. Prince Pooru has just married Chitralekha. King Yayati is murdering his son for the sake of his own youth as well as his sexual pleasure.

King Yayati wants to convince Chitralekha, just married wife to Pooru, about the great sacrifice for the sake of the kingdom and that she should support Pooru in his crisis. He tries to justify his stand, "Please try to understand....I am the king.... I cannot forget my duty by them....Unfortunately, recently, unexpected troubles have started brewing in the corners of my realm....I am dumbfounded when he told me. Even now I am willing to take it back on my shoulder. What father would wish such a fate on his son? Pooru took it on of his own free will. Without a word from me. Without saying a word to me." (63) King Yayati is demanding help from his daughter-in-law. He also explains that Pooru is unable to tackle the situation of his kingdom, so he accept the youth of his son. But she asks him a question, "My help?" (63) Lastly Chitralekha with an interrogating spirit puts a cross question to King and it is quite shocking to Yayati. She asks, "Think. And will your majesty also think about how old I shall be by the time that future is attained? I am here, this minute, sir. And I cannot intarest myself in your unborn future. I married Pooru for his youth. For his potential to plant the seed to the

Bharatas in my womb. He has lost that potency. He doesn't possess any of the qualities for which I married him. But you do. You have taken over your son's youth. It follows that ou should accept everything that comes attached to it" (65, 66). In this way Chitralekha does not agree with the king and finally she commits suicide. The suicide of Chitralekha is an eye-opening event.

In this way, Karnad takes away the mythological magic of the play and presents the king as a man of lust and sensual desires. As Prof. Bedre writes, "Karnad's Pooru does not give his youth out of his love for this father but to escape from the royal responsibilities to which he considers himself unworthy. All the time a mysterious consciousness fills him with the feeling of inferiority that he is a misfit among the Bharat dynasty" (23). Pooru himself admits to his father, "I had not the slightest inclination to follow in the steps of my illustrious forefathers. I found their deeds pompous. I was bored by the hermitage, unembarrassed. I wanted to run away, from all that it represented: that history, those triumphs those glorious ideals" (35). He also strongly complains against his father, "... My forefathers were the great eagles, keen eyed, hovering regally in the clouds. I shall seek to be a worm." This indicates that Pooru does not any have interest in the dynasty. Apart from this, he also confesses his faiture as a husband of Chitralekha and that she deserves someone better than him. These activities and dialogues of Pooru show that he wants to escape from the responsibilities of kingship of the state. He sacrifices his youth for the sake of the kingdom.

King Yayati also plays another trick on Pooru by telling the story of his senior (mother) queen, who has been a rakshasi. Sharmishtha had married Yayati as a revenge because the Aryas had destroyed her home and hearth. She wanted to avenge on the Arya race; so she had made sure that the crown prince of the Bharatas had rakshasa blood in him and, thereby, a half-caste would rule the Aryas. With these various reasons, the king is able to convince Pooru and get his youth. In the play, the Pooru is not presented as he is in the mythology. His sacrifice of Pooru doesn't have any glory in the play. His sacrifice is his weakness as a Arya prince as well as the husband of Chitralekha. When Sharmishtha gets know about the voluntarily accepted sacrifice of Pooru, she says, "No, no, no, you can't. That is utter stupidity! Pooru, the desire for self-sacrifice is a rank perversion" (50). Finally Pooru also agrees and says, "...This is decrepitude. The sum total of Father's transgression..."

To sum up, Karnad's *Yayati* has crossed the limits of myth and become the successful drama of the present. His prince Pooru's sacrifice is the just filial sacrifice for a lecherous father. The act of Pooru is an unheroic one. This is the greatness of the playwright. The lustful and sensual character of the king has been presented by the playwright as the central theme of the play. The differences between the myth and the play are the sacrifice of a son as not a sacrifice but an unheroic activity, and the character of the king is not of noblity. The king doesn't love his kingdom but he wants young hood for the fulfilment of his cannal pleasures. Like his other plays, in *Yayati,* Karnad tries to preserve his special identity as a modern playwright of India.

## Works Cited

Dharwadkar, Aparna. *Introduction. Collected Plays. By Girish Karnad.* Vol.II, OUP: New Delhi, 2005.

Karnad, Girish. "Drama with Distinct vision." *The Hindu.* (Hyd.) Nov. 25, 2007.

Karnad, Girish. *Yayati.* OUP: New Delhi, 2009.

R.T. Bedre. *Collected Essays on the Plays of Girish Karnad.* Creative Publications, Nanded, 2009.

# 18

# Feminine Perspective in Girish Karnad's *Hayavadana*

— K. S. Thirunavukkarasu

Girish Karnad is known for his versatile genius. It is his greatness that he is one of the greatest dramatists of Indo-Anglian literature. His greatness is hidden in quality in place of quantity. He has only five or six plays to his credit. The best of them are *Yayati, Tughlaq* and *Hayavadana*. Karnad is a film producer, an actor, and a TV artiste and above all a dramatist. Certainly, his *Tughlaq* has been popular far and wide. It is true that he wept when he realized that he would not be a poet, but be only a dramatist. He was deeply influenced by Ibsen, Shaw and Shakespeare. He was highly influenced by trends in Kannada literature and he took legend, history and myth for the plots of his plays. He is a pioneer in the field of new drama and all his plays are actable. Their story is generally borrowed from ancient myths, folk literature, or history. *Hayavadana* is based on a folk theme. Its plot is borrowed from an ancient collection of stories in Sanskrit entitled *Kathasaritasagara*. Karnad's play is narrated by a ghost to an adventurous king.

From an indepth study of the plays of Girish Karnad it is evident that Karnad as a dedicated writer has seen the whole arc of life with unflinching uprightness and has presented the utter truth of life in a language that is destined to survive and move and rule man's heart forever. By a clever manipulation of the old myths and folktales, he is able to serve a slice of reality mixed with fantasy. It helps him not only to reflect the fret and fever of the contemporary world, but also enables him to prepare his readers and audience to face the problems without simply existing quite complacently.

One of Karnad's best known fellow Indian playwrights has been Badal Sircar, the famous dramatist hailing from West Bengal. Badal Sircar, one of the most successful dramatists of contemporary India was born in 1925 in Calcutta. His father, a Christian, was a professor of the Scottish Church School. Through sicar's education endowed him with a fluent command of English he is of the view that it would be an entirely inappropriate language for the particular kind of theater to which he is committed to write.

All the plays of Sicar written in Bengali show a considerable development over the past thirty years or so, since he came to be recognized as a potent force in contemporary Indian Theatre. He being a 'metropolitan writer' (Banfield) of Calcutta, both the themes and the forms of his theatre have developed in non-traditional ways.

In his writing Sircar is not political but he prefers to preserve the integrity that his independence has given him. His passionate response to the suffering and injustices inflicted on the poor has motivated him in writing plays.

Badal Sircar's play *Evam Indrajit* was first presented in English by the Madras players at the Museum Theatre, Chennai, in April 1970. The play:

> is like going on a sentimental journey; a
> nostalgic foray into the recent past of the
> Indian theatre; an encounter with the bitter-sweet
> memories of a struggling sensibility
> trying to strike roots in a barrenland;
> because, after all it is only in relation to
> Indian theatre history that Evam Indrajit
> really makes its presence felt.
>
> (*Three Modern Plays*, Introduction)

The play *Evam Indrajit*, written in Bengali by Badal Sircar and translated into English by Karnad, is recognized as a milestone in the history of modern Indian drama. The play is a dramatic presentation of all the prevalent anxieties, vague fears and undefined frustration gnawing at the hearts of the educated urban middle class.

Vijay Tendulkar exposes the basic contradictions in the lives of the middle class. His consistent, prolonged engagement with human aggression has made him one of the most distinguished social theorists of violence in India.

Tendulkar's *Ardhasatya* (1983) produces a psychology of vulnerability. The protagonist of *Nishant* (1975) is an apparently passive witness who identifies herself with the killers of her husband and his family.

The Indian theatre has come a long way since the emergence of eminent playwrights like Girish Karnad, Badal Sircar and Vijay Tendulkar in recent years. With their singular ability to relate ancient Indian myths to contemporary life, profound sociological concerns and sensitivity to meet the needs of emerging feminine psyche, these playwrights have resuscitated Indian drama to a uniquely new life of its own, and has rendered it singularly in, a fast changing world.

*Hayavadana* is a play on the search for identity in the midst of tangled relationships. Devadatta, the man of intellect and Kapila, the man of the body, are two intimate friends. Devadatta marries Padmini, but Kapila falls in love with Padmini. Consequently, the two friends kill themselves. But the comic touch is seen when Padmini transposes their heads, giving Devadatta Kapila's body and Kapila Devadatta's. This act reveals the ambiguous nature of human personality. M.K. Naik comments on the technique of this play: " Karnad does not succeed fully in investing the basic conflict in the play with the required intensity, but his technical experiment with an indigenous dramatic from here is a triumph which has opened up fresh lines of fruitful exploration for the Indian English playwright".

Karnad's *Hayavadana* is a memorable treatment of the theme of search for completeness. The main plot of Hayavadana is based on 'the story of transposed heads' in the Sanskrit *Vetala Panchavimsati.* A modern source of the play is Thomas Mann's *The Transposed Heads* which the author called 'Metaphysical Jest'. The sub-plot of *Hayavadana*, the Horse-Headed Man, is Karnad's own invention. It serves both as prologue and epilogue to the play.The play opens with Lord Ganesh Puja. Lord Ganesh with a human body and an elephant head aptly suggest the central theme of Incompleteness. 'Haya' means horse and 'Vadana' means face. Hayavadana is a horse-headed man. He is the only son of the princess of Karnataka. He longs for his perfection.Devadatta is endowed with all the accomplishment expected of a brahmin youth. He is comely in appearance, fair in colour and unrivalled in intelligence. Devadatta falls in love with an extremely agile and quick-witted girl, Padmini, the daughter of a rich merchant. Kapila, the son of an ironsmith Lohita, has an attractive body. Devadatta and Kapila are closest of friends. The Bhagavata describes them as

> Two Friends there were,
> One mind, One heart (2)

Kapila arranges the marriage of Padmini with his friend, Devadatta. At the same time, she attracted to the virility of Kapila. Both Kapila and Padmini start drifting towards each other. Devadatta becomes jealous of this and shows in his thought

> Does she really not see?
> Or She deliberately playing this game With him? (22).

Devadatta is a man of intellectual while Kapila is of body. Kapila is more attractive than Devadatta because as the representative of animal energy in human body. Padmini is a victim in the hands of the pulls of physical pleasure. She was very attracted by the ethereal shape of Kapila. She describes the Kapila's body as: "What an ethereal shape! Such a broad back-ocean like Muscles rippling across it" (25).

Devadatta in a sudden outburst of emotions decides to sacrifice his life to Kali. That he is doing so because he was unable to bear the pangs of jealousy. He says: "Good-bye Kapila Good-bye Padmini may the Lord Rudhra bless you (28).

Padmini stumbles on the opportunity of having the better of the two - Devadatta's head and Kapila's body. Her predicament is the predicament of a modern emancipated woman. They went to a great Rishi in search of solution to their problem. The Rishi answers as: "the man with Devadatta's head is the rightful husband of Padmini". The play ends with Devadatta and Kapila fighting a duel in which the heads of both roll again. When the friends are dead, Padmini decides to perform sati.

Karnad's *Hayavadana* deals with the theme of 'Search for completeness. In the case of *Hayavadana*, the horse-headed man, he longs for perfection. He wished him to be a complete man. But, at the end, he turned completely into a horse. Hence, he failed in his desire of completeness. Similarly, Padmini longs for Devadatta's intellectual power and Kapila's physical power. Both are different personalities. So she also failed in her desire of having both Kapila's body and Devadatta's head. Hence, it is correct in saying that Karnad's *Hayavadana* deals with the theme of search for completeness. This theme is suggested in the play itself in phrases such as:

> Search for completeness This mad dance of incompleteness" In essence, according to K. Narasimha Murthy: "Karnad's Hayavadana is a play employing native folk theatre strategies to present man's tragic futile aspiration for perfection or completeness (30).

Padmini in *Hayavadana* is a victim of forces which she can neither understand nor control. She yearns for a perfect man as her husband. She is not satisfied with Devadatta her life partner who is intelligent and skillful but not strong in his build. Further Devadatta is unable to fulfil the physical needs of his wife. Consequently, she turns to Kapila for her physical fulfillment and drives complete satisfaction in her intimate movements with Kapila. Soon after his misadventure in the Kali temple resulting in the transposition of heads of Devadatta and Kapila, she feels that she just cannot live with both Kapila and Devadatta, since such a polygamous relationship is not acceptable to the society at large. Traditional society demands a woman to practice scrupulous monogamy, through only Padmini knows exactly what she expects from each of them. She admires Devadata's mind and Kapila's sensuality while society forces her look for both these masculine tracts if she can, in one man. Padmini, would ideally, prefer to live with a 'complete man', who possesses both the complementary traits of a brilliant mind accompanied by a virile human body, the kind whom she, as it were unwrittingly creates in her excitement at the sudden behest of Kali by transposing the heads of Devadatta and Kapila.

Padmini is a vibrant leader who refuses to play the role of a copy mistress even on her wedding night. On all occasions she holds both the men in her life, under the control, by pampering both Devadatta's intellectual concerns and Kapila's sensual craving for her. Padmini's lack of inhibitions gets established rights at the beginning of the play through the song of the female chorus: "Why should love stick to the sap of a single body? A head for each breast. A pupil for each eye. A side fro each arm. I have neither regret not shame"(11).

Padmini is an emancipated intellectual, who loves her husband as well as her lover for the two entirely different aspects of their personalities. She does not want to play the role of a 'pativrata', She does not want to suppress her instinctual impulse rather she gladly gives a free rein to it.

Padmini is, in fact, a victim of forces which she can neither comprehend nor control. Though she yearns for an ideal or complete man in the person of her husband, owing to mind's dominance over body. She remains frustrated and meets with voluntary death. Eventually on the death of Devadatta and kapila, padmini opts for the ritual of 'sati' the usual options of 'pativratas'.

Hayavadana presents the universal predicament of human beings who yearns for perfection in intimate relationships, especially in marriage. The play seems to drive home a lesson in humility, self-control and submission before fatalistic element in life.

Though both Devadatta and Kapila are friends and love ardently, both recoil from any kind of solution to their conflict. Devadatta is enamoured of the beauty of Padmini, but Padmini is not the first woman in Devadatta's life. He had fallen in love with many other women, earlier in life too. But whenever he is in love with any girl. He feels dejected and depressed. Kapila knows that Devadatta is the only friend who confides everything with him. Padmini proves to be so much far beyond Devadatta's "wildest dreams". Yet he wants to posses her. Again, he is imparactical when he vows to sacrifice his arms to goddess kali and his head to Rudra. When he wants to enjoy a happy married life with Padmini. Padmini is the sixteenth girl Devadatta has fallen in love with. This shows that he perhaps considers Padmini as a mere possession, an object to be owned and adorned and not a human being worthy of sharing the ups and downs of life with. That is why has is careless and foolish when he vows to do away with his vital parts to the goddess.

In contrast to Devadatta, Kapila is bold, and seems to have really fallen in love with Padmini the married woman. He is well aware of the fact that he has been taken in by Padmini. Though he wants to maintain a safe distance form her he can hardly restrain himself from staying close beside her as he is extremely susceptible to padmini's physical charms.

> Kapila (aside). So its off. What am I to do
> for the rest of the day? What am I do for
> the rest of the week? Why should it feel
> as though the whole world has been wiped
> out for a whole week? Why this emptiness
> [...] Kapila, Kapila, get a light hold
> On yourself. You are slipping, boy
> Control yourself. Don't lose that hold.
> Go now – don't come here again for a week
> -Devadatta's bound to get angry with you
> For not coming. Sister-in-law will be annoyed.
> But don't come back. Go, Go!
> [Aloud] Well then – I'll start.
>
> (*Hayavadana* 23)

Both the men are callous towards Padmini's inner feelings as an individual. More really cares for padmini's emotional conflicts through both of them are in love with padmini. In fact, they do nothing to satisfy her or to put her at ease. She is driven to play the role of an active agent and gets pushed, time and again to act and choosen her man/men. Devadatta has already vowed his head and arms to the goddess and kapila is more obsessed with the thought as to want the others may say of him if her marries Padmini, even after the death of Devadatta. In the end the two impractical men in her life kill themselves and it is she who pleads with the goddess to bring them back to life. She has every right to choose between the two now, for it is she who has brought them both back to life.

In the play of Karnad women are portrayed in a pathetic light. Most of them are silent sufferers. They are very submissive to resist the evils composed by patriarchical lords and the masters of their lives.

## Works Cited

Krnad, Girish. *Three Plays: Naga, Mandala, Hayavadana and Tughlaq*. New Delhi: Oxford University Press, 1994

________. *Three Modern Plays*. New Delhi: Oxford, 1999.

Bala, Suman. *New Directions in Indian Drama: With Special Reference to the Plays of Vijay Tendulkar, Badal Sircar and Girish Karnad.* R.K.Dhawan (Ed). New Delhi: Prestige Books. 165-176.

Naik, M.K. *A Study of Hayavadana.* Macmillan: New Delhi, 1976.

Sinha, A.K. *Girish Karnad: New Directions in Indian Drama: With Special reference to the plays of Vijay Tendulkar, Badal Sircar and Girish Karnad.* Dhawan R.K.(Ed). New Delhi: Prestige Books. 104-123.

Srinivasa, K.R. *Indian Writing in English Sterling:* New Delhi, 1984.

# 19

# *Hayavadana*: A Mirror of the Society

— Hasibuddin

## Introduction

Literature as an academic subject, is not restricted to the study of characters, plots and images; it also facilitates us to explore the intellectual atmosphere, the social structures and the moral and emotional predicaments of cultures past and present, familiar and strange. It is a useful resource which provides an understanding as to how settlements were established, illustrates the daily conduct of trade, explores the relationship between diverse people and also depicts the conflicting and heartrending emotions felt by a particular migrant community.

The real value of creative literature is that, by observing the many and varied ways in which novelists, poets and dramatists engage with that world, we can begin to see more creatively ourselves. Girish Karnad is a dramatist of this kind, after going through his play one becomes bound to think about himself/herself. He was born in 1938 in Matheran, in Karnataka, India. After completing his B.A. from Karnataka College in 1958, he went to Oxford for Graduate studies on a Rhodes scholarship. He started writing for Kannada theatre upon his return in the 1960s. *Hayavadana*, written in 1971, was his third play. Karnad has the genius and the power to transform any situation into an aesthetic experience.

> India is a cradle of the human race, the birth place of human speech, the mother of history, the grandmother of legend, and the great grandmother of tradition. Our most valuable and most attractive materials in the history of man are treasured up in India only!
>
> — Mark Twain

## Culture

'Culture' derives from 'cultura' and 'colere', meaning 'to cultivate'. It also meant 'to honour' and 'protect'. Culture is the mode of generating meanings and ideas. It represents the principles and constructs, way of life, art, music, literature, beliefs and attitudes of a particular country or group. It is followed by members within a society to acquire a position making them to function and communicate according to these constructs. The culture of a community includes various aspects: economic, spatial, ideological, erotic, and political. Culture is not a natural thing, it is produced. The production and consumption of culture is linked to power and identity. The production and consumption of cultural artifacts define one's identity. Popular culture is the culture of the masses.

## Identity

Identity is defined as the feelings, characteristics or beliefs that distinguish people from others. A race, community or nation has its own traditions and beliefs that constitute its culture and defines its distinct identity. Thus a nation's identity comprises its culture, art, tradition, music and heritage. People belonging to a specific race, community or nation carry with them the shared experience of their race inherent in their collective unconscious in the forms of myth, legend and folklore. It is their national identity that finds a frequent expression through their arts and culture, their literature.

## Hayavadana

Girish Karnad's *Hayavadana* was influenced by Thomas Mann's

*The Transposed Heads*, which in turn is borrowed from one of the Sanskrit *Kathasaritasagara*, an ancient collection of stories in Sanskrit. Culture defines society and Karnad's plays are a reflection of the culture in our society. Focusing on our folk culture, he takes inspiration from mythology and folklore. With *Hayavadana*, Karnad has taken us back to the myths and legends of the Hindu religion.

The main plot of the play begins with Kapila, who finds his best friend Devadatta downheartedly dreaming about Padmini. Kapila, the only son of iron-smith, is a kshatriya, a wrestler whereas Devadatta, only son of the reverend brahmin Vidyasagara, is a learned brahmin and poet but is physically weak. The world wonders at their friendship. After seeing their friendship, people remember Lava and Kusha, Rama and Lakshmana, Krishna and Balarama. They were one mind, one heart. Kapila goes to arrange Devadatta's marriage to her and realizes that Padmini is as clever as she is beautiful. Although Kapila is attracted to her, he arranges the match, and Devadatta and Padmini are married.

After the wedding, Padmini finds herself getting attracted to the strong-bodied Kapila, and Devadatta is consumed by jealousy. A few months into the marriage, the three travel to Ujjain. On the way, they rest between two temples, one devoted to Rudra (The Howler—a form of Shiva) and the other to Kali. Devadatta decided to offer himself to Kali, but Kapila too is not left behind. The two men behead themselves in the Kali temple. The pregnant Padmini, afraid that she might be blamed for their deaths, then decides to kill herself. However, Kali stops her and offers to bring the men back to life. Padmini rearranges the heads so that Devadatta's head is on Kapila's body and vice versa and asks the goddess to do her magic.

The characters of Kapila and Devadatta are manifestations of the images of different castes in our society. In our society, a Brahmin is learned and wise but physically weak. Likewise, the image of Devadatta is stereotypical of a male brahmin whereas

Kapila, a kshatriya, is a wrestler and is not as wise as Devadatta. Here the caste of the men plays a major role in the portrayal of both the men, which is true of our Indian society where we judge people on the basis of their caste and creed.

Along with the central theme, there is a sub-plot wherein Hayavadana (the horse-man) reflects incompleteness. With the face of a horse and the body of a man, Hayavadana, the off-spring of a celestial being and a princess, loathes and wants to rid of the horse's head and longs to be a complete man. He is symbolic of the identity crisis we face today. Karnad implores Existentialism by intensifying the motif of incompleteness by a broken tusk and a cracked belly— which other way you look at him he seems the embodiment of imperfection, of incompletion.

Existentialism implies the quest of the individual for the assertion of the self despite his limitations and failures. In the play, identity and impersonation have been played up leading to conflicts between the mind and the body. When Kapila and Devadatta's heads get transposed, the identity crisis further deepens and the influence of the bodies on the minds is immense. This brings to the fore a conflict that we face in our lives, if the mind in dependent on the body or vice versa. The conflict between the head and the body, is well expressed in Devadatta's (whose head is Devadatta's but body is Kapila's) words, "I'd always thought one had to use one's brain while wrestling or fencing or swimming. But this body does not wait for thoughts, it acts." But the irony has been brought out very well by Karnad. As we in today's times, often chose body over mind, Padmini too does the same. This reflects the changing preferences in our lives.

In India's cultural and socio context, mind is given more emphasis over matter and is illustrated through Devadatta's remark in the play which says, "According to Shastras, the head is the sign of a man." Karnad represents India's erstwhile socio-cultural practices like Sati when Padmini commits Sati in order to prove her chastity, which was a tradition in olden days.

Karnad reveals the religious sentiments prevalent in our society, psychology and culture by showing the presence of Goddess Kali. *Hayavadana* begins with an invocation of Lord Ganesha, who is generally worshipped first among the gods. In the beginning, Devadatta worships Kali in order to win Padmini's hand for marriage. Later in the course of time, he offers himself to the goddess by beheading himself and his friend Kapila follows suit. The Hindu rituals and superstitions are very well portrayed by showing people offering themselves to Kali. This was a practice that was followed a few decades back. Now people offer goats and animals to Goddess Kali, who is also known as the goddess of destruction. The theme also reveals the *Upanishad* principle that visualizes the human body as a symbol of the organic relationship of the parts to the whole.

The sexuality of a woman has been put forth in a very unassuming way by Karnad. Padmini though married to Devadatta is attracted to Kapila. Her constant existence depends on the presence of either of them. She needs both or either of them for her contentment and resorts to Goddess Kali. Eventually, she finds herself in intense excitement when she combines the head of Devadatta and the body of Kapila thereby according herself a high degree of sexual freedom. Padmini's end portrays the suppression of women in our country wherein they have to time and again prove their chastity. With such references to India's cultural, religious and social context, Karnad does not mean to condemn them but make readers and viewers understand how even with different human values and behaviours, we seem to follow well set norms. He has blended such issues such as love, identity and sexuality with folk culture and his imagination. He provides us with a glimpse of the past as well as its relevance to understanding the contemporary world.

## Conclusion

Karnad's fusion of Indian and Western theatrical conventions reflects the story of the *Transposed Heads* in the sense that one body of dramatic structure is joined with another, but dramaturgical conventions go together much more seamlessly than the dismembered heads as we see in Karnad's tale. Hence, even its basis within *Kathasaritsagara* and The *Transposed Heads, Hayavadana* remains a unique expression of one playwright's desire to reflect his own postcolonial identity and heritage rather than using either a strictly traditional Indian or Western dramatic style.

## Works Cited

Barry, Peter. *Beginning Theory, An Introduction to Literary and Cultural Theory, 3rd Edition,* Viva Books, New Delhi, 2010.

Carter, Ronald and Michael N. Long. *The Web of Words -Exploring Literature through Language,* Cambridge University Press, 2007.

Hurd, Stella & Linda Murphy. *Success With Languages,* Routledge Study Guides, 2006.

Karnad, Girish, *Hayavadana,* Oxford University Press, 28th Impression, 2011.

Nayar, Pramod, K. *An Introduction to Cultural Studies,* Viva Books Pvt. Ltd., 2011.

Said, Edward, W. *Orientalism,* Penguin Books, 2001.

Woolf, Judith, *Writing About Literature,* Routledge, 2005.

Young, Tory, *Studying English Literature,* Cambridge University Press, 2009.

## 20

# Attitude of a Patriarchal Society towards a Woman in the Plays of Girish Karnad

— Madhavi S. Paul

Indian society is not an individualistic society, and especially in the case of a woman her claim to individuality is out of question. The emphasis is more on duty than on individuality, and the resultant effect is repression of individuality.

In the rigidly-formed and tradition-bound societies like India the repression one has to put up with is usually very severe and the resultant suffering often assumes pathetic proportions for sensitive individuals. Among Indians again the women happen to be the worst sufferers as the social norms and moral codes have been so framed as to be particularly disadvantageous to them. (Rajeshwar 1995: 141)

Society can never accept or come to terms with a woman strong enough to be assertive and independent, and even if it does accept a woman as the leader it does so grudgingly and after much ado. A woman can either be a slave or a goddess but never an equal. This extreme in attitude of a patriarchal society towards a woman reveals an inherent fear of feminity which is the ultimate authority in the Indian psyche as represented through the glorification of the 'mother'.

We are born whole human beings, but gender-based division of labour breaks us into male and female fragments. Each fragment retains only half of the human potential. The retained part overgrows to compensate for the other part which remains underdeveloped. These two polarized, deformed fragments are called men and women. These gender deformities are thus caused and gradually 'canonized' by socio cultural programming of sex roles. They are glorified and children are trained to attain them through socialization since their birth. The plight of Hindu women is peculiar. A Hindu wife is honoured as a mother to bear progeny for her husband and as a partner to him in performing religious rites. She cannot thus even think of sex as she feels completely exhausted by the end of the day.

Through this form, Karnad has opened up a dialogue on certain key issues that have plagued mankind since primeval times – they are issues such as fidelity, the appropriateness of parental authority, and the tussle between the Apollonian and Dionysian approaches to life. Karnad makes use of history and legend to throw light on the contemporary problems. Gender deformity not only makes men and women incomplete human beings but enslaves them to the exploitative and oppressive society. Men are exploited and oppressed in the society while women are exploited and oppressed in the house. Men are content with their power in the house while women are content with their power over children and daughters-in-law. Like men, women are also divided and hierarchized class-wise and relation-wise. This causes alienation and antagonism between the women of the higher rungs (rich/higher castes/mothers-in-law) and those of the lower rungs (poor/lower castes/daughters-in-law). Men and women imbibe the exploitative and oppressive culture and perpetuate it. So, they realize the reality. They blame one another for their miserable life and quarrel among themselves. But they are not united and do not collectively try to eradicate the morbid culture that brought about this pathetic state.

Girish Karnad, the well-known Kannada playwright, goes back to myths and legends with a view of making them a vehicle of a new vision. By exploiting the various myths, he shows the absurdity of modern life with all its elemental passions and conflicts, and man's eternal struggle to achieve perfection.

The plays of Karnad highlight some social problems faced especially by women and lower caste people subjected since ancient time by patriarchy or upper hierarchy of the society. *Yayati, Hayavadana, Nagamandala, The Fire and the Rain* etc. amply exemplify the above notion.— Devayani, Sharmishtha and Chitralekha in *Yayati*, Kapila and Padmini in *Hayavadana*, Rani and Kurudavva in *Nagamandala*, Nitilai and Vishakha in *The Fire and the Rain.*

Karnad as a cultural administrator goes beyond this and attempts to provide them their due space and defy the traditional hierarchies prevalent in Indian society. The play *Yayati* is devoted to the study of the decision of the patriarchal social set-up that expects women to surrender to the will of the male decision makers without protest. Karnad also lays bare the class-caste-race conflict in the play, the issue of the perpetuation of slavery upon a race of people. The issue of gender also receives the playwright's attention. It is highlighted especially in manner Yayati treats the women in the play.

Girish Karnad's *Yayati* retells the age-old story of the mythological king who in his longing for eternal youth sought to borrow the vitality of his own son. Karnad has borrowed the myth from the *Mahabharata* and other *Puranas*. In the original *Mahabharata* story, Yayati was one of the six sons of king Nahusha. Devayani, whose love for Kacha remained unrequited, marries Yayati to spite Sharmishtha for whom she nurses childhood jealousy. Sharmishtha is deeply in love with Yayati and subjects herself to a lot of physical and mental torture for love. A son is born to her out of her clandestine liaison with Yayati. Yayati blinded by his insatiable thirst for sensual pleasures dreads old age of his father. Enlightened now, Yayati gives up the throne and retires to forest to lead a life of renunciation with Devayani and Sharmishtha.

*Yayati,* the first play of Karnad which is based on the myth of Yayati in the *Mahabharata,* is highly relevant as far as the socio-psychological study of women is concerned. Devayani, Sharmishtha, Swarnlata and Chitralekha. Devayani, the Queen has to endure every sort of humiliation and becomes insane; Swarnlata is tortured by her husband's unfounded doubts of infidelity, insults and finally deserted; Sharmishtha is an easy prey of Yayati's filthy sexual gratification. Though Chitralekha also faces similar conditions, she emerges as a new woman who boldly challenges the decision of Pooru and false rhetoric of Yayati. She doesn't allow Pooru to enter into her bedroom—who accepts the curse of his father for his moral transgression and becomes old:

> I will not let my husband step back into my bedroom unless he returns a young man (61)

And frankly elaborates the reason of her marriage to Pooru:

> I married him for his youth, for his potential to plant the seed of the Bharatas in my womb. He has lost that potency now. He doesn't possess any of the qualities for which I married him. But you do. (65-66).

Yayati abuses her for these piercing words, "whore" (66). She defies everything i.e. kingdom and high reputation of Bharat dynasty and wants "room" for her. She smiles defiantly and swallows the poison and dies. She prefers to die rather than yield before old conventions and assigned roles set for woman. Her death endorses new woman's quest for emancipation. Sharmishtha precisely explains the condition of women:

> A woman dead (Chitralekha), another gone mad (Devayani), and a third in danger of her life (Sharmishtha). (68).

Jealousy and racial conflict also weakens their lot. It is simultaneously a story, a social satire and the psychological study of a woman. It is a comment on blind faith devoid of any reason.

Women are oppressed and exploited more than men in our society as it remains culturally patriarchal in spite of democracy. Women bear and bring up children: do all the house work and some of them do jobs additionally. Yet they are considered a debit to the family. They are ill-treated and tortured by their husbands and in-laws for various reasons. The theme of disillusionment and alienation in *Yayati* which Karnad works out in the person and career of the central character of the play, finds another effective symbol in Pooru, who is transformed from a symbol of the virtues of filial obedience into an embodiment of the modern wasteland experience. His agonizing search for identity and its frustration offer a starting contrast to the perfect integration of values in Sharmishtha, which makes her the best representative of tradition in the play. The tragedy of Yayati is that he shows neither strong convictions of Sharmishtha nor the total lack of them in Pooru. Even after of penance Yavakri fails miserably to control his lust for vengeance. He fails to vanquish jealousy, hatred and lust.

The issue of gender also receives the playwright's attention. It is highlighted especially in manner Yayati treats the women in the play. The play examines the issues of caste and race. It also questions the patriarchal moral code of our society in which there is an attempt to keep the wife isolated and out of the external world. The husbands try to exert their monopoly over their wives in various ways and when they feel that they have failed to retain their absolute hold over their wives' physical and emotional selves they get emotionally charged and destructive. Sex for these men is a tool, which can be used to avenge and take revenge. In the play Karnad tries to fathom the mystery of evils residing within human beings. He is not interested in the external evils, but the evils residing within man himself.

Girish Karnad's next play *Hayavadana,* Padmini belongs to a family of leading merchant of Pavana Veethi of Dharmapura. She camouflages love of Devadatta; his poetry gets new charm and vitality. She is so fascinating that Devadatta finds her:

> "Beyond my wildest dreams" (14) and swears "if I ever get her as my wife, I will sacrifice my two arms to the goddess Kali; I'll sacrifice my head to Lord Rudra..." (14).

Even Kapila finds "Yakshini, Shakuntala, Urvashi, Indumati—all rolled into one" (16) and warns Devadatta:

> She is not for the likes of you. What she needs is a man of steel. (19).

While talking to Padmini Kapila rightly says:

> I know what you want, Padmini. Devadatta's clever head and Kapila's strong body. (38).

The fact is soon discovered—her temptation to Kapila's muscular body; she is real Padmini of Vatsayana: She has the capacity of complete experience Karnad has described her situation through the symbols in the female chorus. The end of the play is very interesting. The two friends are dead after dual and Padmini performs a sati. It is not a tragic end. It applies somewhat absurd meaning to the alarms. It is very well to say that one cannot have all these qualities in one man, but does it mean that one should not be satisfied with one man? Should a woman hunt after for many virtues, excellent one but for some and yet all difference? Karnad dismisses the quest for perfection on the one hand and on the other pleads for its continuity what probably. The world is indifferent to the desires and frustration, joys and sorrows of human beings.

Padmini's plight suggests woman's vain attempt to unite man as intellect and as flesh in order to further her creative purpose. But these two aspects of the masculine personality are basically at war with each other and hence the attempt ends **disastrously in destruction for both woman and man. Integration cannot be achieved by trying to reconcile the irreconcilable, but by accepting cheerfully the fundamental disharmony is human life. Girish Karnad successfully pictures Padmini's thirst for** completeness, for perfection in *Hayavadana*. Probably what Karnad tries to reveal through Padmini is the predicament of a modern, free and bold woman who is torn between the two polarities, a woman who loves her husband as well as someone else for two different aspects of their personalities Padmini, after the exchange of heads, had felt that she had the best of both men, but slowly reality surfaces. A civilized Apollonian society and its modal code will not accept such a woman. The two men will not accept each other when it comes to sharing a woman and all the three will destroy themselves in the process.

A very significant portion of the play is devoted to the study of the decision of the patriarchal social set-up that expects women to surrender to the will of the male decision makers without protest. The play examines the issues of caste and race. It also questions the patriarchal moral code of our society in which there is an attempt to keep the wife isolated and out of the external world. The husbands try to exert their monopoly over their wives in various ways and when they feel that they have failed to retain their absolute hold over their wives' physical and emotional selves they get emotionally charged and destructive. Sex for these men is a tool, which can be used to avenge and take revenge.

Karnad, in *The Fire and the Rain*, looks at the contentious issues of women in India. Karnad takes up this challenge by juxtaposing female oppression with that of caste. He does not allow the problems to remain incomplete and inconclusive. The play's triumph lies in the treatment of the politics of difference that underlies the paradigms of gender and caste. Self-control is the first step to spiritual realization. The message of the play is that all miseries and wretchedness are the tragic outcome of our submission to evil desires and the most tragic aspect of our life is that instead of using knowledge to conquer evils, we use knowledge to boost and nourish evil desires, passions and appetites which can produce nothing but discord and wretchedness. Karnad constructs a story of passion, loss, and sacrifice in the contexts of

Vedic rituals, spiritual discipline, social and ethical differences between human agents, and interrelated forms of performance still close to their moments of origin, yet the treatment of feminine world, images of women, their subjection and changing status is not less remarkable. Vishakha, an archetypal character and Nitilai, Karnad's invention symbolize the subalternity of women that has been highlighted by the playwright exposing the ugliness in our society restricting their place and creativity in human society.

Vishakha and Nitilai belong to two different socio-cultural backgrounds in *The Fire and the Rain.* Vishakha is the wife of Paravasu, a brahmin, and daughter-in-law of Raibhya, a learned ascetic whereas Nitilai hails from a tribal community. Despite cultural polarities, both experience similar socio-psychological taboos and restrictions and feel bounded. For Nitilai, subjection is more intense—apart from patriarchy her inferior position in social hierarchy deteriorates her standing in the society.

Vishakha loves Yavakri but his decision to get knowledge directly from Gods initiates him into ten years' penance leaves Vishakha helpless, alienated—"sick of silence" (141) and deeply frustrated. Subsequently, she is married to Paravasu who offers up Vishakha's life, first to his sensual appetite and then to his lust for fame.The meeting of Vishakha with her former lover Yavakri infuriates Raibhya who grabs her by her hair and start beating and kicking her. She is condemned as "whore" (127) and "bitch" (138) thereafter left to be handled by her husband. She is an easy prey to Raibhya's anger over his rejection as the Chief Priest by the king. He creates Brahma Raksha to kill Yavakri. Vishakha is bold and acknowledges her meeting with Yavakri before her husband candidly. Nitilai, a tribal girl of 14 loves Arvasu, a brahmin of 18. Both work in a troupe. She is exposed to face the world and know how cruel and ruthless it can be. Only Andhak appreciates their love; the elders of Nitilai's tribe are anxious to interrogate Arvasu. Hers is a romantic love, a world of teenage phantasies ignorant from caste and cultural distinctions. On the contrary, Raibhya condemns her as "savage" (126). When

Arvasu fails to appear before Council of tribal Elders; they decreed,

> Nitilai will marry another boy—of our own tribe (135).

She is handed over to a tribal boy and married against her wishes. She has no say. Her protest touches climax when she runs away from her husband, family and everything for the sake of love. But, as an Indian married woman, she doesn't want to cuckold her husband. She transcends from petty sexual gratification and romantic love and develops pious relationship with Arvasu. Nittilai's brother and husband chase her like hounds. She is frightened of their evil designs. She is offered a ghastly death despite her innocence:

> the husband pulls out a knife, grabs Nitilai by her hair and slashes her throat in one swift motion. He then lets her drop....
>
> She lies there, her eyes open, bleeding, dying like a sacrificial animal. (172).

The killing of Nitilai endorses still today patriarchy and long established social conventions are strong enough to crush women's liberty or any kind of adventurism. But the quest of the woman for emancipation has started.

Karnad's last play *Nagamandala* is based on two oral tales from Karnataka – the tale of Flames which comments on the paradoxical nature of oral tales and the tale of Rani who is treated as a dumb member either in the joint family of her father or her husband. She has neither voice nor choice of her own. In the empty house Rani is locked in, symbolizes the chain of restrictions placed round woman which denies even her legitimate rights and hinders her natural growth even today.

Karnad's *Nagamandala* is a sociological study of Indian women; richly textured dramatic transmutation of two folk tales of Karnataka usually narrated by women while feeding children in the kitchen. It not only exposes the ugliness of a society where woman is considered "second sex", "other", "subject", women are taught in the process of being socialized, to internalize the reigning patriarchal ideology, e.g., male superiority; and so conditioned to derogate their own sex and to cooperate in their own subordination. Patriarchal dominance has prevented women from realizing their productive and creative possibility. The play also suggests remedial measures and slaps the orthodox society by an act of reconciliation between Rani and Naga.

Karnad was well acquainted with feminist ideologies and the havoc wrought by patriarchal ideologies in Indian society. In *Naga-Mandala* Rani—the female protagonist, and Kurudavva—the other female character, both are generic, represent the extreme physical torture and mental trauma, struggle for their identity as a woman, as a wife, and as a mother. Four Flames, Story, and the Man also reflect the sufferings and exploitations of women. Rani is treated in a slavish manner, imprisoned like a caged bird, neither is she allowed talking to outsider nor outsider is allowed to do the same. Despite her chastity and fidelity, she is forced to face the Naga Ordeal. Appanna (Rani's husband), Naga (Cobra), Dog, Mongoose, Three Village Elders and the orthodox society have been used as the forces of subjection. Rani's acceptance of Naga as her own is a curt reply to the question of extra-marital relation in which only males are allowed to go freely, even after getting married, to concubine (as Appanna does) whereas the yardstick of morality is imposed upon women. The Prologue introduces Four Flames, which are animated, symbolic representations employed to report the sufferings of women. The tragic sufferings of women are extended to other female character, e.g., Kurudavva, who is an example of wisdom and philanthropy.

Nobody in the society has eyes to see Rani's laceration at the hands of her philandering husband, but blind Kurudavva alone can see the truth. She extends motherly love and care to Appanna as well as to Rani. She is also the victim of orthodox society where the role of a woman is subservient and marginalized. Except her son Kappanna, there is none to look after her. Even the Village Elders treat her cruelly and unsympathetically while she has lost her only son. *Naga- Mandala*, Karnad commented, express: A distinctly woman's understanding of the reality around her, a lived counter point to the patriarchal structure of classical texts and institutions. The position of Rani in the story of Nagamandala, for instance, can be seen as a metaphor for the situation of a young girl in the bosom of a joint family where she sees her husband only in two unconnected roles—as a stranger during the day and as lover at night. Inevitably, the pattern of relationships she is forced to weave from these disjointed encounters must be something of a fiction. The empty house Rani is locked in could be the family she is married into. (Introduction to *Three Plays: Naga Mandala, Hayavadana, Tughlaq* 17)

By peeling off layers of behavioral traits gradually, Karnad lays bare the class-caste-race conflict in the play. Rani's situation is exactly this. So she is a simple, innocent and ignorant girl. She has grown physically but not matured mentally, she, therefore, behaves as a frightened child in Appanna's presence. Naga gives her love, enjoyment and some education too; so her personality grows. Consequently the little, helpless, diffident girl, she gets transformed into a confident and courageous lady.

*Naga-Mandala* is not only about the male difficulty to trust and love women, but also transcend his narcissism. It seems to be about the socialization process of both men and women, particularly in the Indian society where marriage is, more often than not, the first experience of sex and love for most people. The transition from childhood into adolescence, and then into adult roles has, in India, very different stages and psychological and cultural relationships than in other less tradition-bound societies. *Nagamandala* probes into the female growth into selfhood, and their mature adjustment with the social roles appointed for them by the traditional society.

The play examines the issues of adultery and chastity and questions the patriarchal moral code which believes in the loyalty of a woman to her husband but not in the fidelity of a man to his wife. No hue and cry is raised when Appanna commits adultery openly and intentionally whereas Rani, who commits adultery unknowingly, is compelled to face the trial.

*Nagamandala* is a feminist play. It questions and exposes the gender-biased values and morals of patriarchy which oppressed women for ages. This is effectively done by juxtaposing Appanna and Rani at the village court. Appanna enjoys extra-marital sex openly and unashamedly whereas Rani sleeps with Naga who assumes the form of Appanna. Everybody knows Appanna's relation with his concubine, yet the village Elders tries Rani's case only. Thus, the play uncovers the injustice of the patriarchal moral code which demands the faithfulness of a woman to her husband but not the faithfulness of a man to his wife. Indian culture considers marriage to be the supreme boon of a woman because it offers her salvation through her service to her husband. For her, chastity is superior and preferable to life. This reduces her to a non- living commodity that her father offers as a gift Kanyadan to a man in marriage. She is denied love, enjoyment and education which are indispensable to the growth of her personality. She cannot thus even think of sex as she feels completely exhausted by the end of the day. Therefore Appanna in *Naga-Mandala* visits his concubine though Rani, his wife, is very beautiful. To be cultured, both men and women develop the faculty of adaptation to cultured (but not to Nature,) while suppressing that of spontaneity and so neither enjoys life. Nurturing and intuition help women perform their culturally allotted function, child rearing and house-keeping while controlling and rationality help men perform their culturally allotted function, bread-earning. Adaptation to culture and the lack of spontaneity make both of them obedient to their masters. Thus, men and women have become different, except in their obedience. These differences cause alienation and antagonism between men and women. So, they find each other mysterious and hostile.

The Indian society always follows the 'Manu-Sanskriti.' Women were always given a secondary status for many centuries. They were treated as an instrument in the so-called male dominated society. The real identity of women as an individual remained neglected. Many Indian writers through various literary forms focused this problem. India being a most populous and backward country the attempts made by other writers to focus the issue proved to be of little help. The plays of Girish Karnad staged in Karnataka and after translation in English and the telecasting have proved to be very much influential. All these plays deal with realistic social problems.

## Works Cited

Babu. Sarat, 'The Concept of Chastity and Nagamandala', *The Plays of Girish Karnad: Critical Perspectives,* ed. Jaydipsinh Dodiya, New Delhi: Prestige Books, 1999.

Barry Peter, 'Psychoanalytic Criticism', *Beginning Theory: An Introduction to Literary and Cultural Theory,* New York: Manchester University Press, 2007.

Chandran, S. Subhash. "'*Bali: The Sacrifice*' and Dionysian Life Assertion." *Girish Karnad's Plays: Performance and Critical Perspectives,* ed. Tutun Mukherjee, Delhi: Pencraft International, 2006. 294–303.

Gupta,Santosh 'Nagamandala: A Story of Marriage and Love', *The Plays of Girish Karnad: Critical Perspectives,* ed. Jaydipsinh Dodiya, New Delhi: Prestige Books, 1999.

Karnad, Girish. *Yayati.* trans. (Hindi) B.R. Narayana. Delhi: Radhakrishna Prakashan, 2001.

Mukherjee, Tutun. "In His Own Voice: A Conversation with Girish Karnad", *Girish Karnad's Plays: Performance and Critical Perspectives.* ed. Mukherjee. 27-57.

Rajeshwar M, 'The Inner World of Indian Women: Neurotic Characters of Indian Women Novelists', *Feminism and Literature,* ed. Veena Noble Dass, New Delhi: Prestige Books, 1995.

Yadava. Raju, "Race and Gender in *Yayati,*" *Girish Karnad's Plays: Performance and Critical Perspectives.* ed. Mukherjee. 80-87.

# 21

# Rani's Empowerment in Girish Karnad's *Naga-Mandala*

— S. Somasundari Latha

In our patriarchal society women are considered as inferior. They are known as the 'other'. Women are confined to home and they are kept in absolute ignorance. This helps men to rule them. Man is the centre of power. Both within and outside home men try to dominate over women. There is not much difference between wood and women. Women are treated by the society in two extremes. Either they will be treated as ignorant and inferior or as a goddess. But society fails to realize that they are ordinary human beings with feelings and emotions. In a male-chauvinist society a wife has so much responsibilities and so many restrictions. She is expected to be loyal to her husband though he may have a concubine. The wife cannot question her husband about his infidelity. She cannot have a separate identity. She is destined to live under the shadow of her husband. Shashi Deshpande in her novel *The Dark Holds No Terrors* says how the wife is expected to walk a few steps behind her husband.

> A wife must always be a few feet behind her husband. Women's magazines will tell you that a marriage should be an equal partnership. That's nonsense. Rubbish. No partnership can be equal. It will always be unequal, but take care uthat it's unequal in favour of your husband. If the scales tilt in your favour, god help you, both of you.
>
> (*The Dark Holds No Terror.*135)

Feminism is born because of the belief that women are treated unfairly. The term 'feminism' was first used by the French dramatist Alexander Dumas, the younger, in 1872 in a pamphlet L'Homme-femme. Radical feminism emphasizes patriarchal roots of inequality between men and women. It focuses women's oppression as they are dominated by men. Suppression of women is a social stigma. Simone de Beavoir in *The Second Sex* (1949) observes the asymmetry between man and woman in as much as man inclusively refers to the human, while woman is the other.

Girish Karnad's *Nagamandala* delineates the subjugation of woman and how she becomes empowered and finds her fulfillment. Girish Karnad, the prominent post-independent playwright was born in Matheran, Maharashtra. He got his bachelor degree from Karnataka college Dharwad. Then he went to England and studied at Lincoln and Magdalen colleges in Oxford as a Rhodes Scholar, earned Master of Arts in philosophy, Political Science and Economics. He worked for Oxford University press for seven years (1963-70) and served as Director of Film and Television institute of India (1974-75). He was the chairman of the Sangeet Natak Akademi (1988-93). He established himself as a popular playwright with his Tughlaq. He wrote his plays in Kannada and he himself translated all his plays into English. When he was in Chicago as visiting professor and a Fullbright in 1987-88, his *Nagamandala* was staged at the Guthrie theatre in Minneapolis.

*Nagamandala* (play with a cobra) is based on the oral tales Girish Karnad heard from A.K Ramanujan. In the author's introduction he says: "These tales are narrated by women- normally the older women in the family – while children are being fed in the evenings in the kitchen or being put to bed. The other adults present on these occasions are also women. Therefore these tales, though directed at the children, often serve as a parallel system of communication among the women in the family."[1]

Rani, the central character in *Nagamandala,* marries Appanna and comes to her husband's house, expecting love and concern. To her disappointment, Appanna is indifferent towards her, keeps her inside the house and locks the door outside and visits the concubine. He comes home only to have lunch. He not even talks to his wife. Since his parents are no more, Rani finds it difficult to be all alone in the house. Rani who is the only favourite child of her parents gets scared to be alone in the house. When she expresses her fear to Appanna, "Listen - I feel frightened - alone at night" (28) But he doesn't care her words.

Kurudavva, a blind woman, is the friend of Appanna's mother. Her son Kappanna carries her on his shoulders to Appanna's house since she is eager to see Appanna's wife. To her dismay, Appanna's house locked but they find Rani inside. She feels pathetic about Rani's being caged like a bird inside the house, and offers her magical roots in order to lure Appanna. Love between husband and wife is a natural Phenomenon and is inevitable for a happy married life. Rani's longing for her husband's love depicts women's plight in our society. When the matrimony demands mutual love between partners, what is the necessity to use spell?

Rani, the dedicated wife is scared to give the potion of cooked roots to her husband thinking it may cause his death and pours the liquid into the nearing anthill. Like the queen Titania in *The Midsummer Night's Dream* who falls in love with Bottom, a man with an ass head because of the love-juice called 'Love in Idleness', the king Cobra, comes out from the anthill and on seeing Rani, it falls in love with her.

The cobra takes the shape of Appanna and enters into Rani's bedroom and provides her with all bliss and happiness which her conjugal life fails to give. Though Rani finds her husband to be rude and loveless in the afternoon but kind and affectionate in the night, she is not shrewd enough to discover the truth. This is the plight of women in the joint family system.The split in the male figure between the sullen husband by day and the passionate lover by night is of course, a comment on how women perceive their partners in a cloistered system of unequal marriage.[2]

In Indian mythology cobra represents male gender. D. Kirtinath Kurtkoti observes:

> Myth and folk tales in a patriarchal society represent primarily the male conscious forces and wishes and are patriarchal constructs and man-oriented. [3]

Rani is confused by the indifference of her husband in the day and the affection and concern of him at night. She convinces her by saying that it may be an imagination or a dream that her husband spends his night with her. But as a woman she needs the gentle touch of her husband at night. She bursts out to Naga (cobra) with tears in her eyes:

> Rani: why do you tease me like this? I am sick of being alone. And then tonight, I was terrified you might not come – that what I remembered from last night may be just a dream. I was desperate that you should come again tonight. But what am I to say if you spin riddles like this? (42)

But Naga suppresses her by instructing not to ask him the reason.

> Naga: I am afraid that is how it is going to be. Like that during day, like this at night. Don't ask me why.(43)

How woman loses her reasoning capacity and intellect by becoming emotional in her dealing with man is well depicted in Rani's immediate acceptance of not to look out of the window after Naga leaves her house at night. The inferior status of women is revealed in her saying: "No, I won't. The pig, the whale, the eagle – none of them asks why. So I won't either" (45). It is beyond her capacity to comprehend the situation since she needs Naga's love and concern, she completely abandons her intuition and enjoys Naga's company. Ramanujan observes:

> Rani's emotional relationship with the cobra culminates with the awakening of her consciousness. Her spiritual, emotional, intellectual, physical integration is caused by cobra and she is a liberated woman.[4]

Appanna's violent reaction to Rani's pregnancy brings to light the differences in norms and codes for women in the society. While Appanna publicly questions his wife's chastity, there is no one to question about Appanna's extra-marital relationship. The village panchayat which has proposed a test to prove her chastity, fails to suggest any punishment for Appanna's sin. Except Kurudavva no one understands Rani's difficulty and offers any help. When Rani is given the option to choose between red-hot iron or the Snake Ordeal, Rani chooses the latter as she is instructed by Naga. Rani's claim: "I have not done anything wrong. I am not guilty of anything. What shall I plead guilty to?" (56) reveals her maturity and the blind follower of Naga's words. Rani's ordeal reminds us of Sita's Fire Ordeal in *Ramayana*. It is a tradition that only women are expected to be pure and are tested for chastity. There is no code of conduct for men. Manchi Sarat Babu observes:

> Marriage to be the supreme boon of a woman because it offers her "Salvation though her service' to her husband. For that woman 'chastity is superior and preferable to life'.[5]

It is unbelievable that the cobra slides over Rani's shoulder and moves over it like a garland when she plunges her hand into the ant-hill by swearing that he has not touched any other man except her husband and the king cobra. Karnad exploits the belief of the people by having the Snake Ordeal. Taking Rani as goddess incarnate, everyone falls at her feet and worships her. Though this appears to be dramatic, Appanna knows the truth that there is no physical union between him and his wife. He is not able to bear Rani being glorified by the villager as a divine woman.

> Elder: Appanna, your wife is not an ordinary woman. She is a goddess incarnate. Don't grieve that you judged her wrongly and treated her badly. That is how Goddesses reveal themselves to the world. You were the chosen instrument for revealing her divinity. (59)

Now Appanna is in an embarrassing situation. No one is willing to believe his words. P. Dhanavel says: "Appanna begins to suspect his own sanity, when the elders convince him that Rani is the mother Goddess". In Nathaniel Hawthorn's *The Scarlet Letter*, only the female protagonist Hester Prynne is punished for adultery but not the male partner Arthur Dimmesdale. Though man is the equal partner in adultery, he can be let free. But in *Nagamandala*, Girish Karnad treats the adulterous woman with high esteem. Sathya Dev observes Karnad to be the only playwright in the history of Indian theatre to have treated adultery as normal and treated adulterous woman sympathetically. [7]

On seeing Rani's glory Appanna's concubine feels ashamed of herself and willing to do menial work in Rani's house. By giving birth to a son, Rani becomes a complete woman. She gets whatever she wishes for. Karnad proves himself as a gifted dramatist by not ending the play with this but giving two different endings and leave it to the choice of the reader. Shubhangi S. Raykar observes:

> Usually the idea of a play incubates in his mind for a long time and it is only when the total action of the play is clearly before his mind's eye, then he starts writing a play. [8]

Rani's wish to make her son light the fire for the cobra's cremation shows that she realises the truth. Cleverly Rani confesses the truth that her son has been given the gift of life by the Cobra, as by a father (63). Unlike traditional women, she does not have the sense of guilt. She not even feels tensed but coolly says: "Oh! Poor thing, it is dead!" (63). In the second ending, Rani protects the cobra from being killed by Appanna and asks it to stay in the tresses of her hair for ever. Appanna has to nod his head for whatever she says. Rani has a devoted husband, son and life-long servant to do menial work. She realises her self and attains fulfilment in her marriage life. She is a liberated woman. Maren Lockoo Carden opines:

> The new Feminism is not about the elimination of differences between the sexes; nor even simply the achievement of equal opportunity; it concerns the individual right to find out the kind of person he or she is and to strive to become that person. [9]

Women are considered as torch-bearers of culture. They are burdened with the responsibility to preserve Indian culture and heritage. In the Indian context women remain to be chaste, modest, obedient and loyal.[10] They are the victims of social taboos. In Arundhati Roy's *The God of Small Things*, both brother and sister, Chacko and Ammu have sexual relationship after breaking their marriage and getting a divorce. Ammu is condemned to die a lonely death because of her sexual relationship but her brother is permitted to fulfil his sexual needs with any number of women he likes.

Indian women are no longer ignorant. After Independence there is gradually a change in their attitude. The education they receive gives them the necessary àwareness about their position in the society. The exposure to Western culture educates them about the significance of their individuality, self, identity, rights and needs. Like Rani in *Nagamandala,* women are conscious of their needs and aspire for fulfilment in life. Girish Karnad drives home the changes in the attitude of the women by fusing Indian traditional theatre elements and Western sensibility. M.K. Naik observes:

> His (Girish Karnad) plays have pioneered a style, which unites the elements of traditional Indian theatre, such as 'Yakshagana" and strikingly modern sensibility for contemporary socio-political realities.[11]

Girish Karnad engages in demystifying the old belief and interpreting the oral tradition in order to depict the 'metamorphasis' women have underdone in our society.

P. Dhanavel opines emphasizes Karnad's humanism, derived mainly from his profound concern for the "oppressed" and the "downtrodden", his compulsive return to and reinterpretation of the mythical past and oral tradition, and his "determined demystification of the dominant beliefs and practices". [12] Girish Karnad breaks the barriers of the society by portraying Rani as an emancipated and empowered woman, and strives to end women's subjugation and subordination.

## References


1. Girish Karnad, *Three Plays: Nagamandala, Hayavadana & Tughlaq.* NewDelhi: Oxford University Press, 1994. pp.16-17
2. A.K.Ramanujan, Towards a counter system: Women's tales in *The Collected Essays.* Ed. Vinay Dharwadker. NewDelhi:OUP, 1000. p.445
3. D.Kirtinath Kurtoti, *Contemporary Indian Drama: Indian Drama (A Collection of Papers)* Ed. Annaiag Gowda. Mysore: Literary Press, 1974. p.32.
4. A. K. Ramanujan:'Telling Tales'. *Daedalus* (Fall): 255.
5. Manchi Sarat Babu, *Indian Drama Today: A Study in the Theme of Cultural Deformity.* New Delhi: Prestige Books, 1997. p. 37.
6. P. Dhanavel, *The Indian Imagination of Girish Karnad: Essays on Hayavadana.* New Delhi: Prestige Books, 2000. p. 24.
7. Girish Karnad (1995), Performance, Meaning, and the Materials of Modern Indian Theatre: Interview by Aparna Dharwadker. *New Theatre Quarterly,* 11. 44: 358.
8. Shubangi S. Raykar, "The Development of Girish Karnad as a Dramatist: Hayavadana." *Studies in Contemporary Indian Drama.* Ed. Sudhakar Pandey and Ferya Taraporewala. New Delhi Prestige Books, 1990. p. 46.
9. Maren Lockoo Carden, *The New Feminist Movement.* New York: Russel Sage Foundation, 1971. p. 2.
10. Mrs. Sharmili Raju, *Feminist Angles of Indian Female Writers.* New Delhi: Chand and co, 2001. p. 1.
11. M. K Naik. "From the Horse's Mouth: A Study of *Hayavadana".* *Dimensions of Indian English Literature.* New Delhi: Sterling Publishers pvt Ltd, 1984. p.73.
12. P. Dhanavel, op.cit, p. 11.

## 22

# Dialogues on Gender: A Study of Girish Karnad's *Hayavadana* and Habib Tanvir's *Charandas Chor*

— **Deepali Rajshekhar Patil**

Girish Karnad's *Hayavadana* and Habib Tanvir's *Charandas Chor* are plays that proved to be milestones in the Indian theatre. These plays remain significant contributions to the dialogue on gender because they embody several issues and principles largely beyond the trajectory of the realist drama. Primarily, the women in these plays exhibit the boldness to transcend the ethical norms pre-determined by society and assert themselves as seductive as well as desiring females. The unbridled lust in these women attests their non-conformism and disrupts the notions of propriety.

Another common chord that binds these works together is the success the women achieve in asserting their individuality as a result of uninhibited physical desire. The forbidden object of desire seems to cast a magical spell and substitutes the husband in these plays, usually in the guise of the husband or is sought after as a suitable mate. Surprisingly, the women do not owe fidelity to a 'particular male' namely husband, conversely challenging the principle of male proprietorship.

In a country that glorifies motherhood and romanticizes the maternal role, the conceptual fertility in plays such as Hayavadana manifestly detaches itself from the constraints of marital commitment. It is interesting to explore this journey of illegitimate passion to acquire the proscribed objects that establishes the self-absorbed, indulgent nature of the women in these plays. Although the plays most conspicuously depict femininity, sexuality, desire and power; the stranglehold of patriarchy is not ultimately released. It is chiefly the exercise of the ambivalent freedom within the restrictions of patriarchy that forms the subversive thematic elements of these plays.

Based on the conventional story of "The Heads that Got Switched" from *Kathasaritasagara and* modern literary source of Thomas Mann's philosophical tale of *The Transposed Heads* (1940), Girish Karnad offers a beautiful blend of premodern and modern sources that are inextricably transformed to a fully developed parable about conjugality, illicit desire, an "accidental" interference of identity and ensuing crisis which can be resolved only by death. The play's originality springs from the reflexive frames Karnad constructs for the story and the thematic force of its representation of femininity, desire and the treatment of irremediable issues of identity. The story of Devadatta (the well-begotten one), Kapila (the dark one), and Padmini (the lotus woman) reaches complex dimensions when an innocent gesture of Padmini alters her personal world forever. She mistakenly attaches the wrong head to each body and the incongruity sets in. In the human world of Devadatta and Kapila, transposition offers a symbolic but temporary solution to the problem of mind/body dualism. For a brief period of time, Devadatta-Kapila possesses the ideal mind as well as the ideal body, while the other hybrid being, Kapila-Devadatta, is deficient in both respects. Nevertheless, when each man's body reverts to its original qualities, the problem of dualism returns, and the human condition appears as basically one of disunity and imperfection. Devadatta and Kapila *do* represent irreconcilable opposites: two men who were perfectly complementary and inseparable when they were separate become mortal foes when they are forcibly joined together. Padmini's self-serving mistake therefore begins a violent struggle within and between these characters that ends only with the ruin of their lives.

The first capricious female described in the play is Hayavadana's mother, who had insisted on choosing an Arab stallion of celestial origin as her husband at her *swayamvara* and had refused to continue her marriage when her husband regained his proper celestial form. Such an exercise of autonomy by women in mythic antiquity is radically incongruent to the patriarchal control of marriage in the contemporary, modern world. Padmini weds the wrong person because her match is negotiated exclusively by men, and she finds no escape from her unsatisfactory union. The female chorus that forms the backdrop to the action further complicates the gender issues by questioning the authority of monogamy: "Why should love stick to the sap of a single body? When the stem is drunk with the thick yearning of the many-petalled, many-flowered lantana, why should it be tied down to the relation of a single flower?" (*Three Plays* 82). Padmini's marriage follows an unusual logic and becomes a labyrinth of conflict. Momentarily she rejoices her sweet success: "Fabulous body-fabulous brain-fabulous Devadatta" (113). Barred from the moment of triumph, the man who now has Kapila's undesirable head and Devadatta's undesirable body complains that it is not right for Padmini to "just go and live with a man who's not her husband", and that her "fancy" cannot be allowed to provide the solution to their problem- but it does. The exchange of men also takes place in a way that is morally problematic but socially inoffensive. "The search of identity in the midst of tangled relationship is the backbone of the play" (Chaturvedi et al in Tiwari 2007:127). The still "respectable" Padmini continues to reap the joys of marriage and privilege of motherhood, the destabilization of patriarchy is all the more plausible because there is no open challenge to it.

> The ambivalence of Padmini's position in the triangular relationships, however, appears in her many challenges to

> masculinity and male friendship, which create frictions contradicting her apparent power. She dominates both men in shrill, shallow way and resents any sign that their mutual bond might override their interest in her
>
> (Dharwadker 2006: 338-9).

Padmini feels cheated and excluded by the men's suicide at the end for she regards those acts as selfish acts. She was responsible to bring them back to life in Kali's temple and ironically she is the one who leads them to their doom by her self-seeking attitude. The forsaken Padmini in her intense grief feels that the men were victorious and she was defeated, yet she feels the prick of her guilt ridden conscience and she voices her anguish by acknowledging her role in their destruction: "If I'd said, 'Yes, I'll live with you both', perhaps they would have been alive yet. But I couldn't say it. I couldn't say 'Yes'. No, Kapila, no, Devadatta— I know it in my blood you couldn't have lived together. You would have had to share not only me but your bodies as well. Because you knew death you died in each other's arms. You could only have lived ripping each other to pieces. I had to drive you to death. You forgave each other, but again- left me out" (130-31). In Karnad's modern fable about marriage, conjugal passion squanders inevitably into disenchantment and produces craving for other illicit relations, although the males try their best to preserve the sanctity of relationships. It must be understood that though women cannot prevent the eventual downfall, they are not merely catalysts but active agents in the ensuing tragedy.

In keeping with the sovereignty of women is Habib Tanvir's *Charandas Chor* which compared to *Hayavadana* corroborates the flexibility of structure and content, being a syncretic and largely oral text fabricated piecemeal to serve the specific needs and talents of Tanvir's company of tribal performers hailing from Chhattisgarh region. Charandas cuts across the parameters of a romantic hero. He is superbly depicted as the ubiquitous yet uncatchable, even when he is confronted by his nemesis. His superb craftsmanship evokes hilarious laughter when he dupes the constable by posing as a cripple and later as god Hanuman. The major core of the action is rather bizarre in that it grants women both sexual and political power but portrays the irreconcilable male and female worlds because of the collision between male chastity and a rapacious female appetite. In sharp contrast to the disorderly, chaotic male world of the first act is the systematic, perfect hold of the beautiful, unmarried, autocratic rani effortlessly ruling over a feudal kingdom in the next act. Charandas trespasses into this world of reversed genders as he desires to reach the pinnacle of his career as a thief and challenge the rani's authority by making a symbolic theft from the royal treasury. The action follows quite a unpredictable course. Tanvir very effectively brings out this transition in the man-woman relationship that deviates from the acceptable ethical codes.

Charandas belongs to an overwhelmingly male world in which he exercises absolute authority as the unscrupulous thief, trickster, disciple of a truth-seeking guru, a charismatic yet vacillating male who also is the protector of the oppressed. His authoritarian demeanor intercepts with rani's absolute monarchy. This strange interlude follows an unpremeditated course.

Charandas succeeds in arousing rani's interest and then her desire as she now looks upon him as an exceptional suitor rather than as an imperfect mate who should be substituted. This unexpected surrender to passion leads her to relinquish her own nature in two significant ways: she readily accepts the role of a vulnerable lover and wife that is followed by her feeble attempts to conceal her emotions and subsequent embarrassment from her male courtiers and subjects.

Unlike other women who would have easily exercised power and control over their male partner, rani's course of love leaves her utterly powerless and saps the vital chords of enthusiasm from her life. Rani is exposed to frustration rather than fulfillment in her quest, not because Charandas is unresponsive toward her, but because his idiosyncratic oaths create the major hurdle in their way. In an unusual manner the obsessive woman is not desired in turn due to the irrationality of male codes.

Charandas' refusal in the garb of a humble peasant to accept the food served in the gold platter heightens the irony of the situation. This symbolic gesture is the harbinger of the later denial by him to accept rani's offer of marriage. It is preposterous even for a maid servant at the court to contemplate about his serious offence. She clearly voices her discontent:

> Servant: How can any man not agree to such a thing? When you ordered him in font of everyone to do certain things he did not agree ... Now when you say a thing like this in private, how can he possibly not accept it?
>
> (*Charandas* 74)

Rani's suffering is further aggravated as not only does Charandas refuse her hand in marriage but also wishes to declare his denial to the world at large. Incidentally even amidst the brief period of courtship, Charandas addresses the rani as "rani dai"- "dai" is a term of respect for an older woman and also refers to a "midwife". With the bitter insight of unrequited love rani relapses from paramour to queen, from the "feminine" back to the "masculine" role. Rani can reinstate order amongst the chaos and gain her own self-esteem only by destroying Charandas, the man she loves dearly.

Like Kapila and Devdatta, Charandas becomes a sacrificial victim, who lays his life at the altar of love. Devdatta and Kapila are more fortunate of the trio considered here, as they at least are blessed with moments of love, though not fidelity. Charandas is the poor victim who has to pay exorbitant price for preserving his male chastity in the face of voluptuous desire. If Kapila and Devdatta die for transgression of ethical codes, Charandas is killed for his conformism to moral codes. Quite curiously in this peculiar battle between a fellowship of ascetic male and sovereign authority of woman, patriarchy becomes immaterial.

*Hayavadana* and *Charandas Chor* exhibit a complete subversion of patriarchy where women topple the male order. 'Sacrifice', 'shame' and 'loyalty' are virtues that define femininity in the Indian context. However both the plays depict women who very easily wreck their own happiness in pursuit of their irrepressible passion. A complete role reversal qualifies the lives in this dramatic universe; men are reluctant and hesitant whereas women are more eager and aspiring to quench their erotic desires. In these plays women seem to exercise absolute power and rule their destinies.

Padmini and Rani however much they try to control their destinies are unable to reverse the patriarchal codes. Momentarily they seem to taste unrestrained bliss and supremacy but unfortunately this joy is short-lived and in the process to catch the fleeting moments of joy they lose their happiness forever. They counteract the rigidity and conformity in every respect but their sexual transgression is an unpardonable offence and once again they are pushed back to the frames of conventional moral codes that govern their lives.

Both the plays implicate that going beyond the threshold of ethical codes could be a momentary relief but can never be an eternal source of happiness. Padmini and Rani are left forlorn to bear their lot and their guilt looms large towards the end. Both feel cheated and betrayed by the men they wish to acquire, but in their attempt to supersede the men, they hardly reckon the consequences. Rani and Padmini are emblematic women who wish to rule their world but become puppets in the hands of the circumstances. Their endless suffering testifies to the fact that regardless of the patriarchal world they belong to, breach of moral conducts calls for nemesis. The newly emancipated women who seek sexual liberty have to pay individual, social price for this deplorable offence. Life becomes a wretched existence for both Padmini and rani without love. Rani may enjoy political autocracy but it comes at the price of emotional deprivation and physical insatiety. Padmini is extinguished by the same flames of desire as she performs the sati. These women have the power to speak, act, and control the fate of men. They become the prize objects for which men willingly or unwillingly sacrifice themselves.

These speculations on man-woman relationships completely changed the psychosexual meanings and challenged the position offered traditionally to women. Such relationships contested the long preserved notions of hierarchy and rendered contemporaniety to gender issues. The plays discussed offer a dialogue and critique on gender issues and project the role of women in an entirely different light that demands serious reconsideration of sexual liberty and the price that is tagged with desire. The women in these plays, self-indulgent and articulate desire men they cannot legitimately have; each one accomplishes her yearning, but only provisionally, and like the queen bee, destroys her male partner in the process. Dharwadker rightly observes, "Such plays as Karnad's *Hayavadana*... and Tanvir's *Charandas chor* establish radically new relations between textual and the performative, the traditional and the contemporary. While adhering to the representational conventions of a ritualistic form, each play develops a serious psychological or socio-political thematic that explores the continuing resonance of myth and ritual in the changed sociopolitical circumstances of the present" (Dharwadker 328).

## Works Cited

Chaturvedi, Roopesh and Dubey Rohini. "Mechanism of Girish Karnad as a Dramatist" in *Contemporary Indian Dramatists*. Ed. Shubha Tiwari. New Delhi: Atlantic Publishers, 2007.

Dharwadker, Aparna. *Theatres of Independence*. New Delhi: Oxford University Press, 2006.

Karnad, Girish. *Three Plays*. Translated by Girish Karnad. New Delhi: Oxford University Press, 1994.

Tanvir, Habib. *Charandas Chor*. New Delhi: Pustakayan, 1997.

23

# The Rise of New Women in the Modern Indian English Drama: A Study of the Plays of Girish Karnad and Mahesh Dattani

— Abhinandan Malas

The modern Indian literature in English has followed a new course in the recent times that has redefined the space of women in Indian society. The presentation of the women in the modern Indian context has revealed several issues in the modern Indian theatrical scenario which are related to society and which are affecting the space occupied by women in society. In the modern Indian literary scenario women are presented as more active, responsive, interactive, discursive, bold and free to express and evaluate themselves in the patriarchal society.

Girish Karnad and Mahesh Dattani have emerged as two major playwrights of modern India who have explored, through their theatrical and thematic innovations, the psychological and social developments of women in India in the modern context. Karnad often presents his characters in the modern context by placing them in the domain of Indian mythology and history. He has borrowed several of his themes from the Indian history and mythology and has introduced several characters which are modified and developed according to the problems that are prevailing in modern India.

Mahesh Dattani, on the other hand, has placed his characters in the present scenario and has dealt with such problems which are occurring in society but are often ignored and suppressed by it. His women characters are more expressive and bold in the physical level than that of Karnad's but in both the playwrights we see the revolutionary ideas and concepts are being presented by them. While Dattani's characters are bold and to a large extent aggressive in their attitude on the physical level, Karnad's characters are generally reserved, sometimes lacking in dynamic action, but are determined, resolute and more forceful on the psychological level that help them in establishing their own identity and create their own space for existence which stand strongly in opposition to the patriarchal oppression thus discovering a horizon for the Indian women to start a new discourse which recognizes the rise of new women who redefine the post-independence literary and social scenario.

In this paper I focus on the development of these new women in the plays of Girish Karnad and Mahesh Dattani and intend to make a comparative study of the two thus examining and exploring the new feminine discourse that has redefined the Indian society and literature as a whole. The Indian feminine discourse creates a new arena through the writings of these two playwrights which establishes the Indian literature on women on new paradigms and reciprocates to and also differentiates itself from the other issues as well. In this paper I also focus on how the of women presented in the plays of these two dramatists interact with other problematic issues that are also presented in these plays and how the latter are influenced by the former as well.

Women play a very significant role in presenting human psychology, class conflict, ideological problems and the demarcation of the line of its conflict with the patriarchal society which are depicted in the plays of Karnad and Dattani. In Karnad the feminine discourse runs mostly on the psychological level where the inner sexual and personal desires are expressed through the development of some situations that largely reflect the outward manifestation of the unconscious of the female character. In such instances we see that the development of the plot and the action of the play are controlled by the female desire which negates the presence and influence of the patriarchal society and creates a new space where the feminine discourse exhibits a free play of ideologies and concepts that are independent of the influences of phallogocentrism and in turn dominates the male discourse and modifies it according to its own need.

Karnad's *Hayavadana* and *Nagamandala* are the prominent examples in the instance. Both these plays deal with the outward manifestation and presentation of the female unconscious that contains the feminine libido that forces the male discourse to get modified according to its own need. The action and the development of the conflict takes place basically on the psychological level which are presented through apt and subtle development of the mysterious atmosphere and the milieu of magic realism that develop and secure the space for the feminine discourse to proliferate.

In both Padmini (*Hayavadana*) and Rani (*Naga-Mandala*) we get the new woman who transcends the barrier of patriarchy and concept of chastity and morality and try to enforce their own identity as empowered women who can go to any extent to establish their feminine identity and exercise their sexual freedom without getting tainted spiritually and morally. Thus they modify and redefine the male-concepts of chastity and morality. Padmini and Rani are both Karnad's new women who relocate themselves in the male discourse and reestablish themselves as new identities without getting influenced by patriarchy.

*Hayavadana* deals with a triangular love relationship between Devadatta (the upper-caste Brahmin), Padmini (Devadatta's wife) and Kapila (the lower-caste Dalit). Padmini's love for both these men indicates the prevailing incompleteness in society and the expression of female desire. The action of the play begins in the city of Dharmapura where we see Devadatta and Kapila are two close friends living in this city. Devadatta is the son of a wise Brahmin Vidyasagar. He is wise intelligent, educated, fair and handsome but lacks muscular body, physical beauty and the attractive features of his friend Kapila. Kapila is the only son of an ironsmith named Lohita. He is dark and plain to look at but is unmatched in physical strength and skills.

Devadatta falls in love with Padmini and marries her. The conflict arises when Padmini, unable to suppress her female desires gets attracted towards Kapila. Meanwhile Padmini becomes pregnant and the three of them decide to go on a short visit to Ujjain. Padmini gets greatly impressed by Kapila's physical charm, strength and skills during the journey. Devadatta becomes aware of Padmini's intense longing for Kapila. Devadatta cannot withstand his wife's love for another man, nor can he say anything to his dearest friend Kapila. He sacrifices himself before Goddess Kali. When Kapila finds it he also sacrifices himself. Now the plot takes an interesting turn. When Padmini sees both of them dead she wants to escape defamation prepares to sacrifice herself. Goddess Kali appears and grants her the blessing that if she puts the severed heads to the respective bodies then they will become alive. In a hurry Padmini transposes the two heads. This act complicates the whole theme of the play and also its characters as well. Devadatta with Kapila's muscular body becomes the perfect man whom Padmini has always desired for. On the other hand all is lost for Kapila who is having the weak body of Devadatta.

Now, this act of transposing the heads of the two men by Padimini apparently seems to be her mistake out of nervousness. But, a detailed study of her unconscious points out her deep designs behind this act that actually manifests her secret desire to possess an ideal husband who will be having the intelligence of Devadatta and the physical charm and ability of Kapila.

Earlier (when the heads were not exchanged) we have seen Padmini's desire for Kapila. Padmini finds more adventure, more libidinal force and more security in Kapila than her husband Devadatta who is a sophisticated person far away from the earth. This creates a difference in the attitude of Padmini for both the men. Unknowingly Padmini gets attracted towards Kapila due to his physique and character for which his class is responsible. This becomes clearer after the heads are exchanged between Devadatta and Kapila.

The atmosphere of light and darkness creates a semi-realistic situation where the unconscious of Padmini finds suitable ground to display itself and as a result of that the desire of a woman for the ideal husband comes into play. Padmini's Oedipal love (desire for the father) is fulfilled and her shock (due to the lack she witnessed as a child in the mother) is compensated with the hybrid individual with the head of Devadatta and the body of Kapila. Therefore, her act of transposing the two heads is an act of expression of her desire.

In *Nagamandala* the expression of the inner desire of a female becomes more prominent, explicit and bold. The play is related to the oppression of a womn in Indian society and her desire to break away from the shackles of patriarchal exploitation to have extramarital affairs (which becomes a necessity and not an evil) to establish her own identity in society. While talking about the play Aparna Bhargava Dharwadker says:

> By making Rani almost a pure embodiment of feminine simplicity, innocence, and powerlessness, Karnad pares his drama of gender relations down to an elemental level. Marriage for Rani means the loss of the secure world of childhood and parental love, and she has to reimagine that the world in her fantasies merely to keep herself from psychic collapse.
>
> (Karnad, *Collected Plays*, Vol. 1 XXX)

In the play Rani, already married to Appanna, unknowingly establishes physical relationship which Naga (the cobra in the shape of Appanna) and begets a child by him. Rani's husband Appanna has been very cruel to her, keeping her locked the whole day in the house and having the physical relationship with another woman. The cobra falls in love with Rani due to the effect of the root given by Kurudavva to her and which (in the form of a paste) was eaten up by the cobra without Rani's knowledge. Confusion occurs when the cobra takes the form of Appanna (Naga) and starts making love to Rani every night during Appanna's absence. Rani fails to identify the cobra. The identity of Naga and that of Appanna have overlapped with each other thus creating a state confusion among the husband and wife. It is interesting to see that like *Hayavadana* the lovemaking of the Naga and Rani occurs in the semi-dark atmosphere where the real situation and the unconscious of the individual get blended up to create a magic realism where we see the unconscious desire being expressed and fulfilled.

It is difficult to think that Rani cannot differentiate between Appanna and Naga. It seems to be an aggression on the part of Rani against the oppressions of the patriarchal society of which her cruel husband is a true representative. She takes a revenge on Appana who is himself adulterous and cruel. Rani's libido and her feminine identity manifest themselves through the Naga who becomes a symbol of the phallus, the object of female desire. Rani succeeds in proving her chastity and purity through the snake ordeal before the villagers. Appanna becomes her slave. This shows the subversion of the male patriarchy through fulfillment of the female desire and the establishment of the feminine identity that creates the space for the development of the feminine discourse and is in turn recognized by the male-dominated society itself.

While Padmini tries to fulfil her unconscious desire in secrecy Rani does it in public. Rani emerges as a development on the character of Padmini and seems to be more bold, desperate and aggressive. In *Hayavadana* Padmini ultimately ends in a dilemma between the social norms and her desire. While the two men fought to death she performs 'sati', thus, failing to go fully with her unconventional love and desire to establish her own space in society where she can freely choose her mate and can even control and modify the concept of chastity and morality. But that seed of defiance against the patriarchal supremacy in her grows through Rani in *Nagamandala* and Rani fully exercises her will and freedom to redirect the social discourse according to the norms of feminism.

The ending of *Nagamandala*, in contrast to that of *Hayavadana*, happens with a positive note for the establishment of the female identity and to create a space in the male discourse. There are two endings to the play. In the first ending we see the Naga committing suicide after seeing Rani reconciled to her real husband. According to the second ending the Naga (in the form of the cobra) is saved by Rani and she hides him in her long hair forever. This second ending to the play brings out the bold feature of the theme of the play. It shows that while having her husband in the form of a slave Rani also accepts the Naga as her lover. This is a clear case of adultery according to the patriarchal society. But, Rani has redefined the norms of chastity and purity. Her passing through the snake ordeal successfully and her acceptance of the Naga shows that Karnad is conventionalizing the female desire and the feminine adultery which seems to be quite normal and which challenges the unjustified practice of male supremacy over sexual conduct in society. She emerges as the real Queen or the Rani. Rani and Padmini are both Karnad's new women. But, while Padmini falls short from establishing her sexual supremacy and feminine identity Rani makes it real.

In his another important play *Bali: The Sacrifice* Karnad presents the ideological conflict between the Hinduism and Jainism. Sacrifice (*bali*) in Hinduism is challenged by the Queen who is a Jain and a follower of nonviolence. On the other hand the Queen Mother is a devotee of Hinduism and a supporter of 'bali' (sacrifice). The King converts into Jainism after his marriage to the Queen but is unable to come to terms with the new faith. The Queen is always in psychological conflict with the Queen Mother on the question of bali (the blood sacrifice). One night she indulges in physical relationship with a low caste Mahout. The act of adultery committed by the Queen is an act of aggression or revenge on the ideologies of violence in 'bali' or the blood sacrifice. It is not that the Queen is not satisfied with the King or she is adulterous. The indulgence in extramarital affair is a protest against violence, and in this case the Mahout, a dalit, plays an important role as a medium for the expression of that protest. This act of the Queen points out her desire to break away from the shackles of the religious morality practiced by the Mother Queen and followed by the King. It is interesting to see that in this play the conflict develops between two women the Queen is the Queen Mother. While the former tries to establish her own female identity through her religion the latter stands as a representative of the patriarchal society. Her courage and protest make her a new woman who is not dictated by the ideologies of any discourse.

It is interesting to see that in all the above cases Karnad uses the sexual conduct and the hidden desire of the female unconscious to establish the female identity and the supremacy of the female discourse over the male discourse. In the other plays like *Yayati* and *The Fire and the Rain* as well we see the use of physical relationship and the sexual conduct as strong motifs to put forth women as independent and dominating discourse. In *Yayati* Sharmishtha (the Rakshasa princess and an attendant to Devayani) seduces Yayati (the king and also the husband of Devayani) to establish her own identity as woman equal to Devayani, a brahmin (Sharmishtha's former friend and at present her mistress). In this case as well we see the development of the female discourse through the conflict of two women and the male becomes only an instrument in the development of that discourse. Sharmishtha establishes her right by forcing the king to indulge in physical love with her. The act of the king on the other hand is not so illegal in the sense that he only performs his dharma. From that point of view it is obvious Yayati has not committed anything wrong. While talking about the issue Dr. Falguni P. Desai observes:

> Devyani thought Yayati had violated his Dharma, when he married Sharmishtha. She was right in her own way. But if a man is bogged by a woman for Dharma's sake to pour in the seed he must do so, as a king & a Kshatriya Yayati followed his Dharma in doing so....Sharmishtha asks from Yayati her ritu right, ritu embrace, so that her ritu may not be in vain and in such circumstances Yayati rightly follows his dharma and grants her an offspring by practicing world's highest holy law of their union.
>
> (Desai 51-52)

Yayati had to marry Devayani because he caught her by her right hand while saving her life. So that was Dharma. Sharmishtha takes the same course of Dharma to replace Devayani and establish her own space and identity. Thus, while Devayani can achieve her right to become the queen through dharma, Sharmishtha can also claim her right in the same way though belonging to the lower class. The class difference also becomes an important question in this regard. By replacing Devayani as a sexual partner of Yayati Sharmishtha also abolishes the differences of classes that exist between the two women. Like Rani Sharmishtha's boldness includes her in the category of new women that is presented by Karnad in his plays. While Padmini fails to transcend the barrier of her dilemma and sacrifices herself, Rani and Sharmishtha refuse to become the suffering soul and transcend the norms of society, establish their feminine identities and modify and redefine the male discourse according to their own need. Padimini showed the courage to take the first step to fulfillher desire and establish her feminine identity but retreats back due to social conventions.

Fate also goes to the other way for her. But Rani and Sharmishtha fight the discriminations done against them and delineate their own space in the social discourse thus challenging the male supremacy. Sacrifice becomes an important thematic devise in *Bali: The Sacrifice* as well.

Like Padmini the Queen (Amritamani) also refuses the social ideologies thrust upon them and sacrifices themselves which can be considered as a form of protest. Nittilai, a low caste woman, also sacrifices her life to escape the ordeals of male domination in *The Fire and the Rain*. Nittilai is Karnad's 'new woman'.

The character of Nittilai (a low class girl) is a creation of Karnad and it does not exist in the "Vanaparva" of *Mahabharata*. Through her Karnad creates a space for the marginalized classes to interact with the mainstream society. Arvasu (a Brahmin and Nittilai's lover) is not accepted by the people of Nittilai's clan. Nittilai is forced to accept another man. But she cannot ignore her longing for Arvasu. But she is married and cannot transcend the social norms either. She returns to Arvasu and continues to share his sufferings not as his lover but as his sister. After being found with Arvasu she is killed by her husband.

The character of Nittilai is different from the other 'new' women characters presented by Karnad in his plays. She is not desperate like Padmini, not violent like Sharmishtha and not bold like Rani. She is a silent sufferer. She acts as a listener. Through her Karnad creates a space where the people of the different classes can interact with each other so that the problematic issues that arise due to class differences can be solved. Nittilai is courageous. She also respects the social norms as well. She is a truly new woman who becomes the symbol of non-violence, acceptance and sacrifice for love and humanity as well. The character Vishakha in the same play, on the other hand, reflects the violent attitude of Sharmishtha and the boldness of Rani. She is also a new woman who can indulge in extramarital affairs to fulfil her sexual desires and also to exercise her sexual freedom but at the same time also maintains her own identity as a woman without being dominated by the male-society.

Nittilai, in spite of being married to Paravasu, indulges in physical relationship with her childhood lover Yavakri (Paravasu's cousin). This is an attempt to exercise her sexual right. This also depicts her desire to make the protest against the oppressions of the patriarchal society of which Paravasu and Raibhya (Paravasu and Arvasu's father) are the implementing instruments. But, when she comes to know the real intention of Yavakri who wanted to take revenge against Raibhya and Paravasu for the latter (Paravasu) being elected as the chief priest for the ongoing religious ceremony Vishakha immediately goes against him and helps the Brahma Rakshasa to kill Yavakri. Thus, Vishakha's self-respect is hurt when she comes to know that Yavakri has used her as an object to meet his own ends. She immediately makes arrangement to kill him and sides along with her husband. Vishakha is free and defies any kind of barrier. Unlike Nittilai she transcends the norms of chastity to exercise her sexual freedom. On the other hand Nittilai demarcates her own space through acceptance, nonviolence and self sacrifice. But, both emerge as Karnad's new women who possess the attitude to challenge and change the phallogocentric society.

In the plays of Karnad the thematic motifs and the development of the characters lie in the incidents taken from Indian history, myth, folktales, Sanskrit epics and other such sources. But the issues that are dealt with and the presentation of the characters relate to the modern postcolonial Indian context where they become very relevant and prominent. The presentation of women as sexually expressive, bold and challenging and existentially threatening to the male domination creates the tradition of 'new women' who are redefining the Indian social and literary discourse as a whole. On the other hand another important Indian playwright in English, Mahesh Dattani has emerged as an important literary exponent in the Indian social, political and religious context who provides the marginalized classes a voice of protest and expression. No doubt the women also come into that category.

There lies some differences in the presentation of women between the plays of Mahesh Dattani and that of Girish Karnad.

First, Dattani places his characters in the modern scenario where they are in direct confluence with postcolonial Indian society. In Karnad we have seen the characters are related to the modern context through their symbolic presentation in myth, history and tradition of the country. Secondly, while Karnad's women characters are mostly emancipated through the establishment of their sexual identity and freedom and by challenging and subverting the male discourse, the female characters of Dattani are presented and placed in certain conflicts that deal with certain issues like, child abuse, gender discrimination, incest, homosexuality, national and international interests, communal conflicts and many such other bold issues which are often ignored and suppressed by society.

The identity of a woman in the plays of Dattani are established not through direct conflict with the society but by resisting the onslaughts of the latter through acceptance and by emerging as an individual who ignores the oppressions and discriminations of society and defines her own domain and forces the society to accept and recognize her. In Dattani the women characters are not so bold like the issues that are discussed by Dattani. But they stand as a strong resistance to the patriarchal domination. Instead of going into any kind of conflict with society they establish their own identity thus largely influencing society.

In the plays like *Tara*, *Thirty Days in September*, *A Special Season* (*Ek Alag Mausam*), *Final Solutions* and *On a Muggy Night in Mumbai* the women are placed in various situations where they are subjugated by society, they suffer, resist and often emerge as new women. The play *Tara* deals with a sensitive thematic motif which is related to gender discrimination against a girl child and the suffering of a physically challenged individual. In the play Dattani depicts a serious crime committed by the patriarchal society against a girl child. Tara and Chandan were born as conjoined Siamese twins with three legs, one leg common to both of them. The third leg had a better chance of survival with the female child. But, their mother and the influential maternal grandfather forced the doctor to give the third leg to the male child Chandan. The leg survived only for few days and both were left with a single leg each and Tara got an improper health which led her to premature death in her childhood. Tara says about herself and her brother Cahndan:

> TARA. The way we started in life. Two lives and one body, in one comfortable womb. Till we were forced out…
>
> (Dattani vol I: 325).

Here Tara points out the mother's womb which she depicts as the safe and secure space for their existence which is free from the threats of social complexities. Tara suffers. Her father neglects her talent in study and gives more importance to Chandan. Tara cannot bear the shock that it was her mother Bharati who opted to give the third leg to the male child. The struggle and discrimination run parallel in Tara's life. She has no grudge for her brother Chandan. She accepts the discrimination shown by her father to her. She is talented and courageous but her ill health drives her gradually to extinction. In his critical work *The (Un)twinkling Star: Who Takes Tara's Shine Away?* Subhash Chandra says:

> Tara is killed by the social system, which controls the minds and actions of the people. (67)

She has the tenacity to counter the attacks that she receives from society. She protests and hits out at the other children like Roopa who mock and laugh at her physical disability. She stands as a symbol of courage, patience and determination. She surpasses social boundaries and establishes her own identity. Her tragic death cannot destroy the space that she has created as a female which forces the patriarchal society to come into terms with her and recognize her as an individual. Padmini (*Hayavadana*) fails to establish her true identity as a feminine self in the male discourse and sacrifices herself because she cannot accept the domination of society either. Tara, through death, makes a space of her own in the male discourse which modifies the social discourse as a whole. She is Mahesh Dattani's new woman who refuses to submit to the discriminations of society and becomes a martyr.

While Tara silently tolerates and resists the oppressions of society, Smita (in *Final Solutions*), Aparna (in *A Special Season*) and Uma (in *Seven Steps around the Fire, The Swami and Winston* and *Uma and the Fairy Queen*) are more expressive, aggressive and strong in resisting the patriarchal discourse and creating their own domain. In *Final Solutions* Smita is totally different in nature from her mother Aruna. Smita, like her father Ramnik Gandhi, is sympathetic towards the two Muslim boys Javed and Babban. In fact all of them are friends from before. She disapproves her mother's Hindu orthodoxy and is ready to listen to the problems of these people who belong to some minority class and are severely oppressed and discriminated against by society. While her mother and the grandmother are shocked at the presence of these two boys who, they think, can make everything impure in a Hindu house Smita proves these anxieties and fears to be futile and mere superstitions and tries to make the people of the house and also society as well, realize that these discriminations are all socially created to serve the purpose of some particular sections. Smita emerges as a bold woman and through her Dattani presents the need of a listener who can listen to the problems of the oppressed classes so that a space can be created where both the parties can interact with each other and a solution can be reached. Like Nittilai (*The Fire and the Rain*) Smita also acts as a listener.

A bold attempt to defy the male domination and to establish a woman's own space of existence is seen in *A Special Season* (*Ek Alag Mausam*). The story deals with the consequences of illegal sexual relationships and the evil of the disease called HIV AIDS which has grown along with the modern society of India. Aparna's husband is having extramarital affairs and as a result of that he gets infected with HIV AIDS. Aparna also gets that infection through her husband while she is pregnant. As a consequence of this she is forced to abort her child. This proves to be a great shock for her. She leaves her husband and starts serving the HIV infected children in a nursing home named Jivan Jyoti. This act of leaving her husband comes as a protest against the domination of the male that asks the devotion from the female but himself indulges in illegal affairs.

Moreover, Aparna considers her husband to be responsible for the death of her child. She shows the courage to defy the social norms and develops an affair with George, another HIV patient, in whom she finds a person on whom she can rely. This is bold step and a serious crime according to the norms of society and morality. But, Aparna shows this courage to protest the evil practices of male-society. She is like Rani (*Naga-Mandala*) who subverts the patriarchal society and opposes the evil that it brings with it. The difference is that while Karnad presents Rani's emancipation through sexual freedom, in case of Aparna the fulfilment comes through human relationship and purity of the soul.

In George, Aparna finds someone loving and caring who will never betray her. She is truly a new woman. Through Aparna Dattani presents the issue of HIV AIDS and the people suffering from it. Aparna's struggle to live in spite of knowing her imminent death identifies her with Tara. Her struggle demands the attention of society for a HIV patient as well as for a woman.

In the three plays *Seven Steps around the Fire*, *The Swami and Winston* and *Uma and the Fairy Queen* the character Uma is a PhD scholar in Sociology, wife of the superintendent of police Suresh Rao, and the daughter of a vice-chancellor. In all these plays, we find Uma in the role of a detective who is in search of the truth and is always trying to discover something new. Her adventures as a detective lead her to the domain of the eunuchs, the question of national and international issues, the problem of terrorism and the menace of religious fanaticism. She is bold, courageous and innovative. It is true that Dattani chooses a female character as a detective for his whodunits which depicts an opposition to the tradition of presenting a male in such situations. Uma is no doubt Dattani's new woman. It is interesting to see that Uma is childless. That lack is compensated by the discovery of truth that she makes in every play which is equally creative like a childbirth.

In his important play *Thirty Days in September* Dattani deals with the menace of incest and sexual abuse of a female child. The character Mala, now an adult, is having a distorted past which is marked by the sexual abuse she went through as a child in the hands of her maternal uncle Vinay. Once the virginity is lost it becomes an obsession for Mala to indulge in illegal physical relationships repeatedly only to make herself suffer due to the sense of guilt. Her childhood was lost when she lost her virginity. This turned her into a frustrated individual who lost control over her life. While explaining her predicament regarding her code of conduct (especially sexual behaviour) in society Mala says:

> MALA. I don't know why. I just don't understand...Please don't ask me why I do it. It's just a game...not a game. No...it's...I know it's wrong. What I am doing is terribly wrong! But it means a lot to me. I like it. That is why I am a bad person. I have no character...
>
> (Dattani vol II: 18)

Mala, like Tara, has lost her right to lead a normal life. But unlike *Tara* this play ends with a positive note where we see that Mala ultimately succeeds in eliminating her traumatic past and finds her love in Deepak and reconciles with her mother Shanta. Mala emerges as a bold woman who can ignore the male hegemony and defy the distortions imposed upon her by the patriarchal society. Like Rani (*Nagamandala*) Mala silently modifies and redefines the norms of chastity. She rejects the burden of shame that she received from society and ultimately gains full control over her life. Like Aparna and Smita she is Dattani's new woman who is not ready to be dictated by patriarchy and they can develop their own discourse and can create their own space of existence where they can locate their feminine identity.

There are other women characters in some of Dattani's plays who have shown the courage to defy the social hegemony and define their feminine domain. In *Where There is a Will* Kiran Jhaveri is the new woman. She can control her home as well as her office. She has experienced the exploitations done to her family by her father and her husband. But she has defined her feminine domain. She has succeeded in bringing her boss Mr. Hasmukh Mehta under her control. After his death she has become the caretaker of Mr. Hasmukh's family and his company as well. Through her the family gains freedom from the dictates of Mr. Hasmukh's will. In *Morning Raga* Swarnalatha succeeds to become a singer by defying the barriers of social conventions that do not allow women to become singers. Swarnalatha's concert is successful and her dream to become a Carnatic singer is fulfilled. The play depicts the music or the Raga that develops in confluence of the tradition and the modernity, the orient and the occident, the old and the new, the mother and the child. In *On a Muggy Night in Mumbai* Dattani is dealing with the issue of homosexuality and the threat that the homosexual people are facing in modern Indian society. In this play Deeapli is a lesbian and she is proud for being that. The boldness lies in the fact that a woman is ready to declare her own stance from the feminine point of view without being influenced by the threats of the mainstream society.

Thus, it is an established fact that both Girish Karnad and Mahesh Dattani has redirected the discourse of Indian literature to define anew and magnify the domain of the feminine discourse. The 'new women' depicted in these plays are bold in their representations and concepts and are courageous enough to influence the male-discourse and can create a parallel feminine discourse which resists the oppressions of the patriarchal society and compels the latter to consider the former seriously and often subverts the male hegemonic system and turns it into an instrument to serve their own purpose and meet their own end.

## Works Cited

Chandra, Subhash. "The (Un)twinkling Star: responding to Dattani's Tara." *The Commonwealth Review* 13.2: 60-68. Print.

Dattani, Mahesh. *Collected Plays.* vol I. New Delhi: Penguine Books India, 2000. Print.

_________. *Collected Plays.* vol II. New Delhi: Penguine Books India, 2005. Print.

Desai, Falguni P.. "Girish Karnad's *Yayati.*" *Contemporary Vibes* 4.16 (Jul-Oct 2009): 52. Print.

Karnad, Girish. *Collected Plays.* vol I. New Delhi: O.U.P., 2010. Print.

# 24

# Indian Dramas in English: A Feminine Perspective

— Rupali S. Bhave

## Introduction

The woman in India is confined to 'the triple role' of daughter-in-law, wife and mother, yet another form of gender discrimination in the customs of Indian families. Even nowadays in the traditional Hindu families, women are supposed to take their meals after their husbands, elders and children have finished eating. Such a habit and spirit of sacrifice is inculcated in women since childhood as a part of *Stridharma* (Duties of women). At times, a woman is required to eat her husband's leftovers, which is deemed a great prasada. (Shashi Deshpande *Feminism in India*)

Gandhiji acclaimed the concept of *Ardhangini*, enshrined in Indian culture, and accepted the fact that men and women are complementary to each other, and one is never a whole without the other. He accepted the Hindu scriptural view, which conceived *Prakriti* and *Purusha* as one, man and woman as one in the concept of *Ardhanarishwara.* Women have been assigned diversified roles in Indian society – on one aspect she is the Adishakti, the source of all power, and on the other hand she is the virtual doormat, lying prostrate at the feet of her "patidevata" (husband-god) and performing the "stridharma" (the duties of a wife) which led to ultimate self-effacement. This complex role of women in Indian society— both the "Grihalakshmi" and the coquette —have been depicted with clarity in *Indian Drama in English*.

> In childhood a women should be under her father's control, in youth under her husband's and when her husband is dead, under her sons, she should not have independence...
>
> (*The Laws of Manu* 5.148)

The importance of human experience, denied of female voice is a tilted, distorted one man, right from the beginning, have had every advantage in telling us their own stories. They had education, a much higher degree, to articulate and voice their dominance. But women had no education, nor were they strong to voice. Right from Christine de Pisan to Mary Wollstone Craft, from Simone de Beauvior to Jane Austen and beyond, women have been demanding their rights in a male-centric world. Feminism is a protest movement launched by women of the West for equal social, political, legal, moral, cultural rights with men. It is an anti-masculinist movement of the women, by the women and for the women.

The rise of Feminism in Europe, which was in the seventeenth and eighteenth centuries, is related to the economic prosperity of the new bourgeois resulting in the use of servants to perform the domestic work. In the nineteenth century, Feminism remained as a protest movement against the suppression of women's right, against ego-centric worldview. In the twenteenth century, it expressed itself in the Suffrage Movement. The development in technology and mode of production and the rising demand for female labour have formulated the structure and texture of the suffrage movement. Mary Austell and much later, Virginia Woolf, viewed that, "Education alone can expand woman's consciousness of the world and ensure her place in the society." "Beauty is the struggle for living, for survival. Through many struggles we have to create a sense of value." Dang Tu Mai, Vietnam

## The Condition of Women in Three Eras

### *The Ancient Era*

In ancient times Aryans were the main inhabitant of India. These people were mainly brahmins who used to give the status of goddess to the women. Women enjoyed the status of Lakshmi (goddess of wealth) in the households. A famous Sanskrit *shloka* (form of Hindu verse) signifies the status of women in that era, *"Yatra naryastu pujyante, ramante tatra devta"* meaning, "The place where women are worshipped, gods themselves inhabit that place". The women of ancient times had immense power, this is evident from a South Indian legend that once a king accidentally killed the husband of a woman and she had such powers that she burnt the whole kingdom to ashes.

An incident in *Ramayana* is a proof of this. When Lord Rama was performing *the Ashvamedha yajna* his wife Sita was not with him and he had to use the gold idol of his wife to compensate for her absence. Ancient Indian women had a say in each and every aspect related to their lives. They had the right to choose their own life partners. The process of choosing the life partner of own choice was known as *Swayamvara* in which grooms assembled at the house of the bride and she chose the one whom she liked. Maharishi Veda Vyasa's *Mahabharata* and Maharishi Valmiki's *Ramayana* bear testimonial to this. In the *Mahabharata*, Draupadi's father arranged for her *Swayamvara* and Arjuna (a Pandava prince in exile) successfully managed to fulfil the conditions and became eligible to marry her. Even the model women of Tretayuga (second out of four ages of Hindu mythology) Sita also had Swayamvara in which kings of different states participated and Lord Rama won her over by breaking the Shiva Dhanusha (Hindu God Shiva's bow). Not only just princely women but also the common women were given the same rights. Women were so important that many of the major battles were fought for them. The fiercest battle of ancient India, the kurukshetra war was fought for the honour of Draupadi (wife of

Pandavas, ruler of Indraprastha). The Kauravas (ruler of Hastinapur) insulted her in the court and this led to the enmity between the cousins and resulted in the most devastating battle in ancient India. Another example of women power is evident from the cause of death of the most learned man of his time, Ravana. He was the best scholar of his time and was the master of all the four *Vedas* of Hindu religion and had immense powers. Even gods were not able to defeat and kill him but a woman was able to bring his doom. Ravana captured Sita and tried to mary her forcibly which led to his destruction. Women were not just confined to domestic arena but they were also part of religious teachings.

In ancient India, women like Gayatri, Maitreyi, Anusuya were renowned seers of their time which shows that women had the right to religious teachings. They were not prohibited even from learning. They could learn whatever they wanted. The status of women of the Vedic era began to decline with time. Gender inequality started creeping into the society. Slowly thier status degraded to such an extent that they were not given the freedom, which was available to even the Shudras (lowest caste of ancient Hindu society). They were not given the basic rights. They were debarred from religious practices. They began to lose their political freedom as well. As the Vedic age progressed, the status of women became worse. And till the time of the *Smirits* (religious scripture of Hindus) the condition became so bad that women were not allowed free access to education but were given education related to just domestic purposes.

### *The Medieval Era*

Medieval India was not a women's age; it is supposed to be the 'dark age' for them. Medieval India saw many foreign conquests, which resulted in the decline in women's status. When foreign conquerors like Muslims invaded India they brought with them their own culture. For them woman was the sole property of her father, brother or husband and she did not have any will of her own. This type of thinking also crept into the minds of Indian people and they also began to treat their own women likewise. One more reason for the decline in theer status and freedom was that native Indians wanted to shield their womenfolk from the barbarous Muslim invaders. As polygamy was a norm for these invaders they picked up any woman they wanted and kept her in their harems. In order to protect them Indian women started using *purdah* (a veil), which covers the whol body. Due to this their freedom also became affected. They were not allowed to move freely and this led to the further deterioration of their status. These problems related with women resulted in changed mindset of people. Now they began to consider a girl as misery and a burden, which as to be shielded from the eyes of intruders and needed extra care, whereas a boy child would not need such extra care and instead would be helpful as an earning hand. Thus a vicious circle started in which women were at the receiving end. All this gave rise to the following new evils.

*Sati:* The ritual of dying at the funeral pyre of the husband is known as *Sati* or *Sahagaman.* According to *Medhatiti, Sati* is like committing suicide so one should avoid this.

*Jauhar*: It is like *Sati* but a mass suicide. *Jauhar* was prevalent in the *Rajput* societies.

*Child Marriage*: It was a norm in medieval India. Girls were married off at the age of eight to ten. They were not allowed access to education and were treated as the material being. The plight of women can be imagined by one of the *shlokas* of Tulsidas where he writes, *"Dhol, gawar, shudra, pashu, nari, ye sab tadan ke adhikari"*, meaning that "animals, illiterates, lower castes and women should be subjected to beating". Thus women were compared with animals and were married off at an early age.

*Restriction on Widow Remarriage:* The condition of widows in medieval India was very bad. They were not treated as human beings and were subjected to a lot of restrictions. They were supposed to live a pious life after their husband died and were not allowed entry in any celebration because it was considered to be a bad omen.

*Girl Education:* The girls of medieval India and especially Hindu society were not given formal education but an education related to household chores. A famous Indian philosopher, Vatsyayana, wrote that women were supposed to be perfect in 64 arts which included cooking, spinning, grinding, and knowledge of medicine, recitation and many more.

Though these evils were present in medieval Indian society yet they were mainly confined to the Hindu society. As compared to the Hindu society other societies such as Buddhism, Jainism and Christians were a bit lenient. Women in those societies enjoyed far more freedom. They had easy access to education and were more liberal in their approach. According to these religions gender was not the issue in attaining salvation. Any person, whether a man or a woman, is entitled to get the grace of God. During the time of king Ashoka women took part in religious preaching. According to Hiuen Tsang, the famous traveler of that time, Rajyashri, the sister of Harshavardhana was a distinguished scholar of her time. Another such example is the daughter of king Ashoka, Sanghmitra. She along with her brother Mahendra went to Sri Lanka to preach Buddhism.

The status of women in Southern India was better than that in North India. While in Northern India there were not many women administrators, in Southern India we can find some names that made women of that time proud. Priyaketaladevi, queen of Chalukya Vikramaditya ruled three villages. Another woman named Jakkiabbe used to rule seventy villages. In South India women had representation in each and every field. Domingo Paes, famous Portuguese traveller testifies to it. He has written in his account that in Vijayanagar kingdom women were present in each and every field. He says that women could wrestle, blow a trumpet and handle a sword with equal perfection. Nuniz, another famous traveler to the South also agrees to it and says that women were employed in writing accounts of expenses, recording the affairs of kingdom, which shows that they were educated. There is no evidence of any public school in northern India but according to famous historian Ibn Batuta there were 13 schools for girls and 24 for boys in Honavar.

*Devadasis:* This was a custom prevalent in Southern India. In this system girls were dedicated to temples in the name of gods and goddesses. The girls were then onwards known as Devadasis meaning Servants of God. Some kings used to invite temple dancers to perform at their court for the pleasure of courtiers and thus some Devadasis converted to Rajadasis (palace dancers) prevalent in some tribes of South India like Yellamma cult. The plight of women in medieval India and at the starting of modern India can be summed up in the words of the great poet Rabindranath Tagore:

> O Lord Why have you not given woman the right to conquer her destiny?
> Why does she have to wait head bowed?
> By the roadside, waiting with tired patience,
> Hoping for a miracle in the morrow?

### *The Modern Era*

The status of women in modern India is a sort of a paradox. If on one hand she is at the peak of the ladder of success, on the other hand she is mutely suffering the violence afflicted on her by her own family members. As compared with the past, women in modern times have achieved a lot but in reality they have to still travel a long way. Their path is full of roadblocks. The women have left the secured domain of their home and are now in the battlefield of life, fully armoured with their talent. They had proven themselves. But in India they are yet to get their dues. The sex ratio of India shows that the Indian society is still prejudiced against females. There are 933 females per thousand males in India according to the census of 2001, which is much below the world average of 990 females. There are many problems which women in India have to go through daily. These problems have become part and parcel of life of Indian women and some of them have accepted them as their fate.

## The Main Problems of Indian Women

*Malnutrition:* Generally in India, women are the ones who eat last and the least in the whole family. So they eat whatever is left after men folk are satiated. As a result most of the times their food intake does not contain the nutritional value required in maintaining the healthy body. In villages, sometimes women do not get to eat the whole meal due to poverty.

*Poor Health:* Malnutrition results in poor health of women. The women of India are prejudiced from the birth itself. They are not breastfed for long. For want of a son they want to get pregnant as soon as possible which decreases the caring period to the girl child whereas the male members get adequate care and nutrition. Women are not given the right to free movement which means that they cannot go anywhere on their own if they want to and they have to take the permission of a male member of the family or have to take them along. This results in decrease in women's visit to doctor and she could not pay attention to her health as a result.

*Maternal Mortality:* The mortality rate in India is among the highest in the world. As females are not given proper attention, it results in malnutrition. They are married at an early age which leads to pregnancies at a younger age when the body is not ready to bear the burden of a child. All this results in complications, which may lead to gynaecological problems, which may become serious with time and may ultimately lead to death.

*Lack of Education:* In India women's education never got its due share of attention. From the medieval India women were debarred from the educational field. The lack of education is the root cause for many other problems. An uneducated mother cannot look after her children properly; she is not aware of the deadly diseases and their cure, which leads to the poor health of the children. An uneducated person does not know about hygiene; this lack of knowledge of hygiene may lead to poor health of the whole family.

*Mistreatment:* In India violence against women is a common evil. Not just in remote parts but in cities also women bear the brunt. They are subjected to physical and mental violence. They are the ones who work most but are not given their due. They are nowhere safe, neither at home nor at workplace. Every hour a woman is raped in India and every 93 minutes a woman is burnt to death due to dowry problem. There are many laws such as The Hindu Marriage Act of 1955, The Hindu Succession Act of 1956, The Hindu Widow Remarriage Act of 1856, The Hindu Women Right to Property Act of 1937, The Dowry Prohibition Act of 1961, to protect women. Punishment is severe but the conviction rate of crime against women is very low in India.

*Overworked:* Indian women work more than men in India but their work is hardly recognized as they mainly do unskilled work. Their household chores is never counted as work. If a woman is working in a field to help her husband it will also be not counted as work. A study conducted by Mies in 1986 states that in Andhra Pradesh a woman works around 15 hours a day during the agricultural season whereas a male on an average works for around seven to eight hours.

*Lack of Power:* In India a large percentage of women do not have power. They cannot take decisions independently, not even those related to their own life. They have to take the permission of male members for each and every issue. They don't have any say in important household matters and not in matters of their own marriage.

*Marriage:* The family mainly fixes the marriages in India. The scenario in villages is very bad. The girl is not consulted but is told to marry a guy whom her family has chosen for her. They are taught to abide by the whims and fancies of their husbands. Going against the wishes of the husband is considered to be a sin. In marriage the husband always has the upper hand. The groom and his parents act as if they are obliging the girl by marrying her and in return they demand a hefty dowry.

*Dowry:* It's a serious issue. Courts are flooded with cases related to death due to dowry harassment by husband and in-laws. In ancient times women were given *Stridhan* when they departed from the house of their parents. This amount of money was given to her as a gift which she can use on her and her children but her in-laws did not have any right on that amount. This amount was supposed to help the girl in time of need. Slowly this tradition became obligatory and took the form of dowry. Nowadays parents have to give hefty amounts in dowry, the in-laws of their girl are not concerned whether they can afford it or not. If a girl brings a large amount of dowry she is given respect and is treated well in her new home, and if she does not bring it according to their expectations then she has to suffer harassment. Due to this evil practice many newly wed women of India have to lose their lives.

*Female Infanticide:* As women were supposed to be, and in some areas of India are still considered to be a curse by some strata of society their birth was taken as a burden. So in past times they were killed as soon as they were born. In some of the Rajput clans of Rajasthan a newborn girl child was dropped in a large bowl of milk and was killed. Today with the help of technology the sex of the unborn baby is determined and if it is a girl child then it is aborted. In all this procedure women do not have any say, they have to do according to the wishes of their husbands. Even if a women does not want to abort she has no choice

*Divorce:* The divorce rate in India is not so high compared to Western countries but it does not mean that marriages are more successful here. The reason behind the low level of divorce rate is that it is looked upon down by the society. It is regarded as the sign of failure of marriage, especially of women. She is treated as if she has committed some crime by divorcing her husband. In some communities, like the Muslim one women did not have the right to divorce their husband, they were divorced at just the pronouncement of "I divorce you" by their husband thrice and they could not do anything except to be mute spectators. Recently the Muslim Law Board has given the right of divorce to women. After divorce a woman is entitled to get her *Mehr* for herself and her children's sustenance. In Hindu society women get maintenance for themselves and their children after divorce.

## Views on Women in Indian Dramas by Various Dramatists

Rabindranath Tagore has created a web of songs, music and dance via his dance dramas like *Shyama, Chitrangada, Chandalika*, and *Notir Puja*. These are an integral part of Bengali culture worldwide and in far-off places like England and America, and the prabashi Bengalis try their best to keep the tradition alive. Tagore was an icon of Indian culture. He was a poet, philosopher, musician, writer, and educationist. He became the first Asian to become a Nobel Laureate when he won the Nobel Prize for his collection of poems, *Gitanjali*, in 1913. He was popularly called Gurudev and his songs were popularly known as Rabindrasangeet. He lived for 80 eventful years in colonial Bengal, and his views about women changed over time.

His short story "Laboratory," written a few months before his death, expresses his latest views on women and gives shape to the "new woman," whom he perceives as arriving in India in the near future. In so doing, he urges women to find an identity of their own, and realize that wifehood and motherhood are but fractions of their whole being.

This paper proposes to explore his vision and views on women as reflected in his short stories. He had devoted considerable thought to women. "Laboratory" marks his matured and almost his last deliberation on women. While Rabindranath was never comfortable with strident assertions of women's rights, and was not kind to those who were known as feminists (Tagore, *Chithipatra*), he showed a remarkable understanding of woman's psyche, perceived the injustice of an unequal social structure, and advocated for greater freedom and decision-making power for In addition to his remarkable stories about young girls (of which "The Postmaster" is a masterpiece), women in the family and the larger society. The Bengali Renaissance brought with it a new approach to the concept of women in society. In the flood of writings, inspired by the various movements that sought to redress the condition of women in society, like widow remarriage, abolition of sati, abolition of child marriage and *kulinism*, the initiatives taken for women's education, the whole socio-cultural and familial view of women underwent a drastic change.

Much has been said about the way Tagore views his women in his poems, essays, novels and drama. Yet it is the dance dramas of Tagore, a genre quite unique in his time and milieu, which portray the radical nature of his conception of women and the maturation of their selfhood. His dance dramas, especially the three most popular among his readers, *Chitrangada*, *Chandalika* and *Shyama*, also foreground the theme of female desire, a tabooed subject in his times, indeed even now in Bengali writings. In these three dance dramas, Tagore's modern views about women and their selfhood by voicing their desires as women are conspicuous in its presence. Thus they amply illustrate the feminist inclinations that his women portray. Significantly, in dance dramas the he explores the intimate links between dance and the processes of female identity formation in Bengal. Dance dramas open up a space in which representation of Indian women through bodily performance troubles notions of cultural purity and origin and offers instead 'impure' but nevertheless powerful cultural texts.[1]

In all three dance dramas, the women are fully conscious of their desires as a woman, and they do not shy away from acknowledging desire; indeed they even travel great lengths to fulfil their desires. *Chitrangada* was a retelling feminist dance drama. In *it* the situation is significantly different. Chitrangada, the warrior princess, falls in love with Arjuna, the warrior prince. But Arjuna rejects her as she is Kurupa, a woman devoid of feminine charms to attract him. So with the help of Madana, the god of love, Chitrangada dons the mask of Surupa, the beautiful, seductive woman ready to entice men like Arjuna. Yet she is suffocating under this guise of the 'true woman'- the eternal feminine; this façade, this veneer of lies that hide her essential and true identity of an intelligent, valourous woman. The crux of the story lies in the point that Chitrangada makes Arjuna wait before revealing her true identity, her essential self shorn of all lies, in the famous speech which has become the credo of Tagore's vision of women:

> *Ami Chitrangada,/ Ami Rajendranandini/ nohi devi, nohi samanya nari/ pujakori more rakhhibe urddhe, se nohi, nohi/ hela korimore rakhhibe piche, se nohi nohi/jadi parshe rakho more, sankate sampade/ Sammati dao jadi kothin brate sahay hote, pabe tumi chinite more/ aaj shudhu kori nibedan-/ Ami Chitrangada, Rajendranandini.*
>
> (I am Chitrangada, I am the daughter of a king, /I'm neither a goddess, nor an ordinary woman,/ if you worship me from afar, I 'm not that/ if you ignore me leaving me behind, that is not me/ if you keep me beside you in all dangers, wealth / if you promise to let me be beside you in all hardships and penance,/only then would you know me for what I am / today I give you only my name/ I am Chitrangada, a princess).

Chitrangada is not just an erotic playmate of youth; she is also his soulmate in life and beyond. Tagore's idea of femininity shows a remarkable fusion of Western and Eastern ideas in his reconstruction of the character of Chitrangada here: the older Indian idea of wife as a partner in the duties of family life (sahadharmini) had developed, under Western influence, into the romantic concept of a comrade in perilous action. Tagore envisions Chitrangada as an ideal consort of the man of her choice- a woman true to her own identity, conscious of her desires, aware of her potentials, ready for her vocation – not only understanding her partner's needs but aware of her own needs as a fulfilled person. Chitrangada becomes the exemplary woman in tune with her own identity, her desires and her womanhood. She possesses the power and agency to determine her own fate. In Tagore's reputed novel *Gora* (1910), Sucharita and Lalita, the two main female characters, held their personal views on marriage. Rabindranath believed:

> By natural instinct women are creative and graceful. It is women who make the home, which is no way less valuable or easier than running a business. The motivating force that shapes a home is a woman's love. Love is not merely an emotion of the heart. It is a force like the force of gravitation. (*Rabindra Rachanabali,* Vol. 10: 546) The purdah over their faces has vanished, and along with it has gone the purdah that kept their mind away from exposure to the outer world.
>
> (*Rabindra Rachanabali* Vol. 13: 380)

*Shyama* is a story about a court-dancer (Shyama), falling in love with a foreign merchant (Bajrasen). The drama starts with Bajrasen, a noble merchant, acquiring a priceless set of jewels called 'Indramonir Haar' (a precious necklace) from 'Subarna Dwip' (Subarna Island) looking for a suitable bride. Soon, he is seen being chased by a royal guard. They come across Shyama, the royal courtesan, and her acquaintances. Strikingly beautiful Shyama is pursued by many but her heart sets on Bajrasen at the very first sight. The royal guard arrests Bajrasen and Shyama starts plotting how to rescue the object of her affection and soon comes up with a brilliant plan. She manipulates one of her suitors, Uttiyo, to take the blame of the crime Bajrasen has been arrested for. Thus Bajrasen is saved. Shyama and her beloved elope to a land where no one knows them. However, eventually the truth is revealed and Bajrasen is appalled by Shyama's treachery that had apparently caused an innocent young man his life. Unable to deal with the guilt, Bajrasen rejects Shyama. Heartbroken, Shyama leaves her lover. Bajrasen is torn between strong feelings of guilt and undying love for Shyama; in the back of his mind he's aware that the purpose of Shyama's despicable act was to save his life. The story of 'Shyama' may be set in the ancient times, but its message and appeal is still relevant. *Shyama* is a sad story of eternal love, temptation and manipulation in the name of love.

Tagore spoke on the subject of 'Woman' in one of his American lectures, published as *Personality*.[2] He said: "Woman is endowed with the passive qualities of chastity, modesty, devotion and power of self-sacrifice in a greater measure than man is,"[3] the very attributes that feminists regard as imposed on women by patriarchal systems. But in his lecture, Tagore was not suggesting the attributes are weaknesses, rather that the world needs the stability that is inherent in woman's nature. "All her forces instinctively work to bring things to some shape of fulness (sic),—for that is the law of life".[4] The idea of 'the law of life' links to Hogan's understanding of dharma:

> It is the dharma of water to flow, of heavy objects to fall to earth .... It is the nature of humankind to act according to principle. Hence, for men and women, dharma means duty, what I should do—not only ... "morally" but in respect of every social link.[5]

Vijay Tendulkar is one of the most prolific Indian playwrights who has enriched the Indian drama and theatre by picturizing the varied problems of native life in Maharashtra. Women play a central role in Tendulkar's plays. His female characters are mainly from the lower and middle classes: housewives, teachers, mistresses, daughters, film extras, slaves, and servants. These women bring not just variety of social station but also a broad range of emotions into the plays: "from the unbelievably gullible to the clever, from the malleable to the stubborn, from the conservative to the rebellious, from the self-sacrificing to the grasping."[6]

*Kanyadaan* (Daughters gifted away 1983) is also indicative of Tendulkar's variations in his dramatic creations. In this play, he portrayed a dalit writer as a drunkard, wife beater, manipulator and blackmailer. *Kanyadaan* is a good play with which to enter the trouble area of public and critical response to Tendulkar's play. *Kamala* (1981) is a tropical drama inspired by a real life incident. Like most of his sympathetic women characters, Kamala does not have the spirit to rebel against her present condition. In the play *Silence! The Court is in Session*, Tendulkar questions the imposition of patriarchal values on women and its restrictive norms.

Girish Karnad (1938) is a significant name in Indian English drama. He has enriched the Indian drama by his dramatic skills. His originality as a dramatist lies in his extraordinary skill of using myth, history and folktale to make the drama lively and thought provoking. He has received wide recognition and many awards including Padma Shree in 1974 and Padma Bhushan in 1992. His well known plays are *Yayati* (1961), *Tughlaq* (1962), *Hayavadana* (1970), *and Nagamandala* (1972).

The play *Yayati* reinterprets an ancient myth from *Mahabharata* in modern concept. *Tughlaq* is his best historical play where he mingles facts with fiction. He projects the curious contradictions in the complex personality of Sultan Muhammad-bin-Tughlaq. In the play *Nagmandala*, the conflict is between patriarchal and matriarchal views of society. It is about the life of Rani, a typical Indian woman in male dominated society. She is married to Appanna, a wealthy village youth. The focus in the play is on sexual liberty of to sexes: male and female. In order to counter mail dominance, Karnad adopts a strange device in which King Cobra gets sexually involved with Rani and ultimately she becomes pregnant. Like his other female protagonist, she is encouraged to pass through chastity ordeal. Regarding the position of Rani, Smita Nirula holds, "Rani is never free to express herself, to be herself. She is either daughter, wife, lover or mother. She is a woman used, abused. She can either live as a whore or a Devi."

Michael Madhusudan *Dutt* was a man most famous for being associated with the Bengali renaissance movement. He was born on the 25th of January, 1824 in Sagardari, Jessore district, now in Bangladesh. He was the pioneer of Bengali dramas and well known for his poems as well— *Meghnadh Badh Kabya*, *Sharmistha*. Written in western style, *Sharmistha* was the first original Bengali play. This play written in 1858 was based on the story of Yayati, Devyani and her mate Sharmistha. *Padmavati*, a play, composed in blank verses, was a successful attempt by him. This drama based on Greek mythology was composed in 1860.

Mahesh Dattani is one of the leading and contemporary playwrights in English. He is the first playwright in English to be honoured with the Sahitya Akademi Award. A director, actor, and writer, in 1986, he produced first play *Where There's a Will*. Since then he has never looked back. There is a long chain of plays written by him as *Tara(1990), Night Queen, Final Solutions, Dance like a Man* and many more. His plays deal with the social and gender issues. One of his films *Dance like a Man* has won the award for the best picture in English awarded by the "National Panorama".

These plays embody many of the classic concerns of the drama world and deal with the social and contemporary issues. His plays are "about the marginalized sections of our society: minorities, women, gays, and hijras (eunuch)." His plays not only bring up gender issues and the liberty fixed to women in a patriarchal society, but also they deal with gender biases and prejudices which influence the lives of girl-children even amongst middle class educated society. His plays focus actual life problems and sometimes cause controversy. Dattani once said:

> The function of the drama, in my opinion, is not merely to reflect the malfunction of the society but to act like freak mirrors in a carnival and to project grotesque images of all that passes for normal in our world. It is ugly, but funny.[7]

*Tara* is a play deals with the theme of gender discrimination and social consciousness in modern society. It is the story of every girl child born in society whether urban or rural. Tara is a touchy play which shows the partiality towards the male child in highly educated and an upper middle class Bangalore society. The story of the play is about the twins who are born with three legs and blood supply to the third leg was from the girl baby. The father, the mother of the twins and the doctor decide to fix the third leg on to the male baby's body so as to make male baby complete. The decision was taken to make male child physically fit and complete was not on the basis of medical ground but was influenced by the grandfather, a politician. Male domination reflected in the role of grandfather who donates all his property and wealth to the male child. In our society, male child is considered as an asset and female child the liability. This is mainly due to certain misconceived religious beliefs and the problem of dowry. This discrimination against the girl child by family member shows attitude and mentality of the society. It is tragic that the mother is also support in the act of attaching the third leg to the boy's body. It is our cultural heritage that boy is always superior to girl. The common method of obtaining higher death rate for girl children than boys is neglecting the girl child during early childhood.

Dattani sees Tara as a play about the gendered self, about coming to terms with the feminine side of oneself in a world that always favours what is male.[8]

This play raises a few questions of discrimination, i.e. religious prejudice, gender discrimination. This play is not only deals with gender issues and the treatment of girl child in a male dominated society, but also this deal with gender biases and prejudices which still affect the lives of several girl-children even amongst educated, urban families.

The root problem of discriminatory treatment being meted out to girls lies in the status of women in society. He has presented the strange reality of women playing a secondary role to man. Male are seen as the providers and the role of the girls are neglected. This dirty practice is still present in some part of India. The drama also suggests supremacy of Patel when he insists that proper division should be made in the gender roles.

Tara's parents are educated even then they had made such discrimination. Bharati's father can also be considered responsible for this catastrophe. Bharati had been influenced by her father's decision Bharati is scared about the prospect of her daughter; she says:

> It's all right while she is young. It is all very cute and comfortable when she makes witty remarks. But let her grow up. Yes, Chandan the world will tolerate you. The world will accept you- but not her! Oh! .......when she sees herself at eighteen or twenty, thirty is unthinkable and what about forty and fifty! Oh God! (349).

She also tries to show her love by the act of donating kidney to Tara, which ultimately turns useless. He establishes that mother and daughter relationship proves secondary to the orders of patriarchy. He revealed the issue of gender discrimination in this play. The social norms, economic values and cultural elements have been answerable for the inequality against the girl child. Tara is a victim of this social system, which controls the minds and actions of the people. In Indian society, woman is variously presented as a mother, wife, daughter and sister even goddess. *Manusmruti* and *Dharma*-shastras have laid down specific rules for the conduct of women. The women were treated to secondary position in all walks of life. The literacy rate of women has improved. Now a day, they are given secondary status in household, offices, social and public places. Women are exploited and harassed in Indian society. Woman is subject to violence and harassment everywhere.

The position of women in the Indian Society since the ancient age has been commanding, except for the colonial pressures such as the invasion of Mughals, the British etc. which changed the system of the country. Static models of Hindu women as marginalized and muted subjects have in recent years been enlivened by a body of work that investigates the ways in which women both subtly and overtly resist, contest, and re-imagine these roles. Women have never been independent and women's happiness was considered dependent on male control, as mentioned in The Code of Manu, one of Hinduism's oldest foundational texts (John Raines: 2001, p.1). Women have to have good education to do resist and to find spaces for liberation and gender.

## Works Cited

1. Bardhan, Kalpana, *Of Love, Nature and Devotion: Selected Songs of Rabindranath Tagore*. New Delhi: Oxford University Press, 2008
2. Rabindranath Tagore, 'Woman', in *Personality: Lectures Delivered in America* (London: Macmillan, 1919), pp.169-84.
3. Ibid, p.173.
4. Ibid, p.171.
5. Hogan, p.214.
6. Shanta Gokhle, "Tendulkar on his Own Terms," in Geeta Rajan and Shoma Choudhry (eds), *Vijay Tendulkar*, New-Delhi: Katha, 2001.
7. Elizabeth Roy, Freak Mirror and Grotesque Image. *The Hindu*, 15 March 2002.
8. Mahesh Dattani, *Collected Plays*, Penguin, New Delhi, 2000p-288.

# 25

# Indian Drama in English: A Feminine Outlook

— N. Sumathi

In six decades of our Independence, there has been a slow but steady movement towards a greater democratization of the social set-up. Democracy implies the empowerment of the silent and subdued sections. Women too have been subdued. Are women deprived of the right to sail alone in the ocean of life? How do they negotiate the conflicting demands of desire versus duty; needs versus wants; the comfort on the conformity and the perils of living life on their own terms? These baffling questions are in search of a perfect answer from a thorough research on *Indian Drama in English: A Feminine Perspective*.

It is true that a woman is weak physically but emotionally and mentally she is strong enough to compete with man. Once she gets into the robe of different roles as a daughter, a sister, a wife, or a mother, she goes through a number of experiences and hardships that nurture and leave her ripe with saintly wisdom as the years pass on. The more difficult and important roles are those of a wife and, a mother. As a mother, playing a biological role, she attends to her children and shares feelings every moment in their lives. Man's duty lies in merely satisfying his needs and going on to work. He does not like sharing household chores. This happened because the society has deeply engraved the notion that housework is a fitting position only for women. The woman therefore, has always been urged to lay aside all her natural caprice, her love of self-indulgence, her vanity, her indolence, in short, her very *self* – and assume a new nature. She is forced to spend her mental and moral capabilities in devising means for promoting the happiness of others, while her own happiness is blissfully neglected by others. She is expected to have proverbial humility, monumental patience and an untiring devotion to her husband. Thus she is assigned a remote and secondary existence. The complex role of women in society is being portrayed in Indian dramas so diligently by the stalwarts like Sri Aurobindo, Rabindranath Tagore, Krishna Mohan Banerjee, T.P. Kailasam, Girish Karnad, Mahesh Dattani and so on. The aim of this presentation is to study the cause of the "feminine", i.e. both the female position and psychological situation as depicted in the selected plays of Girish Karnad.

Unlike a short story or a novel, a play is a work of storytelling in which actors represent the characters. In another essential, a play differs from a work of fiction: it is addressed not to readers but to spectators. To be part of an audience in a theatre is an experience far different from reading a story in solitude. Expectant, as the house lights dim and the curtain rises; we become members of a community. The responses of people around us affect our own responses. We, too, contribute to the community's response whenever we laugh, sigh, applaud, murmur in surprise, and catch our breath in excitement. In contrast, when all alone we watch a movie by means of a videocassette recorder – say, a slapstick comedy – we probably laugh less often than if we were watching the same film in theatre, surrounded by a roaring crowd. Of course, no one is spilling popcorn down the back of our neck. Each kind of theatrical experience, to be sure, has its advantages. Drama being an audio visual medium has been very effective and powerful genre in World Literature.

Drama has always been an integral part of culture, highlighting and evaluating moral commitments, religious convictions, philosophical approaches, social and political changes, and psychological aspects of women of the time. Hailed as the 'Fifth Veda', drama in India has had a rich and glorious tradition. Bharata ascribed a divine origin to drama and considered it as the fifth Veda. There is almost a global coverage in the total content of Sri Aurobindo's dramatic literature. In matters of plot construction and characterisation Sri Aurobindo's debt to Elizabethan drama is undeniable. The use of the English blank verse is flawless and in the right tune with the characters and situations. But at the same time we do not miss the impact of Sanskrit playwrights like Bhasa, Kalidas and Bhavabhuti as Dr. K.R.S. Iyenger observes, "But all five plays are stepped in poetry and romance, recalling the spirit and flavour of the distinctive dramatic type exemplified in different ways by Bhasa, Kalidas and Bhavabhuti. Though, of course all have Aurobindonian undertones."

Another dramatic voice on the Indian literary scene that demands attention is that of T.P. Kailasam. He wrote both in English and Kannada. Though Kailasam is regarded as the father of modern Kannada drama, his genius finds its full expression in his English plays such as *The Burden* (1933), *Fulfilment* (1933), *The Purpose* (1944), *Karna* (1964) and *Keechaka* (1949). He has a real genius and love for the drama. G. S. Amur holds a very high opinion about T.P. Kailasam. Amur rightly remarks, "A talented actor who appeared on the amateur as well as the professional stage, he brought to the writing of drama an intimate knowledge of the theatre. It is for this reason that his plays whether in Kannada or English, have a uniform technical excellence." The concept of motherhood for most nationalist writers was associated with the crucial role of procreating and rearing a special breed of men. This role extended to energizing the menfolk to reconstruct the 'motherland'. In Kailasam's play *The Brahmin's Curse* there is Radha who assumes such a role for Karna, and in *The Purpose*, it is Ekalavya's mother. Surely, this aspect of Kailasam's plays calls for further study.

Girish Karnad is certainly a name that strikes a chord of recognition for many. A known playwright, he is also a critically acclaimed movie actor. Starting his writing career with *Yayati*, Karnad has moved on to give many more thought provoking and symbolist plays richly steeped in myth and local culture. A highly learned and intellectual person, Karnad's plays are his mouthpiece to act as an impetus to thought regarding many of the contemporary issues plaguing man and society. For four decades he has been composing plays, often using history and mythology to tackle contemporary issues. His plays have been translated into several Indian languages and directed by eminent directors.

There has been enough literature-oral and written, glorifying the women characters that treat them as slaves and this tradition is being observed faithfully. Pooru's wife Chitralekha, though she opposes her husband exchanging his youth for the old age of his father, is unable to prevent it. In a male dominant society, the words of the women do not have any value. As a normal young wife, Chitralekha wishes to bear a child. So, in her fit of anguish she even wishes to offer herself to Yayati; but then realizing the blunder she commits suicide. "Through her Karnad explores the futility of being born a princess who finds reality too much to bear and kills herself" (Raju 84).

Jayadipsingh K. Dodiya has pointed out that "No Indian woman will accept to be with other man". The real crux of the problem is that society in its present form will never accept it. Chastity is a word, confined exclusively to women only. This reduces her to a non-living commodity. But she is denied every privilege that a man enjoys. This, in reality, it is not the fate of Chitralekha alone but of all women. She finally commits suicide for she sees no other escape from the unjust patriarchal order, where she has to unduly repress her feelings and desires in the name of *pativrata* (dutiful and dedicated wife). In the same play, there is another character Swarnalatha, the maid confidant, who comes from a low class and who too like Chitralekha does not receive the love of her family and husband, because the latter believes her to be unchaste.

A woman in Indian society in considered good only if she is chaste. Though Swarnalatha is chaste, she cannot make her husband believe her and finally in order to free her husband from the dilemma, she falsely acquiesces to the lie. Indian society fails to accept woman as a human being with natural desires. She cannot win people's hearts with love but only by performing miracles and being a goddess. So is the case with Chithralekha who is expected to forgo all her desires, her needs—emotional and sexual, and become a *Devi* of supreme sacrifice. But Chithralekha crosses the limits of all the so-called "morality" and hypocrisy and claims directly for her sexual rights.

Through the character of Padmini in Hayavadana, Karnad visualizes another problem faced by Indian women. 'Chastity' and 'loyalty' are concepts limited to women alone. Chastity is such a value invented by patriarchal culture and it is one of the most powerful yet invisible cultural fetters that it has enslaved women for ages since the dawn of patriarchy. The *Ramayana* in which Sita undergoes the fire ordeal to prove her chastity to Rama has been a cultural guide to Indians for more than two thousand years. Every mother along with father and other elders enslaves her daughter to patriarchy by teaching her verbally and non-verbally that chastity is more important than life and that its loss, which brings an unbearable social stigma, is worse than death. Many women lose their lives to protect their chastity and many other women bear in silence all the oppression and violence of their sadistic husbands. If any brave woman violates these values, she is not only looked down upon but also culturally excommunicated. It is clear that the concept of chastity is gender biased and that women care more for chastity than men.

Literature is replete with examples of women who meet with destruction because they try to cross the threshold. Those who happened to cross so, and acquire voice were scared of the wide, dark, animalistic devouring world outside and beat an undignified retreat to get inside the threshold. But a large number of them remain committed, passive, servile and silent, bearing and rearing children, and gratifying the sexual needs of their husbands. Elements of discontent, unfulfilled desires and aspirations, unequal demands made by the other are stillborn and reborn. Men and women imbibe the exploitative and oppressive culture and perpetuate it. So, they fail to realize the reality. They blame one another, quarrel among themselves and make their life miserable. They do not try to eradicate the morbid culture that led to the pathetic state.

Karnad's characters however accept failure stoically and embrace their fate. When the impossible cannot take the shape of reality and opposites cannot be reconciled, for Karnad's character the only alternative is death. For example, Padmini in *Hayavadana* walks boldly to her fate and emerges thus as a strong character. Padmini, the lead character of the play, though married to Devadatta, is attracted to Kapila, her ascetic husband Devadatta's best friend. The play is a surreal love story underscored by urgent, driving questions of postcolonial politics and identity.

Karnad's play concerns Padmini, a young woman who falls in love with the robust Kapila. When Padmini switches her paramours' heads in a tragicomic accident, Karnad confronts the audience with a dilemma: which man is Padmini's husband, the one bearing his head, or the one possessing his body? Both Devadatta and Kapila contend with feelings of incompleteness. The switch seems, at first, ideal for Padmini. However, conflicts arise as the two mismatched individuals try to reconcile the disconnect between their minds and their bodies. The play takes a philosophical turn as the audience is asked to consider whether it is the physical or the intellectual components that create identity. However, the very fact that Padmini is shown in the play as married to one person and unapologetically craving for another person takes this play back into the domain of Indian thought that was lost 1,000 years ago due to external intervention. Padmini clearly reflects that she is an entity caught between two different identities of association. She symbolizes the incompleteness of human desire. She fails in getting reunification of the mind and the body in Devadatta and Kapila. Now she expresses her wish to accomplish her search for completeness through her child. Therefore, she requests the Bhagavata that her son should be brought up as the son of Kapila by the hunters in the forest for five years and then as the son of Devadatta, he should be handed over to Vidyasagara, her father-in-law and revered brahmin. Thus she wants to provide both physical and mental training for her son so that he may attain perfection in life. The issues of gender and the place of women in literature are the most important aspects of feminist discourse. The reason for this is that in any society and culture, male is regarded as the norm, the central or neutral position from which the female is a departure.

Karnad's *Nagamandala* (1988) is a play taking its inspiration from the popular myth and oral stories centering around the King Cobra, 'Naga' but raising issues that hold true as much of our times as of yester years. It discusses issues about man-woman relationship, position and identity of a woman, about psychology and the impact of social and cultural modes on the feminine psyche. "In fact *Nagamandala*: ...is a powerful portrait of the agony and anguish faced by both men and women in their development into adult roles and social adjustment in a society where the individual is given little space for self-development, awareness and independence as a being" (Gupta, 1999: 249). The dramatist using two very common characters who are more types than individual has tried to shed light on the unequal and lop-sided position of a woman as compared to man in our society. Depicting a typical rural scene, he has very poignantly represented not only the social and cultural hypocrisy and prejudices but also the effect that these forces have on the psyche of an individual.

Rani, the protagonist of the novel is a character whose life the play trails as she evolves from an immature, naïve girl into that of a confident and mature woman. She is a symbol of any woman who is unprepared to face life on her own once she leaves the protective threshold of her parent's home. The reality and harshness of the world beyond shocks and confuses her. At the beginning of the play Rani is introduced as a young bride on the verge of a new life with her husband Appanna.

Like any other girl she too enters this new life with many expectations and trepidations, desires and dreams. But reality knocks her down nonplussed. Appanna locks her up in the house all alone only to return in the day for his bath and lunch. Rani's presence in his life is only as his housekeeper and cook. He does not want her to have any social contacts and interactions, and to ensure her complete alienation he first brings home a watch dog and then a mongoose. This solitary confinement of Rani by Appanna in the house symbolizes the chastity belt of the Middle Ages, the reduction of women's talents to housework and the exclusion of women from enlightenment and enjoyment. (Babu 1999: 239)

Like Rani, her husband Appanna is also a type representing the stereotypical image of a chauvinistic male as per the patriarchal dictates of society, dominating, cruel, selfish and callous. Naga on the other hand is a representation of the matured, caring and loving male, truly a myth in the rigid and tradition bound patriarchal society. Gender discrimination is the basis of all kinds of domination and subjugation amongst the sexes. The marginal position of women in the Indian society as a result has become an integral part of the socio-cultural identity of the country. A woman has no identity of her own, a victim of 'incompleteness' she craves for completeness in her relations, in love but usually finds none. Though traditionally the man-woman relationship is compared to the two wheels of a cart, both equally important, yet in reality the female is always the broken, fragmented wheel clinging to the other (male) for support and survival. This inequality and imbalance is clearly visible in the relationship of Rani-Appanna. Rani has no say in any matter; she cannot even question the behaviour of her husband. A result of years of conditioning that a girl goes through right from birth, Rani also accepts her subjugation submissively. When she does try to plead with Appanna, his response is obviously one of irritation and disregard. "Look, I don't like idle chatter. Do as you are told, you understand?"

> Indian society is not an individualistic society, and especially in case of a woman her claim to individuality is out of question. The emphasis is more on duty than on individuality, and resultant effect is repression of individuality. In the rigidly-formed and tradition-bound societies like India the repression one has to put up with is usually very severe and resultant suffering often assumes pathetic proportions for sensitive individuals. Among Indians again the women happen to be the worst sufferers as the social norms and moral codes have been so framed as to be particularly disadvantageous to them. (Rajeshwar 1995: 141)

Freud in his study of the human psyche has stressed on the tremendous effect that repression has on the individual. The social and cultural norms always stand in opposition to the natural instinctive urges of the individual, which are then repressed in order to confirm to the pre-decided socially and culturally acceptable roles. So society, 'the creative agent' as Eric Fromm refers to it is the factor responsible for conditioning, moulding and creating the individual characters into pre-set moulds and types. According to Freud there is always a return of the repressed. External factors, situations and society can repress an individual's longings and desires but it cannot totally extinguish them. Thoughts, emotions and desires which are repressed and are not able to find a free outlet of expression, gets imbedded in the 'unconscious' of the person finding a covert form of expression and wish fulfilment through dreams and myths. The underlying assumption is that when some wish, fear, memory, or desire is difficult to face we may try to cope with it by repressing it, which is, eliminating it from the conscious mind. But this doesn't make it go away: it remains alive in the unconscious, like radioactive matter buried beneath the ocean, and constantly seeks a way back into the conscious mind, always succeeding eventually. (Barry 2007: 100)

Rani is a victim of severe repression and alienation. Confined and left alone without any companionship and comfort, she starts hallucinating. Her innermost desires of love, companionship and comfort find an expression through her various dreams that reveal the severe state of repression and depression that she is going through in her isolation. In her state of mental and emotional anguish, the line between illusion and reality is blurred. Isolated and confined to live a life detached from any social interactions, and emotionally deprived, Rani takes refuge in her dreams about her parents. Rani tries to fill the emptiness of her life with the love of her parents. A dutiful wife as she has been conditioned to be, Rani obeys the dictates of her tyrant husband without a word, but her true feelings find an expression in her dreams wherein she imagines herself being locked up by a "demon" in a castle. The demon is none other than Appanna who locks her up in the house.

Rani's dreams show the inner workings of her psyche, they are an expression of her inner most desires and yearnings suppressed in her unconscious. Highly symbolical in nature her dreams are symbols representing persons and ideas lying hidden in her unconscious. When Rani dreams of her parents for the first time, she imagines an Eagle taking her to them. An Eagle, which is a bird of prey, symbolizes strength and courage. A bird also represents flight and freedom, which expresses Rani's yearning for release from her confinement. She seeks not only solace but also strength for survival from her parent's love. Rani, being a naïve and innocent girl is totally unaware of the ways of the world and realities of life and relationships. Though unknowingly yet instinctively she craves for Appanna's love, her prince who in reality is a beast. So she takes refuge in the dreams of a prince who will rescue her from her distress.

In her endeavour to find love and companionship Rani finds the much-needed comfort of a mother in Kurudava. Interactions with Kurudavva and her support puts a balm on Rani's tortured and tormented psyche, and at last she finally finds a glimmer of hope in her otherwise lonely and gloomy life. This promise of love and hope represented by Kurudavva who shows Rani the path to a better future is symbolized by the Whale in Rani's dream who rescues her from the clutches of the demon. Whale symbolizes the motherly love and protection, the image of which is conjured up in Rani's mind after her meeting with Kurudavva.

Similar to the dreams of Rani, which are personal in nature, myths are the expression of the primordial experiences of a race inherited as the 'Collective Unconsciousness'. Symbolical in nature they disguise the truth not only to maintain the social and cultural order but also to give expression to hidden instincts whose open expression can pose to be a threat to social order and conduct. Particularly in a patriarchal society myths represent the male perspective in need to suppress female individuality. Superstitions and supernatural elements play an important part in the composition of a myth. The aphrodisiacal root given to Rani by Kurudavva is one such superstition that gives an interesting twist to the turn of events in the play. This hold of superstitious belief can also be seen in the heavily prejudiced view of Kurudavva regarding the women in her son Kappana's life, and also in the life of Appanna. Both men neglect their duties and abandon their mother and wife respectively to gratify their physical needs, but still superstition points the guilty finger towards the women who are said to have magical powers to lure and entice the men. Women who live outside the limits decreed by society are either loose women or supernatural beings like

Kappanna's enticer whom Kurudavva describes as, "A temptress from beyond...A yaksha woman..." A man does not need to explain his reasons for gratification of his sensual pleasures but a woman's instinctual need is ignored, and their desire is considered a transgression of moral codes requiring supernatural justification. The Naga in the guise of Appanna presents a choice for Rani, a choice to live a fuller and happier life. It is her expression of desire and also the fulfilment of her wish for love, her desire to live life fully and with satisfaction. If Appanna is the demon then Naga is the prince in Rani's life.

A source of energy, the Naga represents the positive element, the cultural leader, and harbinger of a social change, generating a transformation not only in the character of Rani but also in the society at large. A representation of the true life force, Naga is the source as well as the preservation and regeneration of life. Considered from a realistic point of view, Naga represents the modern, new woman's right to choice, the right to choose a life overcoming all obstacles to her happiness. It symbolizes the breaking of barriers, crossing of the lines that intend to imprison a woman and distance her from her surroundings as well as her own 'self'. More an initiator than a leader, Naga actually initiates Rani on to the path of transformation.

## Conclusion

Constructing a female framework by deconstructing the man-made language is one of the most important goals of feminist readers or critics. Here, if one looks for feminine perspective with reference to Karnad's creation of women, it goes beyond the expectations of women. Chithralekha, Padmini, Rani and Kurudavva are the representations of adi shakthi, pathi devtha, grihalaxmi, an epitome of love, courage and humanism. The emotional and intellectual development of these protagonists and minor characters like Swarnalatha, Kurudavva suggest both the limitations and the possibilities of life as lived by both women and men, for the woman's experience is a paradigm for human experience, the feminine sensibility for the human sensibility. The problems of constructing oneself amid the pressures and restrictions of society make the plays not only the markers of the new sensibility but also indicate the nature of experience and the inner life.

## Works Cited

1. Santosh Gupta, 'Naga-Mandala: A Story of Marriage and Love', *The Plays of Girish Karnad: Critical Perspectives*, ed. Jaydipsinh Dodiya, New Delhi: Prestige Books, 1999, p.249.
2. M. Sarat Babu, 'The Concept of Chastity and Naga-Mandala', *The Plays of Girish Karnad: Critical Perspectives,* ed. Jaydipsinh Dodiya, New Delhi: Prestige Books, 1999, p.239.
3. M. Rajeshwar, 'The Inner World of Indian Women: Neurotic Characters of Indian Women Novelists', *Feminism and Literature*, ed. Veena Noble Dass, New Delhi: Prestige Books, 1995, p.141.
4. Peter Barry, 'Psychoanalytic Criticism', *Beginning Theory: An Introduction to Literary and Cultural Theory,* New York: Manchester University Press, 2007, p.100.
5. Sudhir Kakar, 'The Inner World', rpt. *The Indian Psyche*, Oxford University Press, 1996, p. 59.
6. V. Rangan, 'Myth and Romance in Nagamandala or their Subversion', *Girish Karnad' Plays: Performance and Critical Perspectives*, ed. Tutun Mukherjee, New Delhi:Pencraft International, 2006, p.79.
7. R.A. Singh, '*Feminist Mode in Commonwealth Literature*'. Prakash Book Depot, 2001, p.47.
8. X.J. Kennedy, *Literature: An introduction to fiction, poetry, and drama,* Little, Brown And Company, Boston, Toronto, 1987, p.835.
9. Quoted from *The Criterion: An International Journal in English* ISSN 0976-8165.

26

# Reflection of Suppressed Status of Woman in Indian Drama in English: A Socio-Cultural Study

— Seema Dhoble

## Introduction

Whenever we come across the word feminism or the concept of feminism in India, naturally a set of movements aimed at defining, establishing and defending equal political, economic and social rights, and equal opportunities for Indian women takes shape in the mind within a fraction of second. The male and female dichotomy of polar opposites with the former oppressing the latter at all times have been discussed and put forth in literature and in every form of it, be it poetry, drama and fiction.

The purpose of the present paper is to see the causes of man-woman distinctions in the socio-cultural context and to suggest a caution to be taken but, those man-woman distinctions should not be perceived as discriminations. The cry for equality should not be allowed to change into a demand for sameness. Instead of posing a straightforward blame on the 'male' in the society one has to analyze the different issues which create the 'male-dominance' through the customs, traditions and rules and regulations (made by man only) of the behavioural pattern.

The paper further discusses the role of social norms, social institutions like marriage, religion, family and gender in the formation of individual psychology, personality, growth and development. To explore the masculinity or feminity in the Indian context one has to study how the psyche is shaped within a specific cultural framework.

Man and masculinity is created by society; God creates both equally, with equal preferences and priorities. It is social that institutions and conservative attitude increase the discrimination a lot. A girl is always taught how to be a 'girl', passive, shy and inferior— and a boy is taught how to be a 'boy'— independent, active dominant, superior and a power holder.

It is not a quarrel between man and woman and not even the race for the conclusion of who is superior, but an attempt to give a new insight into the problem.

It is good to say that a human being is a 'social being' or one cannot live without society. But along with the social development, society starts building shackles around the individual. And mainly women become the victim of this because it was the males only who made laws and rules for their convenience or according to their will and wishes.

The following model discusses the above-said fact with reference to some classic literary works:

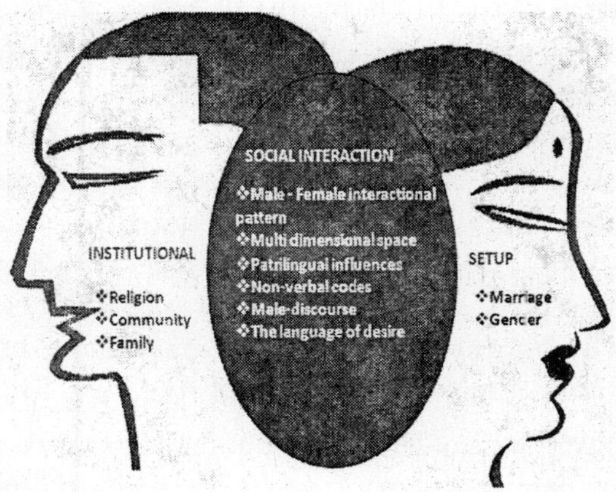

## The Model

The two masks attached to each other and in opposite direction symbolically highlight the position of the male and female. The institutional set-up is placed on both the masks as they both are socialized in the same environment. The oval-shaped circle is nothing but the intersection area where they both (male and female) come together. It shows the interactional pattern between them. It suggests how the socio-cultural norms established by social institutions affect the life of an individual whether it is he or she. It also highlights the interaction between male and female partners in the family, and puts forth the conflicts which arise due to constant interference of social aspects that hamper the smooth flow of personal communication.

## Institutional Set-up

### *Religion, Community, Family, Marriage*

Community, religion and, family become sites of identity for individual. In several Indian texts, whether novel or drama, these become the identity markers for characters. These sites provide a framework to explore various strands of feminism in different literary works. Religion has its important role to play in the process of socialization or in the life of an individual. But the reality of religion exists only for the believers. Many a time the set beliefs which are given by religion are made into superstitions by people of the society. The followers of these beliefs mould them according to their convenience or for their personal selfishness. These moulded beliefs become the traditions of society and though in modern time they prove to be 'dead conventions', some people use and follow them for their personal advantages against others in the society, group, community, family etc, e.g., in the name of religion and beliefs of dharma women are kept as illiterate, marginalized and 'the suppressed'.

Marriage is a sacred and legal bond between two persons of opposite sex. Family and marriage are the two social institutions connected to each other. They are identified with another social institution, i.e., community. The working of these social institutions affects in different ways on the male and female characters in a literary work. e.g. (1) Karnad's *Nagamandala* is a feminist play. It presents the problems of a married status of a e.g. 1) Karnad's *Naga-Mandala* is a feminist play. It presents the problems of a married status of a woman in her relation to her husband and family. He picturises the tragic consequences of subordination of married woman to her husband. (2) *Nirmala* by Premchand is a classic narrative of woman as a victim. Due to poor economic conditions, Nirmala's mother could not pay the amount of dowry and Nirmala was married to an elderly widower, who had sons of Nirmala's age. Hence the story reveals the consequences of this mis-matched marriage.

Nirmala's marriage with Munshi Totaram explores the masculinity in the Indian marriage system.

The superiority of male over female nourishes the male-ego in the Indian context. In every human being there is a cultural psychological space that lies between universally shared wishes of the inner world and the specific restrictions placed on them by a particular society. The treatment given to male and female in India and in different social institutions in the Indian context increases the discrimination between males and females. Unfortunately among them marriage is the most unavoidable and sensitive institution.

> In the family of Nirmala-joint, rich and socially famous Nirmala is accepted as 'Navvadhu' but she is taken only as 'vimata' (step-mother). Though in that role she wants to put herself honestly the social assumptions or social views for 'vimata' of a family and the family members lead her towards the destruction.

Hence, each individual in the family should first see and prioritize his/her soul responsibility towards another member in the family and rather consider the social obligations.

Marriage signals the end of independence— if they were ever independent in their father's house. Marriage does not guarantee the safety of home or a clear identity for the women. Marriage makes unreasonable demands on the woman, and offers little in turn. In the Hindu context, notions of chastity, service to the husband and motherhood work toward an erasure of the woman's needs, desire and even identity. She subsumes her identity under that of the family's.

Governed by regulating framework of self-sacrifice, the woman puts up with several miseries and abuses within marriage. The woman's education, ambitions and desires are far less important than her role as mother, daughter- in-law and wife. The ways in which a woman is controlled by the institution of marriage becomes a clear theme in many Indian writers.

**Gender Consciousness**

Globally, communities interpret biological differences between man and woman to create a set of social expectations that define the behaviours which are 'appropriate' for men and women, and determine their different access to rights, resources, power in society and even health behaviours.

In the given model, gender also becomes a prominent aspect in the analysis. Gender consciousness, discriminations, differences create many conventional ideas which become unfortunately the traditions. The practice of these traditions (blindly) becomes a root cause of crises in the families or specifically in the life of an individual.

The socialization of members and especially girls leads to women themselves accepting their secondary role in family. "For a long time academics have been studying the process of socialization, however it only meant understanding the traits of masculinity and femininity. [The process of socialization in the patriarchal society provides truth for the famous observation of 'Simone de Beauvoir', 'one is not born rather becomes a woman.'

Gender roles are conceived, enacted and learnt within a complex of relationship.]" (L, Dube. 2001, 88)

When this discussion travels from gender discrimination towards sexuality it is observed that the woman embodies the boundaries of licit and illicit forms of sexuality, as she is the guardian of the nation's morality. Further by bestowing her with spirituality—the notion of 'Shakti, 'in the Hindu tradition, for instance—the woman's sexuality is effectively erased in favour of a 'pure' ideal. e.g.

(1) Karnad's *Nagamandala* questions patriarchal moral code which demands the faithfulness of a woman not the faithfulness of a man to his wife. Appanna openly and unashamedly commits adultery but nobody objects to it, the village elders who sit in judgment ask Rani for 'Divya' and prove herself. Nobody believes the innocence of Rani. She sleeps with Naga without knowing its identity. If she had discovered the real identity of Naga she would not allow him to enter in her bedroom. As a typical woman, she is frigid and despises sex. What she craves for is an affection which Naga gives her.

(2) Nirmala is brought up as inferior to her brother in her mother's house. And after marriage she realizes that her marriage is another enclosure that restricts the movement of her 'self' towards a perception of herself as an independent human being. She becomes the icon of Hindu womanhood's self-sacrifice. Her marriage with Munshi Totaram, an aged widower, highlights only a woman in her and kills a human being who dwells actually in her heart. In her life the root cause of the crisis is masculinity. Her sexual experiences with her husband make her situation absurd.

Nirmala constantly avoids the company of Munshiji, her energy is spent in trying to avoid him. Munshiji tries to win her heart but all this only inspires disgust in Nirmala. This is a realistic example of mismatched marriage. One can imagine a girl's inner psyche who has step son of her own age. In Indian culture marriage is not only a social institute but it has a firm religious foundation. Religion projects it as a holy union of two souls but society moulds it according to its own convenience. Economic statuses of both the parties, i.e., class, caste, family structure automatically become more powerful than an individual.

The story of Mansaram and his downfall starts with Nirmala's affection for Mansaram as a mother which is taken as a relationship of a boy and a girl of same age. She tries to tell Munshiji that how she is very fond of children and even children are also accepting her as their mother but Munshiji has taken this otherwise.

Munshiji is a fine representation of Indian male ego shaped by Indian society. On the one hand he wants to marry a girl for the sake of his children and on the other he feels jealous about whom his son has affection and love.

The concept of purity of characters has been associated with women since ancient days. Chastity is a patriarchal concept that has been used to oppress and weaken for ages.

The victim of this discrimination is obviously women in India because they are assumed low and weak in the status. With the emergences of modernity there starts a conflict for sameness or equality. The male who stands opposite to the female is made by society only. Hence, the change should take place in every aspect of society (i.e. family, marriage, caste system, practice of religion etc.) as well as more emphatically in the mentality of the people and not only in the male members.

Finally it can be asserted that the opinion by Cherre Moraga hit the nail on its head:

> If women's bodies and those of men and women who transgress their gender roles have been historically regarded as territories to be conquered, they are also territories to be liberated. (P.K. Nayar 2008, 116)

## Social Interaction and Interpersonal Relationship

This framework throws light on the effect of socio-cultural elements on the interpersonal relationship and interactions of the characters. It discusses the complexities and conflicts that arise due to social and cultural engagements and interventions.

Language is an important symbolic resource for creating and communicating personal and social meaning and literature is the storehouse of such meanings.

We learn our language and its linguistic items by listening to others. Our international patterns are created in the social environment around us. So when the social process of an individual is taken for analysis, it becomes important to analyze it linguistically.

The following international patterns are considered for linguistic analysis:

1) Male- female interactional pattern
2) Multidimensional space
3) Patrilingual influences
4) Non-verbal codes
5) Male discourse
6) The language of desire

### 1) Male– Female Interactional Pattern

Males and females are treated very differently in the cultural systems. As far as language is concerned, same languages provide distinct forms for use by male and female speakers. They speak differently or they have different priorities and purposes in conversation.

Men are more concerned with power and women with solidarity, for example, Conversations are negotiations in which people try to achieve and maintain the upper hand if they can, and protect themselves from others attempt to put them down and push them around. Life then, is a contest a struggle to preserve independence and avoid failure.

In Contrast, conversations are negotiations for closeness in which people try to seek and give confirmation and support, and to reach consensus. They try to protect themselves from other's attempts to push them away. Life, then, is a community, a struggle to preserve intimacy and avoid isolation. (R.A. Hudson 1996, 141)

For Example:

1) Nirmala by maintaining silence wants to preserve the status of her family and in the constant insult and humiliation by her sister-in-law she tries to protect herself there in the house. So, for an Indian married woman though she has her own language to fight for saving and establishing her self-dignity she tries to learn the language of suppression derived from the culture or society.
2) The interactional pattern between Rani and Appanna itself is strange and suppressive. Appanna is a representative of typical Indian husband who regards his wife as his property and adopts a possessive attitude towards her.

Females give priority to solidarity, and concentrate on building and maintaining the social bonds that hold communities together; for males, priority goes to power the struggle for independence. In other words, the interactional pattern puts the responsibility of form bonding and maintain groups (though she likes it or not) solely upon the head and shoulders of women. It is only the female who has to see for family bonding and social status of the family, and learn the language which proves beneficial for this task. The male, though he is there in the social group, always wants to enjoy the independence through male-dominance.

**2) Multidimensional Space**

Everybody has his own viewpoint in looking at society, so to speak. A person construct a more or less unconscious mental map of the community in which he lives, in which the people around him are arranged in a multidimensional space. The particular map which each individual draws will reflect his own personal experience, so people with different sociolinguistic backgrounds will be led to construct correspondingly different maps relevant to language and society.

People can be classified more or less independently according to the dimensions of age, region of origin, social class and sex. Each person, if put in the constructed model of this multidimensionalspace, tries to identify and locate himself in it. Language is only one part of the picture, but a particularly important part because it gives us a very clear structural set of symbols which we can use in locating ourselves in the world.

> The people around us belong to a variety of social types and we have to decide where we ourselves being among those types. If different types speak differently we can use our own speech to signal this choice. In other words, at each utterance our speech can be seen be as an 'Act of Identity' in a multi-dimensional space. (R.A. Hudson 1996, 12)

When this linguistic tool is used to interpret both the texts, one can come to know that both the protagonists, Nirmala and Rani are inhibited from locating themselves in the structure of the multidimensional space. Their own mental maps of the community in which they live are not at all considered by others. Nirmala and Rani have complete perception of their respective situations but they can't use the language to change this situation and to locate themselves in their own space. No utterance of speech, no act of identity is seen.

Their marriage, family, husbands prescribe different dimensions without recognizing their mental map of perception. Externally Nirmala, tries to locate her in the dimensions given by her mis-matched marriage, internally she realizes the hollowness of it.

### 3) Patrilingual Influences

In both the novels, marriage is patrilocal (the husband and wife live where the husband was brought up) and there is a rule that the wife should not only live where the husband was brought up, but should also use his language in speaking to their children (a custom that might be called 'Patrilingual Marriage').

Nirmala and Rani have their own personal language but they can't speak in that and even can't use to convince people around them. That's why Nirmala succumbs herself in silence and Rani has to do the 'Nagdivya' to prove herself. Every individual, either male or female, is more or less stable linguistically, with a personal language which defines our place in the social world. But the patrilingual influences compel the females to speak with the language of husband and his family.

### 4) Non-verbal Codes

We express our innerself and outer self through language sometimes verbally and sometimes non-verbally. Language is the fabric of all experiences; it seems to be all-pervasive and permeates our thoughts and actions, concepts and intentions, emotions and intellects, often unknowingly. In the traditional conservative society the word 'silence' becomes synonym for the word 'woman'. It is for both, educated and uneducated. A woman who is uneducated has to keep silence because she is unknown about the realities of the world while an educated woman should maintain silence to show the value of her education. Females in the society are not allowed to express themselves. The voice of woman has always been silenced under the legendary power and dominance.

Nirmala's silence, her inability to speak, her stubborn refusal to speak up at critical moments, her overwhelming anxiety to appear good as distinct from being and doing good, her persistent failure to act as a morally responsible person- all this is of course a condemnation of the institutions which have made her what she is, and compel her to continue to be like that.

"The society and institutions like marriage, family caste, class, and religion have produced a moral cripple in the form of woman like Nirmala whose very passivity and timidity is pathological and immoral.

"Nirmala is made a saintly creature that can sacrifice her being, delete every trace of herself to play her assigned role to perfection with no hope of appreciation or reward. Nirmala has her inner language of perception, she is not explaining verbally but her silence speaks a lot. With her silence throughout her life, she becomes fragile and vulnerable behind the mask of a protective, supportive and disciplinarian house-wife.

"Appanna is a representative of contemporary Indian society and expects his wife to render unquestionable obedience to her husband. He neither comprehends her verbally nor non-verbally.

**5) Male Discourse**

The role of social norms, traditional values, caste and customs, kinship and relationship forms the individual psychology, personality, growth and development. The actions and speeches of Munshiji and Appanna reflect the society in which they are brought up. Many a time the male discourse gets wrongly justified. It is not like 'he is man and he does this only'. Instead of that one should analyze the surrounding in which he has been put or to dissect the locality in which he has been brought up.

Not only male but the whole social group should change the vision to outlook woman, it is not man-woman fight but it is a fight between 'Individual and society'.

**6) The Language of Desire**

The only reality between Nirmala and Munshiji or Rani and Appanna is 'skin-deep love'. Both the males can understand only the language of desire. The basis of their relationship is not mutual love but the desire for sexual pleasure. Appanna openly and ashamedly commits adultery, for him, his action is 'desirable' but for Rani it is a 'sin'. What Rani does is not due to some weakness in her character like Oedipus, who murders his father and marries his mother unknowingly, Rani does the gravest sin of adultery in the ignorance of the real identity of the cobra but the society based on the patriarchal norm takes it as sin.

The male partner is not willing to listen and to understand the inner language of the female partner or language of her heart but very well understands the language of desire and turns her into 'a clown in bed'. In her autobiographical work, *My Story* (1988) Kamala Das questions the sexual aspect of marriage when she asks whether marriage involved turning into 'a clown in bed, a circus-performer' (K. Das 1996, 70)

Thus, it can be concluded that, the play *Nagamandala* reflects upon the contemporary Indian cultural and social life with the use of folktales. It is feminist play not because it is pathetic story of Rani but because it very brilliantly captures the insanity of innocent woman in the background of a conservative patriarchal society of which Rani is no doubt a victim.

The socially realistic novel *Nirmala* depicts the poor plight of female member victimized at the hands of the tyrant male dominating members of the Indian society.

## Conclusion

1) The social bindings and considerations make an individual act accordingly but at last when the individual realizes the truth, it results only in repentance.
2) Society and culture make the family structure for the development of an individual. For a child its family is first society. But the members of the family, by projecting other members wrongly, disturb the health of the family. This small society is also very much responsible for the growth/downfall of an individual.
3) Social norms and religious aspect of culture make all obligations for woman in the name of 'sanskar' and ideal behaviour so it is only woman to put herself in the

framework of morals, ideals, values, sacrifices. Woman does not have the right to break these obligations and irony she can't even complain about it.

4) Though a male has his own perception and sensibilities about issues like marriage of an old man with a young girl, he likes to treat it according to social conventions and norms because:
   i) Social conventions are built for the convenience of 'male'.
   ii) The male-dominated society wants to make females their possession by any ways.
5) The ways in which Nirmala and Rani are controlled by the institution of marriage becomes an important reflection of social consciousness in both the texts.
6) It is not a straightforward blame on the 'male' in society but the analysis of the different social issues which create the 'male' or watering the plant- called 'male-dominance.'
7) Marriage and obvious man-woman relationship in Indian context is still male-dominating and the female is treated as inferior one in the family.
8) Society's selective silence on the issues related to woman's sexuality reveal the hypocrite nature of people as well as hollowness of the social system.
9) Even in 20th century so called modern period, girls are considered to be millstones around her father's neck and he feels it is an offense to give birth to a girl child and the same feeling leads him towards the absurd situation where the very situation results into the final discrimination strengthening the position of male members and weakening or lowering the status of female members.
10) When it comes to feminine perspective in Indian writing in English, it is evident that the suppressive cultural and social elements are responsible for the inhuman exploitation of the Indian women folk.

## Works Cited


1. Das, Kamala, 1996, My Story, New Delhi, Sterling, p.70.
2. Dube, Leela, 2001, *Anthropological Explorations in Gender, Intersecting Fields*, New Delhi, Saga Publication, p.88.
3. Hudson, R, A, 1996, *Sociolingustics,* Cambridge, Cambridge University Press, p.141.
4. Hudson, R, A, 1996, *Sociolingustics,* Cambridge, Cambridge University Press, p.12.
5. Nayar, Pramod, K, 2008, *Postcolonial Literature An Introduction* New Delhi, Pearson Long*man,* p.116.
6. Karnad, Girish. 1998,Three plays- *Naga-Mandala, Hayavadana, Tuglaq.* Oxford India, New Delhi: Paper Backs.
7. Premchand, (translated and with an Afterward by Rai Alok), 2001, *Nirmala,* New Delhi: Oxford India paperbacks.

# Index

*A Doll's House* 178
*A Room of One's Own* 95
Afzal Khan 89
Asif Currimbhoy 170

Betty Friedan 95
*Bravely Fought the Queen* 3, 22, 47, 48, 61

Chandalika 85
Chitrangada 75
Contemporary Indian drama 197
*Contemporary Indian Theatre: Three Voices* 48

*Dance Like a Man* 3, 89
*Do the Needful* 22
Dramatic representation 153

*Final Solutide* 22
*Final Solutions* 36, 89

Girish Karnad 252
G.V. Desani 88
*Gandharva Vivah* 100
*Garudaquran* 20
Gender inequality 29
Global population 19

*Hayavadana* 198, 292

*Indian Drama in English: A Feminine Perspective* 297
Indian English theatre 2
Indian womanhood 167
Indo-Anglian writer 88
*Inquilab* 170

John Stuart Mill 94

K. R. S. Iyengar 144
*Kanyadaan* 162
Kate Millet 29
*Kathasaritasagara* 126
Krishna Mohan Banerjee 88

Linguistic analysis 323
Literary genres 88

M.K. Naik 1
*Mahabharata* 1
Mahesh Dattani 2, 10, 259
Male discourse 323
Male-female interactional pattern 317
*Man of Peace* 88
Manjari S. Isvaran 88

*Meghnadh Badh Kabya* 293
Michael Madhusudan 293
Modern Indian literature 259
Multidimensional space 323
*Murder in the Cathedral* 83

*Naga-Mandala* 196, 198, 240
Non-verbal codes 323

*On a Muggy Night in Mumbai* 36

Patriarchal construction 29
Patriarchal society 243
Patriarchy 29
Patrilingual influences 323
Poststructuralist perspective 37
Pranav nada 1
Pro-feministic attitude 22

Rabindranath Tagore 287

Sakharam Binder 156
*Seven Steps around the Fire* 272, 273
Sexual politics 30
*Silence! The Court Is in Session* 180
*Slumdog Millionaire* 180
Sri Aurobindo 144
Structure and gender inequality 29

*Tale-Danda* 198
*The Coffin and Siddhartha* 88
*The Dissident MLA* 175
*The Fire and the Rain* 198, 272
*The Hungry One* 181
The language of desire 323
*The Parrot* 88
*The Persecuted* 88
*The Sentry's Lantern* 88
*The Subjection of Women* 94
*The Swami and Winston* 272, 273
*The Transposed Heads* 226, 252
*The Vultures* 143, 149
*The Window* 88
*Thirty Days in September* 274
*Tiger Claw* 88
*Tughlaq* 197, 292

*Uma and the Fairy Queen* 272, 273

*Vashishtha Smriti* 102
Veda Vyasa 95

Wedding Album 198
*Where There is a Will* 22, 205

*Yama and Yami* 88
*Yayati* 197, 292